With Child in Mind

University of Pennsylvania Press
STUDIES IN HEALTH, ILLNESS, AND CAREGIVING
Joan E. Lynaugh, General Editor

A complete listing of the books in this series appears at the back of this
volume

With Child in Mind

Studies of the Personal Encounter with Infertility

Margarete Sandelowski

University of Pennsylvania Press

Philadelphia

Library of Congress Cataloging-in-Publication Data
Sandelowski, Margarete.
   With child in mind: studies of the personal encounter with infertility / Margarete
Sandelowski.
      p.   cm. — (Studies in health, illness, and caregiving)
   Includes bibliographical references and index.
   ISBN 0-8122-3197-X (cloth: alk. paper). — ISBN 0-8122-1415-3 (paper: alk. paper)
   1. Infertility—Psychological aspects.   2. Infertility—Case studies.   I. Title.   II. Series.
   [DNLM: 1. Infertility.   WP 570 S214w 1993]
RC889.S26   1993
618.1′78—dc20
DNLM/DLC
for Library of Congress   92-48536
                                                                                        CIP

For my parents

Contents

Illustrations

Acknowledgments

I have many individuals to thank for their assistance in the creation of this book. I am very grateful to the agencies that have provided me with financial support for my research. The studies described in this book were funded by two grants from the University of North Carolina at Chapel Hill (1987–1988), a grant from Sigma Theta Tau, the International Honor Society of Nursing (1985–1986), and a grant from the National Center for Nursing Research, National Institutes of Health (1988–1993). The award of a William R. Kenan, Jr. Leave (1991–1992) from the University of North Carolina at Chapel Hill gave me the time to write this book.

I gratefully acknowledge, for their intellectual and emotional support, and material assistance in data collection, preparation, and analysis, Beth Perry Black, Carolyn Cooper, Betty G. Harris, Diane Holditch-Davis, Linda Corson Jones, D. Geneva Knight, Stacy Miller, and Christine Pollock. I thank the many anonymous reviewers of my previously published papers on infertility and of drafts of this book for their advice and helpful criticism. I am also grateful for the hospitable and stimulating environment provided me at my professional home, the School of Nursing at the University of North Carolina at Chapel Hill.

Finally, I am most indebted to the women and men who consented to tell their stories of infertility.

Permissions

This book contains material that has been previously published by the author:

Compelled to try: The never-enough quality of conceptive technology. *Medical Anthropology Quarterly* 5 (1991), 29–47. By permission of the American Anthropological Association.

Failures of volition: Female agency and infertility in historical perspective.

Signs: Journal of Women in Culture and Society 15 (1990), 475–99. Copyright © 1990 by the University of Chicago. By permission of the University of Chicago Press.

Faultlines: Infertility and imperiled sisterhood. *Feminist Studies* 16, 1 (1990), 33–51. By permission of Feminist Studies, Inc., c/o Women's Studies Program, University of Maryland, College Park, MD 20742.

Without child: The world of infertile women. *Health Care for Women International* 9 (1988), 147–61; Amniocentesis in the context of infertility. *Health Care for Women International* 12 (1991), 167–78 (co-authored with B. G. Harris and D. Holditch-Davis); and Social exchanges of infertile women. *Issues in Mental Health Nursing* 8 (1986), 173–89 (co-authored with L. C. Jones). By permission of Hemisphere Publishing Corporation.

Women's experiences of infertility. *Image: Journal of Nursing Scholarship* 18 (1986), 140–44 (co-authored with C. Pollock); The color gray: Ambiguity and infertility. *Image: Journal of Nursing Scholarship* 19 (1987), 70–74; and Mazing: Infertile couples and the quest for a child. *Image: Journal of Nursing Scholarship* 21 (1989), 220–26 (co-authored with B. G. Harris and D. Holditch-Davis). By permission of Image Publication Office, Sigma Theta Tau International Honor Society of Nursing.

Pregnant moments: The process of conception in infertile couples. *Research in Nursing and Health* 13 (1990), 273–82 (co-authored with B. G. Harris and D. Holditch-Davis). Copyright © 1990. By permission of John Wiley & Sons, Inc.

Living the life: Explanations of infertility. *Sociology of Health and Illness* 12 (1990), 195–215 (co-authored with D. Holditch-Davis and B. G. Harris). By permission of Blackwell Publishers.

"The clock has been ticking, the calendar pages turning, and we are still waiting": Infertile couples' encounter with time in the adoption waiting period. *Qualitative Sociology* 14 (1991), 147–73 (co-authored with B. G. Harris and D. Holditch-Davis). By permission of Human Sciences Press, Inc.

Somewhere out there: Parental claiming in the preadoption waiting period. *Journal of Contemporary Ethnography*, (1993) (co-authored with B. G. Harris and D. Holditch-Davis); and Relinquishing infertility: The work of pregnancy for infertile couples. *Qualitative Health Research*, (1992) (co-authored with B. G. Harris and B. P. Black). Copyright © 1992. By permission of Sage Publications, Inc.

This volume also reprints material from the following sources:

Barbara Eck Menning. *Infertility: A guide for the childless couple*. Englewood Cliffs, NJ: Prentice-Hall, 1977. Copyright © 1977. Reprinted by permission of Prentice-Hall/A Division of Simon & Schuster.

Anna Quindlen. Baby craving. *Life* (1987, June). Copyright © 1987 by Anna Quindlen. Reprinted by permission of the author.

David Rudkin. *Ashes (A Play)*. London: Samuel French, 1974. By permission of Casarotto Ramsay Ltd.

U.S. Congress, Office of Technology Assessment, *Infertility: Medical and social choices,* OTA-BA-358. Springfield, VA: National Technical Information Service, May 1988.

A. H. DeCherney (Ed.). *Reproductive failure*. NY: Churchill Livingstone, 1986.

M. Seibel. *Infertility: A comprehensive text*. Norwalk, CT: Appleton and Lange, 1990.

S. Maitland. *Daughters of Jerusalem*. London: Blond & Briggs, 1978.

1. With Child in Mind

> Stephen is the child I have been attempting to conceive for the past
> seventeen years. Stephen is why Toby and I are involved in the IVF
> program. . . . [But] Stephen is one of the most deformed babies you
> will ever hear about. He has a handicap. He has no body . . . Stephen is
> waiting inside my mind. (Bainbridge, 1982, p. 120)

This book is about people "with child in mind" (Bainbridge, 1982): couples
who want to have children but who cannot ever, or cannot without special
effort, conceive them. It is about people with infertility—people who
encounter this circumstance as a fact of life or as an impediment to their
goals—and infertile people—people who come to define themselves almost wholly by virtue of their encounter with this event.[1] In the book, I
synthesize what I have come to know about the personal experience of
infertility after seven years of formal study with infertile women and couples. I represent their personal stories of infertility—as one infertile man
put it, "the drama of it all [and] the trauma of it all"—with only as much of
the trappings of science and metaphor (Sontag, 1979) as will illuminate, as
opposed to distort or encumber, their experiences. I have tried to produce a
work that is "representative of [the] me" (Viney and Bousfield, 1991, p. 757)
of the people whose stories were my primary sources of information; I
aimed for meaningful as opposed to statistical representativeness.

In the 1980s, infertility emerged as a "rallying point" for concerns and
even as a "rhetorical vehicle" (Brandt, 1987, p. 6) in debates about the limits
of reproductive freedom, the implications of fully planned "brave new
babies" (Andrews, 1989) and artificially made families, and the "transgres-
sive potential implicit in the very existence of [the] reproductive technologies" (Franklin, 1990, p. 226) that promised this freedom and produced
these babies. Yet, in much of the ever-expanding popular and scholarly
literature on the actualities and potentialities of new advances in reproductive technology and of new parenting partnerships, infertile people have
remained strangely unrepresented and even misrepresented: they are often
not allowed a "place in [the] discourses . . . essential to action and the right

to have one's part matter" (Heilbrun, 1988, p. 18). Indeed, some critics of reproductive technology have come very close to asserting that the views and interests of infertile couples ought not to influence health policy regarding this technology (Koch, 1990).

Rediscovering the individual and, more significantly, the "universal singular" (Denzin, 1989, p. 19), researchers and clinicians in a variety of disciplines, especially those involved in a category of inquiry often labeled qualitative, have recently reemphasized the need to privilege the narrative efforts of their subjects and patients: to return the "suffering, afflicted, fighting human subject[s]" to the center of consideration and inquiry where they rightfully belong (Sacks, 1987, p. viii). This new narrative focus in scholarship is part of a larger turn in the social and behavioral sciences toward interpretive methods and away from conventional research strategies that fail adequately to represent personal meaning and the varieties of reality (Guba, 1990; Lincoln and Guba, 1985; Sandelowski, 1991). Narrative knowing (Polkinghorne, 1988) is an essentially biographical and historical form of inquiry that involves capturing people in flux and life events in context. The narrative understanding embedded in most qualitative approaches "carries the weight of context" (Murray, 1989, p. 178) and thereby provides an important corrective to typical context-stripping and reductionistic approaches to human science inquiry that emphasize the measurement of variables instead of the creation of portraits and stories. In qualitative inquiry as a whole, so-called anecdotal data is prized, not disparaged.

Within a narrative framework, research participants are viewed as storytellers who establish and maintain a sense of order in their lives by continually reconstructing life events in the stories they tell about them. These stories constitute the life-as-told and are the researcher's closest access to a life-as-experienced (Bruner, 1984). Moreover, life events are not assumed to have stable objective traits automatically defining their meaning or determining their impact (a factor that may explain, in part, why conventional quantitative approaches to the psychosocial study of infertility often fail to yield meaningful, even if statistically significant, results). Instead, the meaning and impact of an event are presumed to vary over the life of the individual and over the course of history.

What a life event such as infertility signifies to any one person may change depending on the age and developmental stage of the person affected and the biological/historical moment in which it is experienced. A life event derives its meaning and exerts its influence in interaction with other events occurring in the affected person's life and social network. Riessman (1989,

p. 749) suggested that what on the surface appears to be the same "objective" life event may really be different "phenomenological" events.

With the emphasis on advancing a scientific theory, or a professional, political, legal, or moral agenda, infertile people themselves have remained either storyless, or, more typically, trapped in the wrong story—typified, for example, as selfish, desperate, damaged, or easily duped. These depictions often fail to take into account, fully or at all, the heterogeneity of the personal experience of infertility and the extent to which it is shaped by cultural norms and in social interaction. Infertility, medical therapy, and adoption are problematic for infertile people in large part because they are problematic in American culture. In his autobiographical account of disability, anthropologist Robert F. Murphy (1990) observed that there were lessons to be learned from the experience of paralysis about the conflict between the individual and culture. I believe that personal encounters with infertility, like the individual's response to paralysis, also provide a "splendid arena for viewing this struggle of the individual against society" (p. 5).

The struggles of the infertile people in my studies reprise larger themes in Western culture: the tendencies to view as opposite and conflicting the natural and the artificial, the biological and the technological, and to value one over the other. The infertile people described here sought and succeeded (more or less) to reconcile these cultural oppositions. Through their encounters with and experiences of the paradox and "liminality" of artificial conception and artificial family, they often concluded that " 'artificiality' is part of the 'natural' condition of the world," not separate from it (Channell, 1991, p. 151).

As I hope will be evident in this book, infertile people contended with being both inside and outside the cultural norm, wanting to have children but being unable to have them. In their marginal condition, they both incorporated normative "cultural stories" of infertility, technology, and adoption and resisted them by creating "collective stories" of their own (Richardson, 1990). As one adoptive father put it with some exasperation, "Everybody's got a tale." What the women and men who are described in this book wanted was to tell their own tale.

Method

This book is based on my extensive reading of both popular and scholarly (contemporary and historical) literature on infertility, reproductive technology, and adoption. Among the archival materials I used are case files, housed at the New York Academy of Medicine, that belonged to Isidor Rubin, an important physician in the field of infertility between the 1920s and 1950s. Rubin left behind six tightly packed drawers of alphabetized but otherwise uncataloged files of women he treated for sterility in the 1920s and 1930s.

In addition, I also read a set of uncataloged personal letters that are part of the John Rock collection housed at Harvard University's Countway Library. Included in this collection are over one hundred sets (including replies) of letters written between 1943 and 1957 primarily by infertile women to John Rock and Miriam Menkin, his associate at the Free Hospital for Women in Brookline, Massachusetts. These physicians were key figures in the development of reproductive technology. Also included in this correspondence are letters from sterile men, other physicians providing case reports, one would-be grandfather, one woman offering to be a surrogate, and one man offering to become a sperm donor. The letters, from all over the United States, and from Canada, France, Australia, and Mexico, were largely written in response to articles in newspapers and popular magazines (*Your Health, Science Digest, Look, Time, Newsweek, Coronet,* and *Collier's*) that heralded medical progress and promised "test-tube" and other solutions to infertility.

The primary sources of information for this book come from two studies I conducted with infertile people. The first was a study of infertile women still struggling to have children; the second was a study of infertile couples making the transition to parenthood. These studies were designed to elicit women's and couples' narrative accounts of infertility.

Between January of 1985 and May of 1986, my colleague Christine Pollock and I interviewed forty-eight women who perceived themselves as being or having been infertile. This first study was conducted within a methodological framework of phenomenology that emphasizes understanding the necessary and sufficient elements of experience as it is lived (Van Kaam, 1959). Twenty-six women (all white) from private physician practices and twenty-two women (all but two of whom were black) from an infertility clinic serving primarily the medically indigent participated in this study, which remains distinctive among studies of infertility for its inclusion of a nonwhite and non–middle income group. More detailed information about this study is located in the Appendix.

In 1987, my colleagues Diane Holditch-Davis and Betty Harris and I began a research program to study the transition to parenthood of infertile couples, or the pregnancy, preadoption, and early parenting experiences of couples with fertility impairments. This second study was stimulated by the experiences of the women in the previously described study who achieved pregnancy, and it remains among the very few studies to include groups of normally fertile, infertile, and adopting groups and to explore infertility and its aftermath in depth and over time. The Transition to Parenthood (TTP) project was a longitudinal field study that drew from tenets of naturalistic research (Lincoln and Guba, 1985) in which techniques generic to and compatible with grounded theory were employed (Charmaz, 1983; Corbin and Strauss, 1990). Ninety-four couples awaiting a child had participated in this project by the time this book was completed. More detailed information on this study is located in the Appendix.

Organization of the Book

The documentary and literary sources I used form the basis for Chapters 2 to 4 of this book, in which I interpret the biocultural and sociohistorical context for the personal encounter with infertility. Chapters 5 to 13 are devoted to retelling the stories told to me and my research colleagues in the course of the two studies previously described. The presence of the women and couples interviewed prevails in these chapters, but mine is also clearly evident in the interpretive context and the mode of presentation I chose to frame their words and reframe their stories. In general, I arranged the chapters to capture what I interpreted to be key elements of experience and to reprise, in the words of several couples, the special and strange "journey" the study participants took from their first encounter with infertility to its resolution in adoption and childbearing.[2]

In the last chapter, I draw from these women's and couples' descriptions and from (primarily) nursing literature on care to interpret the dilemmas involved in infertility practice and to propose a philosophical framework for care. In contrast to the growing literature emphasizing the larger and future social consequences of solutions to infertility, I emphasize the less often considered present and everyday encounter between the individual practitioner and the patient/client in infertility practice.

Finally, I have been influenced in all of my choices by the fact that I am a nurse with a nurse's commitment to care, a researcher with a researcher's responsibility to add to a body of knowledge, and a writer with a writer's desire to produce an aesthetically pleasing work. Whether I succeed or fail in this book will likely derive from what may very well be obligations and desires in conflict: to maintain a fellow-feeling for others, to tell the truth, and to make the subjects of research the heroes of their own stories.

Notes

1. For the sake of simplicity, I use the term infertile most often as an adjective modifying woman, man, couple, or parent, but I do not intend to define them exclusively by this term.

2. Living childfree after infertility is also a resolution, but because of the purposes of the studies to be described, we did not deliberately seek such individuals. By the end of the first study, however, one woman had decided to remain without children.

2. In Search of Infertility

> Once upon a time, there was a man and a woman. They met, fell in love and married. And very soon they decided to have a family. They made love, and within a year, their first child was born. That one was very soon followed by others. And they lived happily ever after. This is a fairy tale. For millions of people in America in 1987, it is as patently fantastic as Sleeping Beauty. (Quindlen, 1987, p. 23)

Infertility became newsworthy in the 1980s; it was soon the subject of a growing number of medical and academic publications and conferences, popular books and articles, television news features, and autobiographical and fictional accounts. Although there is no period in human history where fertility has not been a concern (DeCherney and Harris, 1986; Sha, 1990), and despite the fact that the overall prevalence of infertility in the United States has remained fairly stable for nearly a century (estimates in any one time period varying from 10 to 20 percent) (Cutright and Shorter, 1979; Mosher and Pratt, 1990; Shorter, 1980, 1982; Tolnay and Guest, 1982), infertility came to be viewed in the last decade as an American public health problem of epidemic proportions. One infertility specialist (Bellina and Wilson, 1985, p. xv) declared:

> If any other disease showed such an overwhelming surge, the National Institutes of Health would have proclaimed an epidemic and thrown medical centers around the nation into a frenzy of research in a desperate effort to stem the tide.

In a recent *Time* cover story (Elmer-Dewitt, 1991, p. 58), more than one million new patients were reported to have sought treatment for infertility in 1990, "six times as many people as were treated for lung cancer and ten times the number of reported cases of AIDS."

The convergence of several factors accounts for the increasing visibility of and the new urgency about infertility in the United States (Aral and Cates, 1983; Mosher and Pratt, 1990). First, there has been an increase in the number of couples of the large "baby-boom" generation who are experiencing the age effects of postponed childbearing: Among a larger number of couples trying to have children there are a correspondingly larger number of couples discovering that they cannot as fecundity, or the physical capacity to reproduce, declines with age. Delayed and then "condensed" (Aral and Cates, 1983, p. 2329) childbearing (having fewer years in which to have a child) in a large number of couples of childbearing age have, accordingly, created the impression that infertility is proportionately more prevalent now than ever before.

A second factor accounting for the perception that there is an epidemic of infertility is the increasing number of individuals and couples both with and without fertility impairments seeking infertility services. Techniques such as artificial insemination and in vitro fertilization are conceptualized more accurately as services than as therapies, since women without fertility impairments themselves—who have either no reproductive partners or partners with impairments—undergo these procedures, and since these treatments largely circumvent rather than cure impediments to reproduction (Elias and Annas, 1986). Also, normally fertile women donating ova undergo the same hormonal stimulation regimens as women in therapy.

The U.S. Congress Office of Technology Assessment (1988) estimated that the increase in demand for these services has probably surpassed any actual increase in the overall incidence of infertility; the number of physician visits for infertility rose from about 600,000 in 1968 to 1.6 million in 1984. Mosher and Pratt (1991) observed that the advent of new procedures has likely led individual infertile couples to see physicians more often than couples did ten to twenty years ago; growth in the number of visits can, therefore, occur with no change in the numbers of couples affected. In addition, couples delaying childbearing have less time in which to try to have a child on their own and may, therefore, seek services sooner, even before the standard medical definition of infertility can be applied to them: the inability to conceive after one to two years of regular unprotected intercourse.

By some estimates, however, only 31 percent of infertile married couples had ever sought medical services (Hirsch and Mosher, 1987; U.S. Congress, Office of Technology Assessment, 1988). White and upper-income couples are more likely to seek services than their black and less affluent counterparts, and they are more visible as couples likely to have fertility impairments, despite the fact that black couples are actually more likely to be infertile and lower-income couples in need have difficulty obtaining services (Henshaw and Orr, 1987; U.S. Congress, Office of Technology

Assessment, 1988). Infertility is commonly perceived as distinctively associated with upwardly mobile professional couples who are better able to obtain recognition for their problems (Halpern, 1989; Quindlen, 1987; Schroeder, 1988).

Also critical to the rediscovery of infertility and the increasing demand for services is the growing number of physicians specializing in the medical care of infertile couples and the greater availability of and publicity given to developments in reproductive technology, especially in vitro fertilization and embryo transfer techniques. Between 1965 and 1975, the demand for obstetrical services declined with the decline in fertility rates, causing physicians to seek other kinds of patients to treat (Aral and Cates, 1983). Membership in the American Fertility Society increased from about 2,500 in 1965 to 10,000 in 1985 (U.S. Congress, Office of Technology Assessment, 1988). Board certification in reproductive endocrinology/infertility became available to physicians in 1974, with increasing numbers of physicians electing to become certified in this field of practice (Aral and Cates, 1983). In addition, there has been a proliferation of treatment centers in the United States over the last decade and intensive and even sensationalized coverage of the latest advances in conceptive techniques in both medical and lay publications.

The increased demand for medical solutions to infertility is also related to the decline in the numbers of healthy infants available to adopt. Few women with unplanned and/or undesired pregnancies choose to relinquish their babies, electing instead to raise their children or to terminate their pregnancies. The legalization of abortion and the increasing social acceptance of single parenthood have contributed to the declining availability of the babies desired by the couples most likely to adopt. In addition, the adoption process itself has become increasingly complex, time-consuming, and expensive as couples must choose from a variety of adoption options, including private arrangements, adoption of an American child through a private or public agency, and international adoption (Bachrach, 1986; Hostetter and Johnson, 1989).

Finally, a renewed emphasis on familism emerged in the 1980s to contribute to a rediscovery of and new sense of concern about infertility. In combination with the evolution of a social milieu conducive to the public airing of intimate problems, the reemphasis on family and a revitalized "parenthood imperative" (Bram, 1989, p. 276) served to create new anxiety about the ticking biological clock and the consequences for women of delaying childbearing to pursue careers (Pogrebin, 1983).

The perception of an epidemic of infertility has created a social context for childbearing in which middle-class couples, in particular, fear and even anticipate being infertile. Women may now consider themselves (as one woman put it) "preinfertile" just by virtue of having delayed attempts to conceive until their thirties. Clomiphene citrate (Clomid), a drug used to induce ovulation, has become the "Valium of infertility" (Mitchard, 1985), not only because physicians often prescribe it but also because women sometimes demand therapy early in their efforts to have a child and even ask their physicians for prophylactic prescriptions of the drug. Couples may consider themselves as having had what one woman described as "a taste of infertility" if it takes them more than two to three months to conceive. Significantly, there has developed over the last decade an epidemic of anxiety and concern about infertility, even if not an epidemic of infertility itself. Women, just by virtue of waiting to try to have children, may consider themselves not yet infertile. Infertile couples have become "the poster children of the 1980s" (Andrews, 1989, p. 17) and infertility, as suggested by the author of the *Life* cover story quoted at the beginning of this chapter, the impediment to an American fairy tale: to live and love "happily ever after."

A Controversial Entity

For all of the urgency about infertility, it remains an entity that defies simple categorization. Infertility is an ambiguous condition, like other conditions on the "margins" of medical knowledge (Comaroff and Maguire, 1981, p. 115). The very term—*in*fertility—suggests a "fundamentally contradictory system of classification" (Steinberg, 1990, p. 90) designating a medically and socially liminal state of capacity, health, and normality. The line between reproductive capacity and incapacity, between health and disease, and between normality and deviance has always been unclear in the matter of infertility, varying with individual reproductive choices, social circumstances, and cultural norms. For example, women have typically been considered physiologically infertile, or normally incapable of having a child, prior to puberty and with the onset of menopause, but they are considered pathologically infertile, or abnormally incapable of reproduction, if they cannot reproduce in the interval of time between puberty and menopause. In the one case, infertility is an "inability" characteristic of human beings at certain phases of their development; in the other case, infertility is an uncharacteristic developmental "disability" (Clouser, Culver, and Gert, 1981, p. 34).

Women using contraceptives are generally deemed capable of procreation (else why use them?) and only temporarily but normally incapacitated reproductively. A woman may be incapable of having a child with one man, but capable of having a child with another man. The designation *infertile* is typically applied to a couple, a unit of more than one, rather than to single individuals incapable of reproducing, because having a child requires male and female contributions and also because fertility is not culturally recognized as an issue for people outside of a heterosexual partnership.

The relatively recent substitution of the word infertile for sterile or barren reflects a desire to use a less stigmatizing label and also a desire to designate a state of procreative limbo. With the advent of in vitro fertilization and microsurgical techniques and improvements in drug therapy and artificial insemination, the vast majority of couples with fertility problems now maintain the potential for conceiving a child. Even the presumably absolute incapacity to reproduce in voluntarily sterilized individuals can be reversed to potential capacity (Siegler, Hulka, and Peretz, 1985; Silber, 1978). Accordingly, infertility is now not so much a matter of not being able to have a child as it is a condition of not yet achieving or maintaining a viable pregnancy. Importantly, in terms of diagnosis and prognosis infertile couples are neither absolutely capable nor incapable of procreation.

As an in-between condition, infertility occupies a somewhat marginal place in the taxonomy of diseases and is variously defined as (*a*) itself a disease; (*b*) a cause of disease; (*c*) a consequence, symptom, or manifestation of disease; and (*d*) an elective condition involving the failure to achieve a culturally prescribed goal or to satisfy a personal desire. Infertility is all of these things, none of them by itself, and more.

INFERTILITY AS DISEASE

Infertility is a clinical term commonly defining a state of affairs in which a couple fails to conceive a desired child after one year of regular unprotected intercourse. Individuals or couples are clinically infertile if they have never conceived (primary infertility) or if they fail to conceive again after having achieved pregnancy regardless of its outcome (secondary infertility). Couples are also designated as clinically infertile if they suffer repeated pregnancy losses.

Locating infertility in the domain of disease serves to underscore the normative aspects of conditions such as infertility. The cultural mandate to procreate in marriage, the longstanding association of fertility with normal adulthood (particularly womanhood), and the prevalent view that reproduction is part of the natural design of the human species are among the factors that make infertility an undesirable condition, place it outside the boundaries of health and normality (if not wholly inside the domain of disease), and prescribe that infertility be medically or otherwise treated (Brown, 1985). In most cultures, people attempt to reverse infertility (Rosenblatt et al., 1973).

Locating infertility in the domain of disease, defined as a physiological malfunction, also serves to legitimate the claims of infertile couples to a share of the social resources allocated to assist people with other body malfunctions. Couples we interviewed complained that infertility was not viewed as a "serious disease" worthy of the resources people afflicted with other diseases can get, and national efforts by infertile couples are under way to have all medical services for infertility included in health insurance plans. The authors of a memo issued in 1990 by a local North Carolina chapter of RESOLVE (the national lay information and support group for infertile couples) state:

> There is absolutely no question that infertility is a disease as defined by accepted medical and legal practices and that it is a part of the process of having a baby. It is unfair and discriminating to treat infertility as separate from maternity treatments and not as the disease that it truly is. *Infertility is a disease not a condition* and should be covered like other diseases! (italics in original)

For many infertile people, the question whether infertility is perceived as a disease is a matter of more than philosophical interest. Their activism for social reform emphasizes the "strategic use" of disease language (Good, 1977, p. 53) to achieve their goals.

INFERTILITY AS CAUSE OF DISEASE AND SUFFERING
Even where a reluctance may exist to define infertility as a disease "in the classic sense" (Sciarra, 1989, p. 3), infertility is, nevertheless, widely recognized as pathogenic, that is, as causing or contributing to physical incapacity or emotional and psychic distress. When defined in terms of a prolonged period of never being pregnant in the period of life when it is normal and expected that pregnancy will be achieved, infertility is viewed as pathogenic by virtue of increasing or extending individuals' exposure to diseases, infectious agents, and other factors (such as contraceptives and environmental hazards) that can impede reproduction. Endometriosis, for example, is commonly associated with women who delay getting pregnant; pregnancy is assumed both to prevent and to ameliorate the disease. Endometriosis, in turn, is commonly viewed as an impediment to conception.

Interestingly, infertility emerges here as both cause and consequence; when it is perceived as the prolonged absence of pregnancy, infertility becomes a cause of disease that, in turn, may cause infertility, alternatively defined as the inability to reproduce.

Also affirming the pathogenic view of infertility is the spate of literature that has emerged in the 1980s documenting the anxiety, depression, marital tension, and other symptoms of psychiatric disease or mental and emotional distress and psychological strain that infertility can cause or to which it contributes (Berg and Wilson, 1990; Daniluk, 1988; Greil, Porter, and Leitko, 1989; Lalos et al., 1986; Mazure and Greenfeld, 1989; Menning, 1980; Pfeffer and Woollett, 1983; Wright et al., 1989). Although infertility is neither a mortal nor physically crippling condition, to the couple wanting a child it becomes a "part of oneself" causing suffering (Clouser, Culver, and Gert, 1981, p. 31), which, in turn, may require medical, psychological, and/or spiritual treatment. Infertility is a "malady" because it causes pain, disability, and loss of freedom and pleasure (p. 36).

Infertility also causes couples to confront issues of (genetic and generational) continuity and mortality and often to develop the egocentricity and shrunken worldview associated with the chronically ill (Gorovitz, 1982). As I describe further in the next chapters, infertile couples, like the chronically ill and disabled, suffer from the uncertainties of diagnosis and prognosis, social stigma, and perceived failures of self and body; and they confront the need to recast their identities and biographies (Bury, 1982; Charmaz, 1983, 1987; Conrad, 1987; Corbin and Strauss, 1987; Greil, 1991). Infertile couples have been described as "heartsick" (Menning, 1980, p. 313), even if not sick in the conventional sense.

INFERTILITY AS CONSEQUENCE OF DISEASE

In contrast to the view of infertility as a pathogenic agent is the conceptualization of infertility as a consequence, symptom, or manifestation of physical or mental disease. Multiple biomedical paradigms of infertility and the many disease processes presumed to cause it exist. There are endocrinological, genetic, developmental, constitutional, environmental, immunological, and psychosomatic explanations of infertility. These factors, operating alone or in combination, have been identified as causing the anomalies and obstructions in the reproductive tract, endocrinological abnormalities, and other biological aberrations impeding conception and the maintenance of pregnancy. Figures 2.1 and 2.2 illustrate the etiologic pathways to infertility as shown in one medical textbook. These pathways are typically conceived

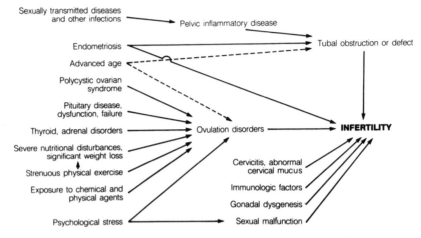

Figure 2.1. Suggested causes of female infertility. (From A. H. DeCherney [Ed.], *Reproductive failure* [New York: Churchill Livingstone, 1986], p. 20. Reprinted with permission.)

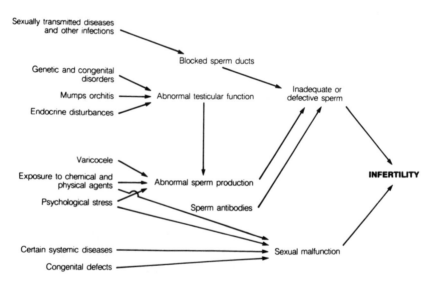

Figure 2.2. Suggested causes of male infertility. (From A. H. DeCherney [Ed.], *Reproductive failure* [New York: Churchill Livingstone, 1986], p. 20. Reprinted with permission.)

in terms of "male," "female," and "couple" factors. In one study (Hull et al., 1985), twenty-three percent of infertile couples had sperm or other male problems contribute to their infertility, forty-one percent had female factors—including ovulatory failure, tubal damage, endometriosis, and cervical mucus problems—contribute to their infertility, five percent had coital problems, and twenty-eight percent of couples had unexplained infertility. Causes of infertility are "suggested" (Berkowitz, 1986, p. 20) or constitute "etiologic interpretations" (Behrman and Patton, 1988, p. 7); they are typically not presented as definitive.

Multiple explanations exist, in turn, for the disease processes believed to cause infertility. Endometriosis, for example, is viewed variously as (*a*) a cancerlike disease, but a benign proliferation and dissemination of endometrial tissue outside the uterus; (*b*) an infection, but a sterile process of inflammation, fibrosis, and adhesions; and (*c*) an autoimmune disorder, with evidence of an abnormal increase of antibodies (Gerbie and Merrill, 1988).

Complicating the etiological profile of infertility is the fact that, in most cases, couples are completely unaware of the presence of any reproductive impairment until they try and then repeatedly fail to conceive. Pelvic inflammatory disease causing tubal obstruction, for example, is often a "silent" process in which symptoms are subtle or nonexistent (Hartford et al., 1987; Rosenfeld et al., 1983). Infertility has not uncommonly been depicted as "masquerading" for hidden but as yet unidentified problems (Sandler, 1968), where causes of infertility remain "unsuspected" and "occult" (Drake et al., 1977; Moghissi and Wallach, 1983). Infertility is, accordingly, a clinical problem where the existence of a disease process is typically inferred from the continued nonoccurrence of an event—conception—rather than from any symptom complex interfering with daily functioning or threatening physical well-being. In many couples, no underlying disease process can be documented at all (Jaffe and Jewelewicz, 1991). Until very recently, such couples were categorized paradoxically as "normally infertile" (Wallach and Moghissi, 1988, p. 799).

When one or more factors contributing to a couple's infertility can be found, they may be neither sufficient nor necessary causes of infertility. Endometriosis, for example, may be the only factor demonstrable as a possible cause of infertility, but many women have the disease with no apparent decline in their childbearing ability (Muse, 1988). In addition, successfully treating a demonstrable cause of infertility frequently does not necessarily treat infertility itself. Clomiphene citrate can induce ovulation in

80 percent of women treated for ovulatory dysfunctions, but only 50 percent of these women will achieve pregnancy (Seibel and Bayer, 1989); of the women who achieved pregnancy with the drug in one study, 22 percent of them suffered a spontaneous abortion (Behrman and Patton, 1988).

With the advent and increasing use of more sophisticated diagnostic procedures, more abnormalities or borderline conditions may be discovered, but their relationship to infertility may remain ambiguous. For example, diagnostic laparoscopy has led to an increase in the reported incidence of endometriosis (Gerbie and Merrill, 1988), but whether this chronic disease is cause or consequence of infertility remains unclear. The same test result may be differently interpreted as indicating normality and pathology, and an organ function once diagnosed as normal (or abnormal) may over time become abnormal (or normal). The evaluation of semen illustrates in particular the significant overlap between normal and abnormal in the matter of fertility and the numerous factors affecting the outcome of test results (Jaffe and Jewelewicz, 1991). Couples have conceived with abnormal semen analyses (Dunphy, Neal, and Cooke, 1989).

Medical tests intended to diagnose fertility impairments may also be therapeutic; medical regimens intended to treat fertility impairments may only be diagnostic. For example, it is not uncommon for women to become pregnant shortly after undergoing a hysterosalpingogram to determine tubal patency (Rozin, 1965). In vitro fertilization techniques, in turn, may be more useful in evaluating the fertilizing capacity of sperm than in producing a pregnancy (Matson, 1990).

In addition, entities that can now be more fully observed or have been discovered by means of new diagnostic technology may neither be causes of a couple's infertility nor abnormal at all. Luteal phase defect, paradoxically the most underdiagnosed and overdiagnosed "paraclinical" (Helman, 1985a, pp. 313–14) condition believed to be a cause of infertility, is a "disease" that may not be a disease at all, but rather a member of a family of dysfolliculogenesis syndromes occurring periodically in all women and more often in some (Blackwell and Steinkampf, 1989). The heightened ability to observe an entity in the diagnostic process may not lead to a correspondingly improved ability to interpret it.

Moreover, infertility is typically treated as a problem of a reproductive partnership or couple, as opposed to an individual, with the ability to procreate varying with the combined fertility index of a given couple at a given moment in time. The location of infertility in a unit of two and the lack of effective treatments for male impairments has led to the rather paradoxical (and controversial) situation of treating women, who may have no impairments themselves, on behalf of the fertility of the couple. Sperm manipulations, intrauterine insemination, and in vitro techniques are increasingly being used to bypass deficiencies in the number and quality of sperm and in the development of therapies for men. Infertility has, accordingly, been construed as a kind of "social disease" arising from the particular union of two individuals (Kass, 1971). Without such a union, there would be no infertility.

In addition to the vast medical literature documenting the immediate physical causes of infertility, there is also an important literature that emerged in the 1940s (to which I refer in more detail in Chapter 3) that emphasizes the "psychogenicity" of infertility (Edelmann and Connolly, 1986; Kipper et al., 1977; Mai, Munday, and Rump, 1972; Noyes and Chapnick, 1964). More recently, a literature has emerged that emphasizes the potentially deleterious impact on fertility of neuroendocrine system–mediated stress (Demyttenaere et al., 1991; Edelmann and Golombok, 1989; Harrison, Callan, and Hennessey, 1987; Harrison, O'Moore, and O'Moore, 1986). In this literature, infertility is a psychosomatic problem, with psychic factors viewed "as pathogens acting upon or expressed in the material body in a patterned way" (Helman, 1985b, p. 3). The biological incapacity to reproduce is, accordingly, viewed as the consequence of an aberrant psychology involving conflicts in sexuality and social roles (Allison, 1979; Andrews, 1970; Benedek et al., 1953; Bos and Cleghorn, 1958; Kamman, 1946; Kelley, 1942; Rommer and Rommer, 1958).

Whether and in what way infertility is cause or consequence of psychological disease or distress continues to be a subject for debate, in part because research on the psychology of infertility remains problematic. First, since infertile people are most accessible to researchers when they are involved in medical regimens, much of our understanding of the psychology of infertility is based on the relatively small numbers of infertile people seeking medical help (Hirsch and Mosher, 1987). Psychological characterizations of infertile people have more often than not been characterizations of the typically white and middle-income couples (and women especially) willing and financially able to undergo medical treatment. Still in considerable doubt is whether the psychological effects of infertility or of the treatment for infertility are being captured in these studies (Pepe and Byrne, 1991).

Second, although the quality of scientific investigations into the psychology of infertility has improved, these investigations are still criticized for being inadequate methodologically, with sample sizes too small for the research designs employed, high subject attrition rates, lack of appropriate comparison or control groups, lack of precision in defining key variables, lack of attention to factors of time, and inappropriate instrumentation (Noyes and Chapnick, 1964; Seibel and Taymor, 1982; Wright et al., 1989).

Third, because researchers have no clear conceptualizations of infertility and of infertile people to guide them in their studies, or else have stereotypical conceptualizations, they have found it difficult theoretically or clinically to interpret their findings. Researchers have discovered that psychological measures designed to detect psychiatric disease may be inappropriate for use with infertile people. Although couples typically experience infertility as one of the most devastating events of their lives, overall no significant differences have been found between fertile and infertile people on various psychological measures of distress and mood (Downey et al., 1989; Fagan et al., 1986; Freeman, Garcia, and Rickels, 1983; Garcia et al., 1985; Paulson et al., 1988). Infertile people typically score within normal limits on these measures and are considered "appropriately reactive" (Mazure and Greenfeld, 1989, p. 253) to the hardships involved in undergoing therapy for infertility. In fact, some researchers have found infertile couples to be very well-adjusted psychologically and even to have better marriages than normally fertile people (Callan and Hennessey, 1989; Cook et al., 1989).

One explanation casting doubt on the "true" normality of infertile couples in these studies is that they repress or deliberately suppress their true personas and real distress to appear normal and socially desirable (Mazure, De L'Aune, and DeCherney, 1988) in order to get or maintain access to medical services. The failure to discern expected differences between infertile and fertile people or to detect expected abnormality is here explained away as a failure in instrumentation or as a kind of failure on the part of infertile people themselves: they dissemble to appear normal. Less often considered are the facts that infertility is a heterogeneous phenomenon capturing a range of experiences and that being infertile by itself may not be a factor that easily distinguishes one individual from another. Importantly, the role of psychological factors as cause or consequence has been an integral component of studies of infertility for the last fifty years, but the dynamics of that role have yet to be clearly delineated.

INFERTILITY AS ELECTIVE CONDITION

Because of the ambiguities of diagnosis and because it can be dismissed as a problem that even without treatment is compatible with good health and life (Kass, 1971), infertility has also been described as an "elective, non-emergent problem" (Schlaff, 1991). Even if it is accepted as a malady, it is one that couples choose by virtue of choosing to try to have a child and, then, by choosing to seek treatment when they discover that they cannot. In an important sense, infertility begins with the desire for, rather than with the inability to have, a child. Unlike entities such as cancer, atherosclerosis, and diabetes, infertility is a condition where the underlying disease process causing it does not necessarily have to be diagnosed or treated for the purposes of life and good health, or even for conception to occur.[1]

This view of infertility as an elective condition is the basis for locating it outside the medical domain as a failure to satisfy a desire (albeit one that is viewed as either biologically innate or culturally prescribed) and as, therefore, not necessarily deserving of the resources allocated to "real" diseases. When physicians treat infertility, they are, accordingly, simply "doctoring desires" rather than curing disease (Ramsey, 1972, p. 1482).

A variation on the elective theme is the idea that women want children and seek medical help to have them largely because they are socialized to do so. In this sense, women's desires and choices are themselves viewed as socially doctored. In some feminist literature critical of Western medicine and reproductive technology (which I discuss in more detail in Chapter 3), for example, infertile women's desire for children and their "desperate" efforts to have them are viewed as socially constructed; women choose to undergo round after round of painful, degrading, often ineffective, and harmful treatments to satisfy a patriarchal mandate (Corea, 1985; Franklin, 1990). Women only "want" children and "want" conceptive technology because they are taught to want them; in addition, women presumably make "patriarchal bargains" when they consent to undergo treatment (Crowe, 1985; Lorber, 1989; Williams, 1990).

Neither women's desires nor their choices are viewed here as authentically their own. Women could choose not to be infertile, or not to suffer from their inability to have biological children, by learning to recognize the oppressiveness of patriarchal constructs that define women according to their fertility status and, then, by choosing not to subject themselves to patriarchal medicine. In effect, women could treat their infertility, not by undergoing medical therapy, but rather by a process of feminist resocialization.

In the elective paradigm, if infertility is a condition often in search of a disease, it is also one that has been denied its categorization as a disease and even its very existence as a real entity. Locating infertility in the domain of desire and choice or emphasizing it as a socially constructed reality may serve to diminish the suffering caused by infertility and to undermine infertile people's claims to sympathy and subsidized health and social services.

A Protean Entity

Infertility is a phenomenon that demonstrates well the vagaries of medical and social classifications of disease, illness, and sickness. The natures of both the disease and the dis-eased continue to remain elusive, as infertility is viewed as both a fixed neutral and natural entity residing in the body and a changing social and historical reality (Good, 1977; Turner, 1987). Infertility is an "illness construct" that has become useful as a device for categorizing symptoms and for organizing experiences that reflects both normative and prescriptive cultural values (Hunt, Browner, and Jordan, 1990; Overall, 1987). Given the many perspectives on infertility, it is likely that there are many infertilities, with infertile individuals differently positioned on multiple dimensions of desire, voluntarism, capacity, and permanence (Toon, 1981).

Whether signifying one condition or many conditions, infertility challenges conventional notions of disease, disability, and illness, frequently inverting and conflating cause and consequence, and diagnosis and treatment; having multiple and ambiguous causes involving major organ systems in the bodies or psychic components in the minds of one or both reproductive partners; and remaining unexplained in a significant number of cases. Although there may be a disease process that is demonstrable, it may be neither necessary nor sufficient as either cause or consequence of infertility. In addition, although infertility may make people (heart)sick, it is often an illness in search of or denied its disease.

Infertility remains mysterious—"a protean pathologic entity of [often] uncertain nature and etiology" (Gerbie and Merrill, 1988, p. 785). The physician charged with the "investigation of the infertile couple" (American Fertility Society, 1991) and with treating infertility has been challenged to be a detective of sorts, an "Ellery Queen" searching for clues and trying to "uncover the culprit" (Buxton and Southam, 1958; White, 1981, p. 38). Figure 2.3 illustrates the various paths physicians may follow in their pursuit of causes.

Indeed, finding the culprit of infertility is a matter of no small import

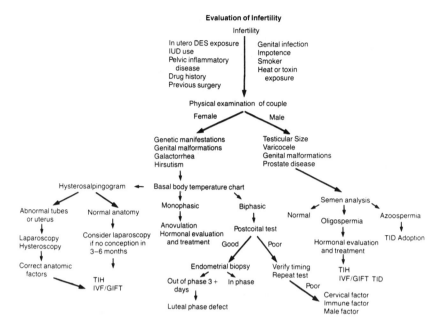

Figure 2.3. Investigation of the infertile couple. (From M. M. Seibel, *Infertility: A comprehensive text* [Norwalk, CT: Appleton and Lange, 1990], p. 1. Reprinted with permission.)

for practice and social policy. How infertility is "framed" (Rosenberg, 1989) determines what social supports, sympathies, and resources are available to infertile people and, even more important, the extent to which infertile people are viewed as deserving of them (Chadwick, 1987; Simons, 1984). American couples experience their infertility within this sometimes contradictory framework of disease, desire, and just deserts.

Note

1. Interestingly, Farquhar (1991) found that in traditional Chinese medicine, an infertile person is considered very sick because infertility is conceptually located at the end of a sequence of increasingly serious problems.

3. Where There Is a Will

Illness expands by means of two hypotheses. The first is that every form of social deviation can be considered an illness. . . . The second is that every illness can be considered psychologically . . . people are encouraged to believe that they get sick because they (unconsciously) want to, and that they can cure themselves by the mobilization of will. . . . These two hypotheses are complementary. As the first seems to relieve guilt, the second reinstates it. (Sontag, 1979, p. 55)

There has been a relatively constant interest in the role of personal responsibility for disease (Knowles, 1977; Reiser, 1985; Rosenkrantz, 1979). The emphases on low-fat diets, regular exercise, the use of seat belts, the perils of substance (tobacco, alcohol, drugs, and food) abuse, and "safe sex" are only the most recent manifestations of the belief that where there is sufficient and appropriately directed will, there is a way for individuals to prevent disease, injury, and premature death.

Although infertility has been characterized primarily as a medical problem subject to diagnosis and treatment, its medicalization has not fully removed the burden of blame or responsibility (Brickman et al., 1982) from infertile couples. In a cultural milieu characterized by the expectation that conception can be prevented, terminated, and initiated at will, and in which individual habits and life-styles have been persistently implicated in the onset of disease, not being able to have a child—even if by default and not by design—is still often viewed as a kind of failure of will. In this chapter, I consider this perceived failure and the persistent tendency to blame couples and especially women for their infertility.

Infertility is recognized and suffered when couples want and try to have a child but cannot, and it is typically depicted as related to certain life-style choices (Clarke, 1991). Several events within human control have been repeatedly identified as causes of impaired fertility. The most frequently cited of these events is the increasing tendency for more socioeconomically advantaged couples, in particular, to postpone childbearing and, thereby, to increase the age-related biological risks of infertility. Delaying childbearing also prolongs the exposure of individuals to contraceptive, occupational, and environmental hazards, increasing the age-specific risk (Aral and Cates, 1983). Other factors often cited implicating infertile couples in causing their infertility are the rise in sexually transmitted diseases, which are particularly associated with early and frequent sexual contact and multiple sexual partners, and certain habits such as over- or under-consumption of food and intensive exercise. In the introduction to the third edition of a well-known medical textbook on infertility, the physician authors emphasized the life-style changes that have contributed to infertility (Behrman and Patton, 1988, p. 1). They observed:

> A different American lifestyle has contributed to the increased number of infertility patients seen by the physician in this decade. Foremost is the change in society's attitude toward sex and marriage. Restraints on sexual intercourse outside of marriage all but disappeared during the late 1970s as use of the birth control pill and intrauterine device became commonplace in teenage women. Legalization of abortion also contributed to this freedom. Coincident with that change was a virtual epidemic of venereal disease, often unrecognized, resulting in increased pelvic inflammatory disease and subsequent tubal sterility. This pattern of sexual freedom, increased pelvic inflammatory disease, and subsequent infertility . . . went unheeded in the United States.

These physicians then cited the changes in marital patterns, including more women in the work force, delayed childbearing, and divorce, that have contributed to infertility and that have challenged physicians to treat women in their forties and to attempt to reverse the effects of voluntary sterilization procedures. They especially singled out the "career woman . . . accustomed to achieving success" but who fails in the reproductive arena. "Not only is she in her late twenties or thirties but she is enmeshed in the stresses of a career that contributes to variations in ovulatory pattern and certainly to her approach to infertility evaluation" (p. 2). Other medical writers have more explicitly linked infertility to "Women's Liberation," which they perceived as having produced "successful PhDs," but also women "desperate" to have a child (White, 1981).

Significantly, the origins of fertility impairments have consistently been linked to personal choices, especially those made by women. Although infertile individuals may not be held responsible for the physical dysfunctions that are the immediate and proximate causes of their inability to procreate, they are often blamed for the personal choices that constitute the ultimate causes of their infertility (Shaver, 1985). Biological dysfunctions may themselves be involuntary, but they are often construed as the result of actions in the voluntary domain.

The physical ability to conceive and carry a child and the desire—as manifested in individual behavior—to have a child, accordingly, constitute the involuntary/voluntary calculus that has distinguished biological failures from "culpable failures of volition" (Rosenberg, 1986, p. 44) as causes of infertility. As Rosenberg observed, the "desire to explain sickness and death in terms of volition—of acts done or left undone—is ancient and powerful" (p. 50), especially when, as in the case of infertility, there is no consensus about the nature and treatment of a disease.

Perverted Volition

Before the middle of the nineteenth century, when the first American book devoted exclusively to (what was then most frequently termed) sterility was published (Gardner, 1856), there were very few English-language books or papers on the subject (McLane and McLane, 1969). Still, as early as 1797 one medical student observed that sterility was omitted as a diagnostic category in then current taxonomies of disease. Suggesting that physicians were not interested in sterility to the extent that they should be, because the inability to have children placed "no lives . . . in danger," he admonished his colleagues to investigate the causes of barrenness with the diligence that the "anxiety of mind" and resulting "evil" associated with "unfruitful marriage" demanded (Walker, 1797, pp. 7–8).

Sterility was viewed not so much as a distinctive diagnostic entity but rather as the result of the leukorrhea, cervical and uterine displacements, menstrual irregularities, bowel and bladder problems, and other medical and gynecological ailments that then plagued both women and their physicians. Frequently appearing in nineteenth-century gynecology texts only in passing, in abbreviated discussions, or in an appendix, sterility was conceptualized as a symptom "only to be reached through the malady causing it" (Atkinson, 1880; Garrigues, 1894, p. 654). If the physician cured this malady, he would also have cured the sterility.

Marital sterility became increasingly important to physicians as a separate diagnostic entity and as a social phenomenon in the latter decades of the nineteenth century. Although mechanical explanations for sterility prevailed (Sims, 1866), the dysfunction provoked continuing disagreements among physicians concerning its cause. Sterility treatments included a variety of cumbersome uterine supporters and pessaries, slow and rapid mechanical dilatation of the cervix, the application of leeches, cervical incisions and amputations, a variety of local and systemic chemical agents, and electrical therapy, all of which caused considerable and protracted mental and physical discomfort (Curtis, 1924; Davis, 1923; Fry, 1888; Hales, 1878; Kay, 1891; McLane and McLane, 1969; Pallen, 1877; Townsend, 1889). One Philadelphia physician (Blackwood, 1878) sarcastically observed that the method for treatment of sterility depended on the "taste," "inclinations," and desire for "gynecological fame" of the physician. He summarized the lack of consensus among physicians about the proper approach to sterility that characterized medical practice (pp. 1–4), noting that

> the variety of causes suggested as productive of sterility . . . the versions, the flexions, the strictures, the irritabilities, the inflammations . . . and the number of operations proposed for the relief of these abnormalities . . . the probing, scarifying, stretching, dilating, incising, cauterizing, and amputating . . . are only equalled by the number and variety of instruments . . . pessaries of every imaginable shape and material . . . which have been invented, modified, and improved upon for the performance of these operations.

Continuing disagreements among physicians about the causes of sterility and the difficulties they encountered in treating their patients allowed new explanations for sterility to appear, explanations that often emphasized human, especially female, agency. Although knowledge existed of sperm deficiencies and of the male role in producing female sterility through transmission of gonorrhea, male sterility was largely equated with impotency, and physicians were reluctant to accept male responsibility, tending to exonerate a man even in cases where only one sperm cell could be shown to be viable (Gardner, 1856; Gross, 1890; Jackson, 1878; Noeggerath, 1876; Peters, 1884; Sims, 1868–1869).

As a social phenomenon, infertility telescoped the concerns of physicians and other social critics about the health of women, the new activism of women, and the relationship of these factors to national growth and prosperity. Women's apparently declining health and its impact on the family and society constituted one of the most important medical, social, and demographic issues of the day (Cassedy, 1986; Gordon, 1977; Reed, 1984). The suggestion of women's as opposed to men's blameworthiness for sterility emerged in the latter decades of the nineteenth century when public attention was directed toward the new educational and occupational aspirations of women and their assertions of independence and claims to political rights and toward the declining birth rate among what many viewed as the most desirable segments of the population.

The idea of female volition as an explanation for sterility entered the

American dialogue at a time when physicians required explanations and an increasing number of women became noticeably disinterested in having large families or in having children at all, willfully preventing conception or impeding the course of an established pregnancy. In addition, aspiring physicians sought to ground medical practice in science and to separate themselves professionally from their many other competitors providing health care services (Ehrenreich and English, 1978). Moreover, a combination of factors related to the profound socioeconomic changes caused by industrialization, urbanization, and modernization contributed to a beginning emphasis on the quality of life rather than on the quantity of children and to the emergence of a new family role for women that empowered them to make decisions about how many children they would have (Hardyment, 1983; Smith, 1979; Zelizer, 1981).

Between 1800 and 1900, the total white fertility rate decreased 50 percent, at least one half of the decline attributable to a reduction of childbearing within marriage. The years between 1870 and 1915 were especially significant because they were characterized partly by increasingly visible differences in the fertility rates of native, white, upper-income women and their poorer, black, and immigrant counterparts, with native white birth rates lagging far behind those of the other groups (Smith, 1979; Van Horn, 1988). Along with the falling white birth rate, elective abortion had become another public reality by mid-century, increasing among married, native, white socioeconomically advantaged women who wanted to delay or to stop further childbearing. The heightened visibility of elective abortion among married women, combined with anxieties about the falling birth rate and concerns about professional status as abortion was increasingly commercialized, led physicians to campaign actively to restrict abortion. Moreover, physicians viewed women's ability to abort themselves or to obtain abortions easily as permitting a dangerous departure from women's prescribed family roles (Mohr, 1978).

Physicians specializing in the diseases of women increasingly viewed gynecologic practice in terms of women's procreative capacities. The success of a socially conscious gynecology, a medical and increasingly surgical domain that located women's health and the welfare of the family and society in the functioning of the female reproductive organs, was founded on the principle that women should be fruitful and multiply and that they should restrict themselves to the roles that God and nature prescribed for them, namely wife and mother. The new veneration of this "true woman" (Welter, 1978), whose maternal nature was biologically and divinely fixed, made the diagnosis and treatment of sterility integral to the medical care of pubertal females and women of childbearing age. Physicians believed that childbearing preserved the true woman, protected her for a time from the physical and emotional ravages of the monthly menstrual cycle, and protected society from decline and extinction (Barker-Benfield, 1977; Green, 1983; Napheys, 1869; Smith-Rosenberg, 1973a, 1973b).

Against the backdrop of alarm over the falling white birth rate and the rising elective abortion rate (miscarriage and stillbirth sometimes also viewed as artificially induced); over the increasingly successful efforts of women to contracept; over the expanding influence of women in the domestic sphere and their increasing forays into the public sphere of higher education, work, and politics; and over the continuing vagaries of sterility diagnosis and treatment, volition became an important explanatory variable in the etiology of sterility. The failure to reproduce at all or in sufficient numbers could more easily be viewed as a consequence of the failure to want to reproduce.

Physicians admitted responsibility for creating many cases of female sterility by poor postpartum obstetric practice and by performing sterilizing procedures to control disease and to regulate what they perceived as some women's aberrant behavior and sexuality. They also regularly argued among themselves about the abuses of such procedures in terms of the life, health, and fecundity of their patients and about the paradoxical practice of curing women's mental and physical dysfunctions by sterilizing them, while at the same time proclaiming biological maternity to be necessary to women's good health (Ashby, 1894; Barker-Benfield, 1977; Longo, 1979).

It was primarily women, however, who stood accused of delaying childbearing and of leading lives and developing habits inimical to procreation. In medical literature, marital sterility was increasingly constructed as a social disease, a disorder of civilization and modern living involving culpable and largely female acts of omission and commission. One Washington gynecologist articulated the role of female volition in the etiology of sterility in what he termed the "habit of sterility, self-caused or physical." The "moral significance of sterility" for him lay in recognizing how men, but especially women, injured themselves by deliberately limiting offspring and engaging in perverted sexual relations. He lamented the use of artifices to limit the number of children born, maintaining that even where the desire existed to have children at some future date, the wilfull induction of temporary sterility often created a "habit," a permanent incapacity that could not be reversed when the desire for children asserted itself. Believing, like most of his medical colleagues, that civilization was harder on women's health than on men's, he advocated a system of education that taught women the importance of maternity. Deriding the efforts of "advanced female thinkers" of the day to expand women's influence in and beyond the home, he complained of the "conjugal onanism" that inevitably resulted from the "restless condition" of modern women who aspired to absolute equality with men. "[This] restless activity, a dissatisfaction with her duties and calling, and a want of reverence for her special vocation, go hand in hand with sterility." Even inherited sterility was for him ultimately a product of human agency because it was closely linked with voluntarily contracted, consanguineous marriages (Bigelow, 1883, pp. 1, 11, 13).

This physician's discussion of the moral or volitional aspects of sterility reflected the very prevalent medical (and other expert male) view that women who reached beyond their appropriate sphere were ultimately to blame for the sterility that constituted such a tragedy to themselves, their families, and to society. A recurring theme in medical and other prescriptive literature on women's health was that too much of the wrong kind of education, as well as the ambitions of women, perverted their biological destiny. Although most women might eventually want to become mothers, their involvement in intellectual pursuits that diverted energy away from the reproductive organs to the brain would lead to conditions that lowered fertility (Haller and Haller, 1974). Medical and other experts on women's progress focused on intellectual rather than on physical labor as the cause of sterility, since their concern was almost exclusively for the declining birth rates in the classes of women most likely to pursue intellectual careers, namely, upper-income women. Despite the fact that the incidence of sterility was at least as great in the poorer classes and among those engaged in strenuous physical labor, physicians legitimated their concern about the dysfunction in upper-income white women by theorizing that physical labor and poverty were favorable to fertility and that indolence and wealth were associated with decreased fertility (Bedford, 1855; Campbell, 1888; Taylor, 1871). A popular treatise on women's diseases summarized the "depreciating habits of civilized life" that predisposed the "civilized" woman, in contrast to the "North American squaw" and the "southern negress," to sterility. These habits, almost wholly in the domain of female agency, included neglect of proper nutrition and outdoor exercise, brain fatigue, improprieties of dress, imprudence during menstruation, and the prevention or termination of pregnancy (Thomas, 1891).

At the beginning of the twentieth century and throughout the Depression era, when fertility rates reached their lowest levels and childlessness rates reached their highest levels, the role of volition in the etiology of sterility continued to be an important feature in the discussions of physicians and other social experts of the dysfunction. Nativist fears of "race suicide" and of what was viewed as the unchecked fertility of the poorer classes and immigrants, and a eugenics movement toward racial improvement prevailed in the opening decades of the new century (Gordon, 1977; Grabill, Kiser, and Whelpton, 1958). As experts continued to emphasize the importance of women's maternal role, childless women were caught up in the wave of criticism created by a convergence of fears of racial decline and deterioration and the continuing activism of women inside and outside of the home, evident in the suffrage movement, increasing divorce rates, and the continuing use of birth control. A moral tone for the new century was set in a paper read before the obstetric and gynecologic section of the American Medical Association in 1901, in which a physician argued that barrenness was largely independent of physical causes. He offered as evidence the gynecologic progress that had been made over the same period when sterility had presumably increased to 20 percent of married women. Tying sterility to divorce, criminal abortion, and women's "egotism," and noting the ease of conception even in the most adverse of circumstances, he proclaimed the causes of sterility to be almost wholly "moral" ones (Engelmann, 1901).

Although physicians concerned about the relationship between women's health and autonomy allowed for the possibility that sterility was not always a matter of choice—that the will to reproduce could exist along with the inability to reproduce—and that male deficiencies of the body or will played a role in causation, many directed their enmity at women, who "under the banner of individualism [were] destroying the machinery of society" (Popenoe, 1926). Using the calculus of ability and desire, socially conscious physicians and other experts warned that if women refused to breed, or succeeded in making breeding a physical impossibility, the end of the race was near. The author of a frequently cited study of 1,000 women in the 1926–27 edition of *Who's Who in America* worried that almost one half of the married women listed there had no children (Cope, 1928). Physicians continued to warn of the "abuse of self in earlier life" (Hoffman, 1916) that caused so much sterility, the alarming number of women trying to prevent conception and to destroy fetuses, and the "industrial conditions" and "social customs" that weakened women (Davis, 1923). One physician opined that life, for both women and men, was no longer governed by "physiological certainty," but rather by social factors impeding maternity that threatened "the very foundation and stability of our country" (Gregg, 1905, pp. 61–62).

Medical experts pointed to the preventable causes of sterility and the human agency involved in the breaking of hygiene laws (Macomber, 1924; Meaker, 1927). In the 1931 edition of *Sterility and Conception,* the physician author reiterated all of the nineteenth-century professional complaints against modern women who transgressed the laws of nature. In a particularly vitriolic attack against American women, he declared them "ultimately responsible" for the perceived American population crisis, saying that they ought to play the exacting role in life their reproductive powers demanded of them (Child, 1931, pp. 12–13). Other physicians well known in the field of sterility noted the susceptibility of the female reproductive organs to damage, a fact of nature and of civilization that placed a greater burden on women than on men to maintain the will and the ability to reproduce (Meaker, 1934). Isidor Rubin, one of the most important and respected clinicians in the area of sterility between the 1920s and the 1950s, commented on the "conspicuous infertility" of women who vied for industrial jobs and executive positions (Rubin, 1954, p. 331).

Some physicians explicitly linked voluntary with involuntary sterility. The author of an influential text on sterility remarked on the "steady stream of emergence from willful childlessness to involuntary sterility" (Berkow, 1937, p. 21). An editorial in the *Journal of Contraception* documented the continuing controversy concerning the percentage of truly involuntary sterile marriages ("Childlessness," 1939). By mid-century, it was sometimes difficult to distinguish between voluntary and involuntary sterility; the idea that voluntary childlessness caused involuntary childlessness served to make all childlessness suspect as a matter of individual will.

Male Volition

Interestingly, the early twentieth-century campaign against venereal diseases, sparked by the progressive impulse toward social reform, diverted some blame from infertile women. This campaign emphasized women's martyrdom at the hands of infected men who did not know any better or who were afraid of making their sexual indiscretions known to their wives. Physician Prince Albert Morrow, a key figure in the fight against venereal diseases, was horrified at the incidence of sterile marriages attributable to men's sexual activities outside of marriage. Calling these men honest but ignorant, Morrow chastised them for taking advantage of women's infantile and blind devotion to them, and he chastised physicians for colluding with their male patients by keeping what was referred to as "the medical secret" from women (Morrow, 1904, p. 46).

Citing key medical figures in the field, such as Emil Noeggerath and Albert Neisser, Morrow located the cause of many miscarriages, ectopic pregnancies, fetal and infant deaths, and sterilizing postpartal infections in the gonorrhea and syphilis wives contracted from husbands. Urging women to interest themselves in the movement for the prophylaxis of social diseases, Morrow reminded them that the burden of shame, suffering, disease, and death lay on their shoulders. He was particularly concerned with prostitutes' "diseases of vice transplanted to the bed of virtue" (Morrow, 1907, p. 22). Sympathetic to prostitutes whom he believed to be products of men's sexual appetites, Morrow held men responsible for the destruction of the health and lives of women and children. Morrow also deplored the rampant male egotism, double standard, and androcentricity of a society that faulted only childless wives for sterile marriages and only prostitutes for the spread of diseases.

Morrow was among a contingency of physicians who felt compelled to continue reminding their colleagues and society that sterility was largely a result of "incapacity and not of choice" and that it was attributable to the male at least as often as it was to the female (Morrow, 1909, p. 626). These physicians argued that criminal abortion hardly played the role in causing race suicide that venereal diseases played. They noted with concern that in no other branch of medicine were patients subjected to such unnecessary treatment as some women suffering from sterility, and they decried the gynecological practice of blaming women for sterility (Bandler, 1920; Brandt, 1987; Burr, 1906; Gilman, 1910/1980; Gregg, 1905; Moench, 1927; Rongy, 1923; Taylor, 1905).

Although medical ignorance and male pride were cited as continuing problems in the management of marital sterility, seldom were men viewed as deliberately thwarting nature's plan or society's mandate to reproduce, since the power to reproduce and to maintain the integrity of the family had always been vested in women. Physicians tended to depict male volition (their own and that of husbands in general) as the reluctant, unwitting, or benevolently misguided aiding and abetting of marital sterility. Men often appeared as the passive accomplices of their birth-controlling wives. The recognition of the male factor in the etiology of sterility may have diverted responsibility for the dysfunction away from women, but it gave them only a brief respite from blame.

Disguised Volition

The idea of female agency in the etiology of sterility assumed a new and more subtle form beginning in the 1940s with the increasing interest in psychosomatic medicine, in Freudian concepts of disease causation, and in maintaining women's primary allegiance to the home and family (Dunbar, 1954; Hartmann, 1982; Kaledin, 1984; Margolis, 1984; Sandelowski, 1984). The dislocations and necessities of the Depression had caused women to choose childlessness or to delay childbearing, and the need for women to assume occupations left behind by men fighting in World War II had exposed women to life-styles and opportunities that had generally only been available to men. The war itself and a nostalgic desire for tradition and family harmony subsequently created a renewed consensus among all classes about the importance to women, men, and the nation of having children.

Along with the baby boom, which began in the 1940s and reached its peak late in the 1950s, came a pervasive cultural belief in the value of having many children and the concurrent belief in the abnormality of having only one or no children. Despite women's apparent adherence to the renewed pronatalist standard, the zeal with which both professional and popular literature prescribed marriage and motherhood betrayed the concern that these domestic goals were not the only ones attracting women. Medical and psychological experts were particularly worried about the health and social consequences of women choosing not to fulfill properly the maternal role (Hartmann, 1982; May, 1988; Poston and Gotard, 1977; Ryder, 1969; Taeuber, 1971; Ware, 1982).

The moral failures of the previous era were recast as psychological aberrations mandating scientific diagnosis and cure. In the new psychogenicity model of disease causation, infertility was symptom and consequence of a complex psychic chain of events that was hidden even from the infertile themselves. Although the connection between women's intellectual and professional aspirations and achievements and poor health and lowered fertility continued to be made with great urgency in both professional and popular literature, infertility now was also depicted medically as a maladaptive disguise for and defense against the hostility toward or fear of reproducing. Psychic factors involving hostility to men and reproduction were included as causes of the structural organic changes, altered reproductive physiology, and aberrant sexual behavior that reduced the chances of conception (Benedek, 1952; Benedek et al., 1953; Bos and Cleghorn, 1958; Deutsch, 1945/1973; Kelley, 1942).

Freudian interpretations of unconscious processes in the causal chain of infertility equated outcome, the failure to reproduce, with unconscious rather than conscious desire or will. Clinicians, therefore, easily and unerringly proved the presence of unconscious factors by assuming that true desire for children in almost all cases would lead to children, while the true lack of desire would lead to infertility. Freudian interpretations modified the causal chain of infertility by making the desire to reproduce an important determinant of the ability to reproduce and, accordingly, cast doubts on the existence of both accidental pregnancy and involuntary childlessness. If a woman did not get pregnant but claimed a desire for pregnancy, then that served to prove that she had really not wanted to become pregnant at all. Similarly, if a woman did get pregnant but claimed a lack of desire for the pregnancy, then that served to prove that she had really wanted it. Either way, women were theorized as controlling reproductive outcomes. Such interpretations, like the overtly moral ones that preceded them, were especially useful in filling the explanatory void created by the persistence of unexplained or idiopathic infertility, where no organic cause could be found or where conventional medical treatments consistently failed to produce a pregnancy. Such explanations also served to explain phenomena that fascinated clinicians, such as "one-child" sterility and the occurrence of pregnancy after adoption, after psychotherapy, and before a medical treatment program was begun (Fischer, 1953; Hanson and Rock, 1950; Heimann, 1955; Jacobson, 1946; Orr, 1941, Robbins, 1943; Rutherford, Banks, and Lamborn, 1951).

Gynecological literature from the 1940s through the 1960s reflects a concern with what some physicians construed to be the mysteries of the female body and psyche. In fact, gynecology and female psychology were inextricably linked to each other because of the assumption that female will, manifested in hyperfemininity, hypofemininity, or female masculinity, controlled female reproductive capacity (Kroger and Freed, 1951). Some clinicians even attributed intentional action to pathophysiological phenomena such as repeated miscarriages and unfavorable cervical mucus, evidenced by the clinical terms for these events: "habitual" abortion and "hostile" mucus. Virtually no behavior of the infertile woman was free of clinical suspicion.

Even douching could indicate an ambivalence toward conceiving, since an overemphasis on cleanliness and body integrity was deemed incompatible with sharing the body with husband or fetus (Ford et al., 1953; Mandy et al., 1951; Stern, 1955). Infertile women were trapped in a psychological catch-22 situation; both compliance and noncompliance with medical treatments, great desire and equivocal desire for children, and hyperfertility and infertility were all viewed as manifestations of a common ambivalence toward maternity (Gidro-Frank and Gordon, 1956; Mandy et al., 1951; Marbach, 1961; Rutherford, 1965).

The discovery of the role of unconscious female agency in the etiology of infertility led to the reemergence of the issue of the advisability of treating all infertile individuals. Although there is no evidence that physicians withheld any treatment from married childless women, even from those women whom physicians had designated as having induced their own sterility by having abortions (Rubin, 1931, 1947), there are indications that infertility was not necessarily viewed as a disorder that mandated treatment. Earlier in the century when cesarean sections posed great risks to women, some physicians had questioned the morality of treating infertile women with pelvic deformities who were certain to face difficult labors or an increased incidence of pregnancy or infant loss (Polak, 1916). Thirty years later, eugenicist Paul Popenoe (1948) mused that society might do better without the contribution of children by individuals whose inability to reproduce testified to their racial inferiority. In a similar eugenic vein, the editor of the first issue of *Fertility and Sterility* asserted that the purpose of the journal and its medical audience was to "improve the quality" rather than merely to increase the numbers of human beings (Tompkins, 1950, p. 1). A decade later, another physician in a popular book on infertility declared that although the dysfunction could be defined as a sickness, physicians could withhold treatment from infertile couples. Stating that money, marital stability, and eugenic fitness ought to determine who receives treatment, he thanked a "provident nature" for ensuring that certain dysgenic and poor individuals could not reproduce (Hamblen, 1960, p. 11).

In the 1950s and 1960s, the assumption that unconscious failure of volition existed could justify delaying medical treatment until the patient completed psychological and motivational evaluations and treatment. Finding out why and even whether infertile women really wanted to become pregnant assumed some importance. One group of clinicians suggested that infertility might protect vulnerable and sick women against the psychic hazards of maternity. Citing reports of high infertility in schizophrenics, they noted the frequent association between reproductive failure and emotional distress, and the potential dangers of inducing emotionally deprived and impaired women to reproduce through medical treatment (Mandy et al., 1951).

Other writers in the medical and psychological literature observed that assisting the infertile to become parents could thwart nature's wishes, given the high incidence of obstetrical and psychological problems in this group of patients. William Kroger, a key figure in the merging of gynecology and psychiatry, warned that aiding the emotionally immature infertile woman to become fertile could "open up the proverbial hornet's nest" and lead to neurotic children, broken homes, and divorce ("Emotions," 1952, p. 383). In a speech to the American Society for the Study of Sterility, he mused that infertility could be "nature's first line of defense against the union of potentially defective germ plasm" and called the successful treatment of infertility a "hollow triumph" if it led to more emotional pathology ("Sterility and neurotics," 1952, pp. 81–82).

Because of the disguised volition paradigm of this time, the inability to have children was likely an especially painful and stigmatizing experience for women. Living in an intensely pronatalist period characterized by a special cultural "aversion" to childlessness (Taeuber, 1971, p. 217), these women were perceived as a "discarded group of blighted women" (Weinstein, 1948, p. 560) who suffered the opprobrium that was then attached to childlessness. The author of a *Ladies Home Journal* article advised her readers that only a small percentage of childless couples did not want children and sympathized with infertile couples whose friends falsely accused them of the selfishness associated with the deliberately childless (Palmer, 1941). In another article of the period, the woman author whose own infertility was medically unexplained observed that women had "inadvertently freed themselves from the cradle" by demanding "emancipation from the kitchen." Consistent with the new focus by physicians on women's unconscious will in the etiology of infertility, she found that she was able to conceive only after she stopped striving for a career and started leading the domestic life prescribed for women ("We wanted a baby," 1946, pp. 28–29). By mid-century, the idea that the infertile were in some measure to blame for their infertility was pervasive enough to cause some medical experts to assert that, to the contrary, infertile people were no more responsible for their problems than individuals afflicted with other diseases (Buxton and Southam, 1958).

The infertile women who wrote to John Rock, a well-known specialist in infertility whose research on artificial methods of conception was widely publicized in the 1940s and 1950s, revealed the desperation, shame, and ridicule they endured. Begging him to use their bodies in experiments or to find women willing to bear their husbands' children, these women wrote of the frustration, marital conflict, and isolation they experienced because they could not have children. One particularly "bruised and battle-scarred" woman, writing him in 1957, remarked that it was hard to keep living and that she was an "outcast with mothers." Raging over the lack of sympathy and help for the infertile, when they were so easily forthcoming for the "armless, legless, blind or deaf," she asked whether "a city of childless people" might be established "where they can hold their heads as high as anyone."

Despite the methodological problems discovered in the psychological literature on infertility, in particular the tendency to view psychological problems as causes rather than consequences of infertility (Edelmann and Connolly, 1986; Noyes and Chapnick, 1964; Wright et al., 1989), the search for the origin of infertility in unconscious processes remains appealing. A more recent variation of the psychogenicity thesis is evident in the (still unsuccessful) search for the neuroendocrine link between stress and reproductive dysfunctions (Brand, Roos, and Van Der Merwe, 1982; Denber, 1978; Edelmann and Golombok, 1989; Reichlin et al., 1979). Commenting on a critique of the psychological literature, one physician advocated improving the methods used to uncover the emotional causes of infertility and emphasized that because the "patient may not be aware that she has any emotional problems," physicians were "at the mercy of [their patients'] unconscious minds [and] willful withholding" (Rutherford, 1965, pp. 105, 114). Researchers have more recently suggested that where psychological studies fail to uncover emotional problems, the difficulty may lie in the failure of instruments to detect subtle emotional changes or in the tendency for infertile couples to repress or suppress their true emotional status (Mazure, De L'Aune, and DeCherney, 1988; O'Moore et al., 1983; Slade, 1981).

The idea of female volition also persists in the convergence of the themes of perverted and disguised volition. Frequent references in medical and popular texts to new opportunities and sexual freedoms for women have forged the century-old link between women's emancipation, their reproductive capacities, and public welfare. Women continue to be reminded of the basic incompatibility of reproductive freedom and health and of the tragedy they court when they delay having the "multiple pregnancies nature undoubtedly intended" (Green, 1977, p. 331). Contemporary psychological literature continues to blur the distinction between voluntary and involuntary infertility by suggesting that infertile women may not really want to become mothers and may be protected by their infertility from unconscious role conflicts (Allison, 1979; Pawson, 1981; Poston, 1976; Van Hall, 1984). Sterilization "regret" and increasing demands to reverse the effects of tubal ligation procedures suggest the adverse role that personal choice and will can play in creating infertility (Grubbs et al., 1985). Popular literature on "baby craving" and "baby hunger" suggests the consequences to women of thwarting the instinct to reproduce (Davitz, 1984; Quindlen, 1987).

Infertility is now portrayed as the "new bedfellow" of reproductive freedom ("New bedfellows," 1980), the price liberated women and upwardly mobile professional couples pay for prioritizing the establishment of careers, the acquisition of material goods, and the pursuit of sexual pleasure over childbearing (Kosterman, 1987; Quindlen, 1987; Waldorf, 1990; White, 1981). Infertile couples are still viewed as "traitors to mankind" and as "fighting nature" (Bellina and Wilson, 1985, p. xvi). Recent observations of the social milieu of infertile couples reveal the stigmatization and victimization they continue to suffer (Miall, 1986; Simons, 1984). (I discuss the social milieu of infertile people in more detail in Chapter 6.)

Misguided Volition

There has also emerged a new kind of failure of volition attributable to infertile women and couples that is best illustrated in some recent feminist literature on reproductive technology. Some feminists critical of the new conceptive technology and certain surrogacy and adoption arrangements imply "misguided" volition, especially on the part of infertile women—a failure of will associated not with causing infertility but rather with seeking to reverse it through means deemed hazardous to the autonomy and well-being of all women. These hazards include the continuing medicalization and expropriation of women's reproductive functions, the further subordination of women to male control, the fragmentation of motherhood, and the perpetuation of social inequalities regarding access to medical therapy and contemporary adoption and surrogacy contracts (Arditti, Klein, and Minden, 1984; Corea, 1985; Despreaux, 1989; Donchin, 1986; Franklin and McNeil, 1988; Holmes, Hoskins, and Gross, 1981; Rowland, 1987; "Special issue," 1985; Stanworth, 1987).

Because they tend to deny the existence of a maternal instinct or innate drive to procreate, these critics have sometimes been led to conceptualize the infertile woman's desire to reproduce as nothing more than the result of the patriarchal mandate that she reproduce. By locating women's desire for children and for therapies such as in vitro fertilization in the pronatalist imperatives of patriarchal culture, they permit women no authentic desire or choice at all. By suspecting women's motivations for children and their inclinations toward medical therapies, and by depicting them as largely products of the social and gendered construction of choices, some of these critics effectively, even if unintentionally, dismiss and trivialize women's desires (Raymond, 1984; Rothman, 1984). As Petchesky (1980, p. 675) observed, "the fact that individuals themselves do not determine the social framework in which they act does not nullify their choices nor their moral capacity to make them."

In addition, some feminists have recently reemphasized the importance of maternity as the basis for women's empowerment and solidarity, the uniqueness of the maternal-fetal bond, and the mother-child relationship as the prototype of all human relationships. They have also revalorized maternity in their debates about the excessive technologizing of pregnancy and childbirth (Oakley, 1986; Rich, 1977; Rothman, 1989; Ruddick, 1980). Yet, at the same time that childbearing and motherhood have been rediscovered as central to women's lives and advancement, infertile women become suspect for wanting and pursuing these experiences.

Some feminist critics have also juxtaposed the putatively inauthentic desires of the socioeconomically privileged infertile woman who is willing and able to pay for expensive medical therapies and adoption procedures with the real needs of less advantaged fertile and infertile women and women denied access to even minimal health services. The infertile woman, whose independent choice of and informed consent for technological and other solutions to infertility are typically denied in this feminist discourse (Corea, 1985; Rothman, 1984), is also paradoxically portrayed as choosing against other women: the desires of the privileged are seen as satisfied by denying the necessities to the underprivileged. The women denied access to conceptive technology because they are too poor or deemed unfit for parenthood (Somerville, 1982), the profound inequities in the delivery of health care, and the practice of making sterilization more available to the less advantaged than are techniques to enhance fertility have been cited to affirm the dubious morality of the privileged infertile woman's choices (Hubbard, 1985). More recently, the plight of mothers coerced to surrender their babies at birth has been cited as evidence of the affluent infertile couple's loss of "moral bearings" in their anything-goes pursuit of a child (Chesler, 1988, p. 125). Infertile couples are depicted as benefiting from other women's tragedies and as depleting resources that should go to the less favored.

Finally, some feminist critics have placed infertile women in a difficult moral position by enjoining them to serve as moral exemplars of a feminist utopia in which sexism, classism, racism, commodification of babies and of women, lack of regard for children, and other social injustices do not exist (cf. Andrews, 1989). These critics are concerned that infertile women prefer to have healthy children of their own, a desire that is virtually universal among women wanting children. They are concerned that white, infertile women prefer to adopt white children, something that is expected in the natural course of events; that they prefer infants to older children, also a developmental progression in nature; and that they want healthy rather than physically, mentally, or emotionally impaired children, another universal desire. The desire of infertile couples for what most other couples want, expect, and get is called into question and interpreted as racist, eugenic, and selfish. Moreover, the desire of a couple to bear their own child or to adopt a child who could have been their own is deemed irrational, obsessive, and suspect only in infertile couples. Normally fertile couples who desire children neither forego, nor are they expected to forego, having their own children in the interests of adopting children already born and without parents. Importantly, infertile couples are asked to be "more virtuous, more selfless, [and] more liberated" than the vast majority of fertile couples (Lasker and Borg, 1987, p. 190), and better able to handle the constraints against which all human beings make choices.

The concerns of these critics with the well-being of women as a social group and with reproductive technology are well founded and have been insightfully argued. Women have been "erased" in the representation and practice of biomedically assisted conception; the fate of eggs and embryos are more widely discussed than the fate of the women producing them (Steinberg, 1990). Women "wanting children badly" (Williams, 1990) and, therefore, "wanting" techniques such as in vitro fertilization (Crowe, 1985) are vulnerable to exploitation, have been exploited, and deserve protection from that exploitation. Yet such protection remains paternalistic when it is based on the presumption that being infertile means being so desperate or so "over-socialized" (McCormack, 1989, p. 89) as to be deemed incapable of authentic informed consent for medical and other solutions to infertility

(Corea, 1985). As some feminist scholars (Birke, Himmelweit, and Vines, 1990, pp. 18–19) have more recently argued: "Understanding where a need comes from does not remove it. Nor indeed is there any difference in the desire for children from any other in that respect. All needs and desires are socially produced."

By finding infertile women's desire for children and their actions in pursuit of them questionable, some feminist critics have unintentionally placed themselves on the side of those who have historically viewed infertile women's motivations and actions as suspect. Like physicians who use women's desperation (cf. Gerson, 1989; Franklin, 1990) to conceive to legitimate further experimentation on them, feminists use it to demonstrate the extent to which women have been oppressed; both groups misrepresent women's desires for their own ideological purposes. Struggling to ensure the right of women to choose against motherhood, feminists have only recently become aware of women who are not free to opt for motherhood. Indeed, the infertile woman who cannot have a child at will threatens the very idea of reproductive choice. By using the infertile woman to illustrate women's continued subservience to patriarchal agendas and control, some feminist critics have inadvertently aligned themselves with those who have over the past century burdened her with their anxieties about women's proper role. The infertile woman remains caught in the cross fire, perceived as both the creator of and martyr to her childlessness.

4. Magnificent Obsession

> Why is she afflicted with this ghastly disease of optimism, of believing that this time, this month, this chance? (Maitland, 1978/1980, p. 262)

Nothing seems to distinguish the contemporary experience of infertility more than its brave-new-world therapeutics. Indeed, as I suggest in this chapter, for the contemporary infertile couple and for those observing and caring for them "the treatment [has] become the illness" (Peitzman, 1989, p. 28).

The rediscovery of infertility over the past decade has largely been a response to the development and availability of new techniques to assist reproduction. Most of the psychologically oriented literature on infertility has focused on couples undergoing medical regimens. This literature explores mainly such factors as the characteristics of infertile couples (Given, Jones, and McMillen, 1985; Hearn et al., 1987; Mazure and Greenfeld, 1989; Sahaj et al., 1988); the experiences of infertile couples with and adjustment to diagnosis and treatment regimens (Berg and Wilson, 1991; Leiblum, Kemmann, and Lane, 1987; Lorber and Greenfeld, 1990; Reading, Chang, and Kerin, 1989; Takefman et al., 1990); the logic of their treatment choices (Callan et al., 1988; Johnston, Shaw, and Bird, 1987); and the personal and social consequences of undergoing medical protocols for infertility (Baram et al., 1988; Freeman et al., 1987; Greenfeld, Diamond, and DeCherney, 1988; Klein and Rowland, 1989; Leiblum et al., 1987; Lorber, 1989; Scritchfield, 1989).[1]

In vitro fertilization, in particular, has become both artifact and symbol of infertility. There has been a proliferation of treatment centers in the United States (Aral and Cates, 1983; U.S. Congress, Office of Technology Assessment, 1988), especially those offering in vitro techniques. The United States IVF-ET (in vitro fertilization and embryo transfer) Registry's membership alone in 1990 included 207 clinics in forty-two states, Puerto Rico, and the District of Columbia, representing approximately a four- to fivefold increase in five years (Medical Research International, 1992).

Although in vitro fertilization is being offered to couples earlier in their treatment careers than ever before, it is still dramatically depicted as an "end-stage treatment" (Plough, 1981), as a "last-ditch" (Johnston et al., 1985, p. 502) "end-of-the-road" (Dennerstein and Morse, 1985, p. 835) attempt to have a "last-chance" baby (Modell, 1989). Cast as the eleventh-hour technological solution to infertility, in vitro fertilization seems to telescope the best and the worst features of contemporary solutions to infertility, including the high physical, psychic, and financial costs of medical therapy, the enormous responsibility placed on couples themselves to get pregnant, and the high hopes and high failure rates of modern treatments. As the product of the newest and most sensationalized means to reverse infertility, the test-tube baby is the iconic representation of the adversity and hope embodied in the contemporary experience of infertility. Couples undergoing in vitro fertilization have become the paradigmatic infertility patients; they are characterized alternatively as obsessed with achieving pregnancy and as "brave" (Jones and Jones, 1991) in their willingness to persist in treatment.

The primacy of therapy over disease is aided by the extensive medical and media coverage given to new and improved techniques that promise a biological child to virtually any couple. A recent cover story in *Time* (Elmer-Dewitt, 1991) heralded (alongside a picture of a fetus sucking its thumb) the "dazzling array of medical breakthroughs [for] curing infertility." The June 1987 cover of *Life* shows the exquisite infant who holds the title as the "world's first 'host womb' baby." Popular representations of contemporary therapy for infertility typically include the promise that "infertility can often be overcome," that doctors now have a "solution for almost every physical problem," and that if a couple "is prepared to try" the techniques available, they have an "80 percent chance of a successful pregnancy within eighteen months" (Angier, 1990).

Despite all of the publicity given to new treatment opportunities, however, whether couples today have any greater chance of having a biological child than their counterparts had twenty years ago before the advent of the "new era" in reproductive technology remains a matter for much debate (Seibel and Levin, 1987). Contemporary infertility therapeutics include (*a*) pharmacological and surgical techniques to eradicate or remedy the dysfunctions believed to be impeding conception or gestation; (*b*) hormonal drugs to stimulate, augment, or control the timing of reproductive events; and (*c*) noncoital procedures to bypass reproductive dysfunctions that cannot be treated or even diagnosed. Most of these treatments—upgrades of old ones as well as new advances—palliate or circumvent reproductive impairments rather than cure them. Moreover, treatment for infertility is frequently empirical as opposed to specifically targeted on a clearly identified cause of infertility, unambiguous causes often hard to determine and fashions in therapy likely to prevail (Sciarra, 1989). Determining the effectiveness of individual therapies for infertility remains problematical for scientific investigators because of the difficulty in conducting randomized controlled experiments, because of the multiple factors involved in any one couple's infertility, and because of the variation and lack of standardization in diagnosis and treatment (Haney, 1987; Leridon and Spira, 1984; Olive, 1986).

The "myth" (Lilford and Dalton, 1987, p. 155) of great medical progress in the treatment of infertility continues to be challenged by the reality that only 50 percent of couples will achieve pregnancy in treatment (U.S. Congress, Office of Technology Assessment, 1988). Medical Research International, the Society for Assisted Reproductive Technology, and the American Fertility Society (1992) reported from outcomes of 175 of the registry's member clinics that the overall live delivery rate achieved with the most publicized and sensationalized of these treatments, in vitro fertilization, was only 14 percent (based on 16,405 retrievals). Ninety-two (53 percent) of these clinics reported less than ten clinical pregnancies.

In contrast, pregnancies occur in the course of treatment that may not be attributable to treatment at all. Pregnancy rates in untreated couples are often similar to those in treated couples (Collins et al., 1983, 1984), and expectant management has been shown to produce pregnancy rates equivalent to medical or surgical intervention (Collins et al., 1983; Schmidt, 1985; Seibel et al., 1982).[2] Some researchers have speculated that in many cases, treatments simply speed up the achievement of pregnancy in "subfertile" couples who in time would have conceived on their own (Fisch et al., 1989). Couples not uncommonly conceive while still in the diagnostic phase before any treatment has begun, a factor suggesting the physically therapeutic value of some diagnostic tests (such as hysterosalpingography, which may remove tubal obstructions) and the psychologically therapeutic value of simply seeking medical help. Couples waiting for in vitro fertilization have been found to conceive at rates similar to those undergoing the procedure (Jarrell et al., 1986; Roh et al., 1987).

Wide discrepancies may exist between the effectiveness of treatments in curing or palliating reproductive dysfunctions and in producing viable pregnancies (Bateman et al., 1992; Holman & Hammond, 1988). Women can be made to ovulate and their fallopian tubes reopened, but they will not necessarily go on to conceive. Moreover, the treatments themselves may cause iatrogenic harm; they are associated with considerable risks to the physical and emotional health of women and couples, including paradoxically the risk of infertility itself (Borenstein et al., 1989; Corea, 1985; Klein and Rowland, 1989).

The frequently minimal chances of benefit and significant risk of harm associated with conceptive techniques have raised questions about the nature of infertility therapeutics—whether they heal or resolve infertility, the morality in offering them, and the meaning of treatment and cure. Whether infertility therapy is therapy at all or is only presented as therapy to "deflect" attention from its still-experimental status or from the need for social reform has yet to be resolved (Caplan, 1990, p. 162; Woliver, 1989). If, as is often asserted, a baby is not necessarily the cure for infertility, infertility "cures" do not necessarily result in a baby, may exacerbate the suffering of infertile couples, and may delay satisfactory closure to the problem of infertility.

New Age and Old World Therapeutics

Modern twentieth-century therapeutics are distinguished from the medical therapeutics of earlier times by a scientific epistemology mandating that the effectiveness of a regimen be evaluated by tests of scientific evidence, rather than by its conformity to a theory, to a preset ritual, or to the demonstration of a physiologic response such as diuresis or catharsis. An agent is defined as effective when it can be shown to alter the natural history of a clinical entity in predictable ways, either by eliminating the primary cause, by replacing some deficient component in the body, or by ameliorating its symptoms (Pellegrino, 1979).

New Age
Infertility therapy can be conceived as both modern and traditional. The in vitro fertilization, embryo transfer, and sperm manipulation techniques available to couples now were in the realm of fantasy and science fiction only twenty years ago. Surgical (including microsurgical and laser) techniques and antibiotics can eliminate primary causes of infertility, drug therapies can replace deficient hormones, and insemination and in vitro fertilization techniques with and without donor gametes can ameliorate the symptoms of infertility by circumventing impediments to conception.

Conceptive techniques have themselves virtually reinvented infertility, transforming it from a condition of deficit to one of potentiality. To be infertile is no longer to be *not*-fertile but rather to be *in*-fertile, a medically liminal state between reproductive capacity and incapacity. Biomedical techniques now exist that permit virtually any couple to have a biological child, or a child genetically and/or gestationally related to one or both of its nurturing parents. While there are fewer truly sterile individuals, or people who have absolutely no opportunity to have a biological child, there are more people with incurable fertility impairments that can be bypassed or circumvented. Couples for whom infertility was once medically prescribed—who were advised not to have children for medical or genetic reasons—now have the opportunity, via gamete donation and surrogate wombs, to have some biological link to a child.

Significantly, infertility has only recently come to mean the potential to have a child of one's own, rather than merely the incapacity to have a child on one's own. With the advent of new conceptive techniques and improvements in older techniques, infertility has been reinvented as an indeterminate condition. The ultimate prognosis concerning any couple's capacity to procreate remains unknown until the technical opportunity to procreate no longer exists. As women in their forties and even fifties increasingly seek infertility services, conceptive techniques have served to expand women's reproductive years by reversing the physiological infertility normally expected in the (peri)menopausal period. Conceptive techniques are, accordingly, altering our perspectives concerning the normality of pregnancy in middle age. Indeed, as suggested in a recent *Time* cover story (Elmer-Dewitt, 1991), there now seems to be no good reason left why a fifty-five-year-old woman should not aspire to or achieve pregnancy. Importantly, so long as there is a medical protocol to try and so long as couples and their physicians agree to keep trying, infertility is, by virtue of its therapeutics, less an incapacity than an ongoing state of being "not yet pregnant" (Greil, 1991), where a couple "can't conceive the simple way," rather than "can't" conceive at all (Waldorf, 1990).

By making infertility a medically liminal category, infertility therapeutics have also made it a socially liminal one as couples live their lives as if they were imminently parents-to-be, making career, housing, and other important life decisions to accommodate yet another attempt at treatment in pursuit of their fantasied baby. The women we interviewed often engaged in luteal-phase activity, behaving as though they were pregnant in case they were pregnant: refraining from smoking, from ingesting caffeinated food and drink, and from strenuous exercise in the second half of their menstrual cycles. With new treatment opportunities, babies may persist in the mind even if they never get to exist in the body (Bainbridge, 1982; Burns, 1987).

OLD WORLD

Yet contemporary infertility therapeutics also recall a premodern era in medical therapy in several ways. Success in therapy is often defined narrowly as the demonstration of a physiological effect, such as the induction of ovulation or of a chemical pregnancy, as opposed to the delivery of a live infant. In fact, there is a concern that infertile couples are being lured into therapy by physiological successes alone, the effectiveness of treatments presented in terms of chemical and clinical pregnancy rates instead of take-home baby rates (Blackwell et al., 1987, p. 738; Jones et al., 1983; Soules, 1985). In addition, modern superovulation techniques recall the "heroic stimulative" therapies of the nineteenth century (Warner, 1986, p. 9). Women are subjected to massive and cyclic doses of hormonal agents to hyperstimulate their ovaries to induce ovulation and in preparation for artificial insemination, in vitro fertilization techniques, and ovum donation. There is also a ritualistic character to medical regimens as couples undergo repeatedly the "rites" (Pfeffer and Woollett, 1983, p. 8) of infertility. Such "rituals of misfortune" (Helman, 1984) or of "adversity" (Murphy et al., 1988), associated with liminal conditions such as infertility, serve to defuse anxiety (if not to reverse infertility) by allowing couples and physicians to take control of a situation often out of human control.

The Therapeutic Imperative

These rituals have become the subject of critical scrutiny as couples and their caregivers find it difficult to determine when enough is enough in the pursuit of pregnancy. Infertile couples have been described as driven (Olshansky, 1988) in the pursuit of pregnancy, as feeling that they have no choice but to undergo certain treatments (Frank, 1989), and even as "addicted" to treatment (Greil and Porter, 1988). Many couples believe that they can beat the odds against their achieving pregnancy and are, accordingly, willing to endure the considerable mental and physical anguish associated with treatment and even, after terminating it, to return for medical assistance when new treatment modalities are developed (Callan and Hennessey, 1988; Freeman et al., 1987; Halpern, 1989; Johnston, Shaw, and Bird, 1987; Leiblum et al., 1987; Modell, 1989).

Infertile couples who persist in treatment for years without success have been described as obsessed, but they have also been described as more highly motivated, determined, and adventurous than their counterparts who "give up" (Waldorf, 1990). They are not sick with their addiction, but rather they are hero-adventurers: pioneers on the frontiers of reproductive medicine. One group of clinicians (Given, Jones, and McMillen, 1985) found that certain personality characteristics—achievement motivation, ambition, and innovativeness—were associated with couples participating in in vitro fertilization programs.

The ritualistic character of infertility therapeutics and the impetus to persist in treatment against considerable odds derive from a therapeutic imperative incorporating mandates from culture, technology, and nature. Perceiving technology as a subsystem of culture, Lechtman and Steinberg (1979, p. 139) proposed that technologies express cultural preoccupations through the "very style of the technology itself." An understanding of technology requires distinguishing between its deterministic aspects (the inherent properties or characteristics of a particular technology that are inescapable and independent of a specific cultural environment) and the deterministic aspects of culture that shape technology. Comprehending the strong therapeutic imperative in the resolution of infertility, accordingly, requires not only an appreciation of the distinctive ways that technology, culture, and nature interact in infertility therapeutics but also a consideration of the properties of conceptive technology that themselves favor repetitive use.

The Mandate from Culture

In literature critical of the conceptive technology comprising modern infertility therapeutics, this technology has typically been viewed from the outside as a material and social manifestation of the premium placed on genetic kinship and on women bearing children and of a general and, sometimes, misplaced faith in physicians and medical technology to resolve a wide range of problems, including ones that are not clearly in the medical domain. These cultural forces push couples and physicians toward technological solutions to infertility.

Feminist critics of conceptive technology, in particular, have emphasized the social determination of infertility therapeutics by espousing a view of it as drawing from and preserving certain arrangements of power and authority (Winner, 1985). For these critics, medical therapies for infertility are the logical culmination of male efforts to regulate women's sexuality, expropriate their reproductive labors, and disrupt female reproductive continuity by fragmenting the experience of maternity. By permitting three different women to be (genetic, gestational, and nurturing) mothers to the same child, conceptive techniques have made women's claims to motherhood potentially as tenuous as men's to fatherhood. Contemporary infertility therapeutics reinforce the cultural emphasis on the importance of having a biological child and the link between normal womanhood and maternity. These therapeutics continue the practice of having women bear the physical and psychic burdens of reproduction by treating primarily women for infertility even when their male partners have the impairments impeding conception. In fact, linguistically representing infertility as a couple's problem is an example of the "rhetoric of equivalence" (Steinberg, 1990, p. 92) that masks the unequal burdens carried by women and men in an infertile partnership. These critics have argued insightfully that the virtually irresistible, even coercive nature of this technology derives from the pronatalist and patriarchal imperatives that have shaped its development, deployment, and use. Conceptive technology offers something to infertile women they cannot afford to refuse (Arditti, Klein, and Minden, 1984; Beck-Gernsheim, 1989; Birke, Himmelweit, and Vines, 1990; Corea, 1985; Donchin, 1986; Franklin and McNeil, 1988; Lorber, 1987; McNeil, Varcoe, and Yearley, 1990; Overall, 1989; Rodin and Collins, 1991; Rothman, 1984; Rowland, 1987; Spallone and Steinberg, 1987; Stanworth, 1987).

Similarly, male physicians are also conceived of as drawn to this technology because it allows them access to something that has always been "closed to men" (Selzer, 1982, p. 155): a greater and more intimate role in reproduction. Conceptive technology continues the heroic, interventionist stance associated with Western physicians and reemphasizes therapy, as opposed to preventive and other nontechnological efforts, as the solution to infertility. Moreover, modern infertility therapeutics created a financially lucrative new practice area and a new source of patients and prestige at a time when obstetrician-gynecologists had to deal with falling birth rates, multiple challenges to their expertise in the care of women, and the encroachments of other caregivers into the domain of gynecological practice (Summey and Hurst, 1986). One prominent physician recently described infertility as a "growth industry" (Haney, 1989). Conceptive technology, accordingly, offers something to physicians they cannot refuse, given the historical propensity for institutionalized medicine to maintain its hegemony in health care.

THE MANDATE FROM TECHNOLOGY

Conceptive technology also can be viewed from the inside as having its own pull, apart from any pronatalist or patriarchal imperatives. Bush (1983) proposed that technologies have "valences," or tendencies to "interact in similar situations in identifiable and predictable ways" (p. 155). Citing the work of Jacques Ellul, she suggested that technologies are not neutrally charged but rather "pull or push behavior in definable ways" (p. 155). To maim or kill, for example, the gun requires a shooter, but the gun by its presence alone raises the level of violence in a situation.

Like the gun, conceptive technology requires human beings to determine and achieve its purposes, but this technology also has an inherent quality of "never-enoughness." This never-enough quality contributes to the often problematic conflation of quality of treatment with quantity of treatment: the equating of good therapy with enough therapy. This confusion of the good with the sufficient contributes, in turn, to the "compelling" (DeZoeten, Tymstra, and Alberda, 1987, p. 624) nature of infertility therapeutics and to the dilemma of deciding when to terminate treatment.

Significantly, the techniques that constitute infertility therapeutics work in ways that compel their repetitive use. Having a life and style of its own (Cowan, 1983; Lechtman and Steinberg, 1979), conceptive technology is charged or "valenced" (Bush, 1983, p. 155) toward repetition, utilizing procedures such as the pharmacological induction of ovulation, artificial insemination, and in vitro fertilization that are "continuing" rather than "one-time" therapies, such as the surgical correction of a tubal impairment (Talbert, 1985, p. 11). Although best current estimates of the effectiveness of continuing therapies for infertility suggest that most pregnancies will be achieved in three to six cycles of treatment, pregnancies may also occur after twenty or more cycles (Behrman, Kistner, and Patton, 1988).

This continuing aspect of infertility therapeutics reprises the natural process of getting pregnant. Few couples conceive a child after trying only one time; both natural and assisted conception demand that couples start and keep trying until they achieve success. Whether on their own or with medical assistance, trying has become for couples who expect to plan and control their reproductive lives an integral and even a culturally naturalized component of getting pregnant (Modell, 1989). Just waiting for conception to happen or not trying may thus appear unnatural, especially in the face of an American antagonism toward wasting time (Dossey, 1982) and an assumption that any goal can be achieved and any obstacle overcome with enough effort (Kaufman, 1988).

Indeed, a distinctive feature of the contemporary experience of infertility engendered by the continuing therapies now available to assist conception is the obligation to keep trying. Infertile couples may now suffer the opprobrium of failure not just because they fail to reproduce but also because they fail to try enough (Beck-Gernsheim, 1989). American couples with the financial means and the medical, psychological, and social profile to be accepted into treatment programs (Haseltine et al., 1985; Johnson et al., 1985; Nsiah-Jefferson and Hall, 1989) now bear a new burden (in addition to infertility itself) distinctively associated with their privileged access to therapy. The relatively fewer or haphazardly offered treatment opportunities available to individuals prior to the 1970s and generally with limited finances underscore the social class and historical significance of this new mandate.

Couples have to choose whether to initiate, continue, or terminate treatment. The new treatability or infertility, in turn, makes conceptive technology all the more "compelling" (DeZoeten, Tymstra, and Alberda, 1987, p. 624) and infertility less tolerable and perhaps more regrettable than when there were fewer available, accessible, and acceptable medical services. "Anticipatory regret" (discussed in more detail in chapter 7) has emerged as a major factor motivating couples to persist in medical treatment, sometimes for years (Tymstra, 1989).

Women have historically demonstrated a willingness to undergo almost any treatment or experiment in the hopes of having a child. One late-nineteenth-century physician commented on the enormous "physical (and) mental suffering" of barren women and on their willingness to submit to "severe procedures in the hope of relief" (Ashby, 1894, p. 260). In their letters to Dr. John Rock (whose research on treating infertility was well publicized at the time) written in the 1940s and 1950s, infertile women regularly offered themselves to him to be "guinea pigs, anytime."

Although the impetus to persist in efforts to get pregnant is hardly new nor exclusively related to modern treatments—women and couples across cultures traditionally seek whatever is available to overcome their infertility (Rosenblatt et al., 1973)—only recently have couples been situated in a time and place in which they can learn about and take advantage of new opportunities to persist. In an important sense, couples encountering infertility today are among the first generation of couples able to make an "illness career" (Conrad, 1987, p. 9) out of the pursuit of fertility.

Therapeutic sufficiency has, accordingly, become an important dimension of medical constructions of appropriate therapy. The new "message" conveyed in medical literature on in vitro fertilization and other therapies is that the goal of achieving a "successful pregnancy" can be reached with "persistence" (Guzick, Wilkes, and Jones, 1986, p. 667). Some physicians have been concerned that couples may not initiate treatment at all or may terminate it too soon (Mao and Wood, 1984; Paterson and Chan, 1987). One group of clinicians implied that failures in treatment could be categorized as (*a*) pure failures of treatment, where women have tried enough; (*b*) psychological failures, where women drop out of treatment too soon; and (*c*) knowledge failures, where physicians do not know the desirable length of treatment (Schoysman-DeBoeck, Van Roosendaal, and Schoysman, 1988).

Concerned about drawing the line on treatment, one physician (Taylor, 1990) suggested a calculus whereby physicians could inform couples when "enough is enough." Illustrating this calculus with the case of a couple where the man is diagnosed with an abnormality in sperm production, he demonstrated how a good try might take up to five years of a couple's life. Specifically, he advised couples to undergo no more than one year of expectant management, in which spontaneous conception could still occur. He then advised them to proceed to in vitro fertilization to assess the fertilizing capability of the man's spermatozoa. If this was satisfactory, the couple could choose for the wife to undergo ovarian hyperstimulation and intrauterine insemination, from which they could expect a 20 to 30 percent chance of pregnancy after six treatment cycles over a period of no more than nine months. If the couple failed to become pregnant, they could then attempt six cycles of gamete manipulation over no more than eighteen months, a procedure with a 40 percent chance of pregnancy. If this failed, they could then proceed to eighteen cycles of donor insemination for up to an 80 percent chance of pregnancy. Importantly, this physician recommended this kind of a program to offset the "obsessive drive" of couples who will not "let go" of treatment (p. 774).

The Mandate from Nature

Through their repetitive aspects, continuing or cyclical infertility therapies naturalize artificial conception by incorporating it into the realm of natural conception, but they concurrently remove infertility from the realm of nature by defining infertility as an impediment to nature's design. Proponents of assisted conception prophesy that what is now viewed as artificial will soon become as unremarkable as nature. In fact, "natural" in vitro fertilization is now distinguished from that achieved with hormonal priming. Infertile couples have expressed their view that assisted conception is ultimately natural, even if it represented an extraordinary, unusual, or "high-tech" departure from typical conception (DeZoeten, Tymstra, & Alberda, 1987; Modell, 1989). For the couples we interviewed, artificial conception was deemed natural because God/nature allowed it to succeed, because it simulated natural reproductive processes, because the child produced belonged biologically (in some form) to one or both of its nurturing parents, and because the pregnancy and birth that followed it were themselves natural processes wholly comparable to these events in spontaneously conceiving couples. Couples and physicians have construed in vitro fertilization as a way of giving nature a helping hand. Significantly, in the matter of medical treatments for infertility, "what is natural is man's artifice" (Fletcher, 1988, p. 44).

Moreover, physicians often use natural conception itself as the standard against which the effectiveness of conceptive techniques is compared. While the chances to conceive for any couple having intercourse during the periovulatory period of a cycle naturally are low (about 20 percent), with therapy a couple who had virtually no chance to conceive could be brought up to nature's standard. Equating the "arithmetic of infertility therapy" (Talbert, 1985, p. 9) with the probabilities of natural conception, some physicians have underscored the comparable inefficiencies of both natural and assisted conception. Of one hundred oocytes, only twenty will proceed developmentally to the delivery of a term infant anyway (Tagatz, 1990). Behrman and Patton (1988, p. 4) marveled at the "natural pregnancy wastage of 69 percent." New techniques for detecting pregnancy at earlier stages have permitted the recognition of preclinical pregnancy losses in both assisted and natural conception that once went unnoticed (Wilcox et al., 1988).

Rather than falling short of nature, conceptive techniques have simply exposed nature's inefficiency. Therapies can, accordingly, be construed as mimicking or duplicating nature to the extent that with certain treatments, take-home baby rates are comparable to those in natural conception. Some therapies are even depicted as improving upon nature. The goal of superovulation therapy is to induce the development of more eggs per cycle than in natural ovulation in order to increase the chance of fertilization, while the goal of techniques manipulating sperm is to employ less sperm for fertilization than is required in the natural process. In addition, the normal pituitary functions of women are sometimes chemically "shut off" on the premise that they "get in the way" of achieving conception (Haney, 1989): nature is fooled and bested by hormonal treatments that induce therapeutic states of pseudopregnancy and pseudomenopause.

Significantly, the impetus for couples to persist in therapy is, in part, a result of locating infertility therapeutics in the natural scheme of reproduction and making infertility seem unnatural. Although naturalizing therapy tends to minimize the higher financial, physical, and psychic costs of assisted as opposed to natural conception, both couples and physicians find comfort in the belief that nature fails in its procreative purposes at least as often as technology does.

Conceptive technology also compels its use in the way it segments the normal, biological process of conception, transforming it from an inchoate event into consciously lived stages of achievement or failure. The "moment" of pregnancy is transformed into a series of pregnant moments (Seibel and Levin, 1987; Williams, 1988). The fragmentation of conception into levels of achievement or failure that are consciously experienced is well illustrated in some women's perceptions of the in vitro fertilization process. As I will describe further in Chapter 8, these women felt themselves to be moving toward pregnancy with each stage successfully passed within a given cycle or with every additional cycle in which the technique was attempted. Achievement at one stage compelled movement to the next. Achievement of a pregnancy, even if lost after only a few days, was perceived as a gain and provided a good reason to begin the process again. If a woman failed to move through all of the stages in the process, at least she knew at what point she had stopped achieving. The in vitro fertilization process was artificial only to the extent that it exposed to the eye and to the consciousness the "hidden" aspects—the milestones and the breakdown points—of natural conception. With a technique such as in vitro fertilization, nature's work could be observed and lived.

A Compelling Therapeutics

The therapeutic imperative in the resolution of infertility draws from mandates of culture, technology, and nature. Western physicians are oriented to acting aggressively to overcome nature's defects, and they and infertile couples often perceive quitting the pursuit of pregnancy too soon as unheroic, as an unwarranted submission to adversity and as giving up on the body.

As will be evident in subsequent chapters, infertile couples often walk a fine line between persistence and obsession. For them and their caregivers, both persisting too much and quitting too soon are to be avoided. Most importantly, with the advent of new technical options, it is quitting rather than persisting that increasingly requires justification. After all, in the quest for a child, if winners never quit, then quitters can certainly never win.

Notes

1. Infertile couples are also most accessible to researchers when they are seeking medical assistance.

2. Interestingly, the pregnancy rate obtained by traditional practitioners in Kenya was found to be similar to the rate of treatment-independent pregnancies in the West (Katz and Katz, 1987).

5. The Color Gray

> **Gray:** Of a color between white and black . . . indeterminate and intermediate in character. (Random House Dictionary, 1967, p. 618)

With this chapter, I begin to re-present the stories told by the women and couples who participated in my two studies. In this and the next two chapters, I emphasize their first and continuing encounters with their inability to have a child and consider how they perceived and managed the ambiguity of infertility, their social interactions, and the paths to parenthood available to them.

No Rhyme or Reason

If medical therapeutics are a distinguishing mark of the contemporary experience of infertility, then ambiguity is arguably its essence. A notable feature in the talk of the infertile women and couples interviewed was their use of such expressions as "in limbo," "on hold," "dangling," and "in a gray area"[1] to describe the uncertainties and indeterminateness of infertility.

One of the most important facets for the study participants of the ambiguity of infertility was explaining the occurrence of infertility: determining how and why it happened to them. For example, of the forty-eight women who participated in the first study, twelve had been given no definitive diagnoses and fifteen had been given multiple diagnoses. Of seventy-five infertile couples in the second study, eleven had diagnoses of unexplained infertility and eighteen had been given multiple diagnoses.

One woman noted her frustration at being told, after five years of trying to have a child, that there was "no reason" for her not becoming pregnant.

> I've been to all kind of doctors. They do tests but they don't find nothing wrong with me. They didn't find anything wrong with [my

husband] either. There's a lot of questions you ask but you just don't get no answers. I just don't know what to do. You get disgusted going to the doctor because every time you take a test and it comes back, nothing is wrong with you. It almost makes you wish that they can find something wrong with you—at least they'll know.

One woman, who had suffered four miscarriages, merely wanted someone to tell her why she was losing them and to tell her what was going on. Another woman, in treatment for four years with no success, noted that she and her husband were in the "unexplained infertility category, which really multiplies my frustration." She asked, "Why can't the doctors look inside with a telescope and say, this is the problem; we're going to fix it? They looked in [my husband], they looked in me, I don't know what else is left."

Sometimes the women attributed the problems associated with infertility diagnosis to the scientific inexactness of a medical field in which physicians disagreed on causes, cures, and prognoses, and in which standards varied for interpreting infertility and even pregnancy test results. One woman, advised of a positive pregnancy test, had suffered the loss of what she thought was a miscarriage only to discover that she was never really pregnant. Another woman, who endured an early loss of a pregnancy achieved by in vitro fertilization, concluded that there were "no definite answers in this area. It's an experiment with everyone" who seeks a physician's help. One woman could not understand how the doctor could tell she had a problem releasing an egg when he had "never really gone inside" to have a look. Still unsuccessful after three years of trying to conceive, another woman felt like "a mouse that they're experimenting with" and that "infertility science" was only "a little step above witch doctors."

Moving back and forth, by choice and by necessity, from general gynecologists to one or more infertility specialists was for these women and couples a fairly common occurrence. Their existing feelings of uncertainty increased when different physicians arrived at different causes for their infertility and suggested different cures and even, at times, denigrated one another's diagnoses or treatment regimens. Women felt "caught in the middle." Even when they were given a diagnosis, some women had trouble believing it or accepting it as an explanation of their infertility because they were "so healthy" and "so active" and "alive" that they felt there was not anything they could not do. For example, women who accepted that they were "poor ovulators" or that they "just . . . couldn't ovulate" or that their husbands had low sperm counts nevertheless recognized "no definitive cause" for their infertility or stated that they had received "no conclusive diagnosis" of infertility. These women demonstrated how gynecological problems and sperm deviations may not necessarily be viewed by infertile individuals themselves as adequate explanations for infertility if, for example, the causes of these problems could not be determined, if these problems did not absolutely preclude conception, and if nothing else was wrong.

Some women also had difficulty accepting a medical explanation if the identified problem manifested no symptoms or, alternatively, if it manifested symptoms that they had always interpreted as normal. Some women, for example, perceived the pain and heavy bleeding associated with endometriosis as indistinguishable from or merely exaggerations of the pain and bleeding of the menstrual cycle, interpreting these symptoms benignly and resignedly as a woman's lot in life. Some women who had dismissed past heavy bleeding episodes as insignificant later surmised that they might have been achieving pregnancies all along but then losing them because of what they now understood to be a deficiency in progesterone production. The process of infertility diagnosis caused women to reinterpret past events and to conclude, as one woman intimated, that things were not always what they seemed.

Sometimes apparently straightforward solutions to infertility turned out to be failures. One woman suggested that infertility was "a hard lesson" in ambiguity. As she explained:

> I realize that I may be one of those women who never has a baby. I think it's better to go through all this with that in mind than to go through it with really high hopes that something's going to work. I was really convinced last summer that I was going to get pregnant on that intrauterine insemination because I really felt like we knew I was ovulating and we knew that the tubes were not blocked and I thought, well, my uterus was tipped, so maybe there was a problem [with] the sperm getting into the uterus and up into the tubes. So I thought, we'll do the intrauterine thing. That's a cinch! I mean you're putting practically the whole sperm deposit right up top. Three times and it didn't work.

Although there was certainty in the role that a problem such as tubal occlusion, for example, played in preventing conception, there was no certainty in the role that a problem such as endometriosis played, even when the diagnosis was certain. A woman could have "a little" or "slight" endometriosis, be relieved of it, and still not get pregnant. In contrast, a woman with "severe" endometriosis could unaccountably get pregnant. One woman remarked that there was "not much rhyme or reason" in infertility diagnosis and treatment since women with complex problems achieved pregnancy while women with no "apparent" problems did not. In addition, one woman concluded after she was told of her endometriosis that the doctor was "speculating." Some women perceived endometriosis itself to be an "ambiguous" diagnosis, "debatable," its severity determined by the doctor's "mood." These women also viewed it as a "rubber stamp" diagnosis.

The Perils of Presumptions

Contributing to the ambiguity of infertility was the fact that both women and men typically entered into reproductive partnerships with each other with the presumption of fertility, taking for granted their ability to have a child together when they wanted one. Factors that served to affirm a couple's silent presumption of fertility included having regular menstrual periods, lacking any gynecological aberrations or other medical problems, coming from a large family, having had a child, having avoided sexual promiscuity, and a prevailing cultural view that conception was easy to achieve and hard to avoid. For the women who found themselves still without the child they wanted, merely achieving a pregnancy (no matter what its outcome) could serve for a time to maintain the presumption that nothing was really wrong. In addition, having no reason for the infertility, having a reason that could be minimized, or having a physician's assurance that there was no real problem served to neutralize for these couples the threat of infertility. If any doubts about fertility existed, they were usually exhibited by women and induced by such factors as menstrual dysfunctions or a generalized fear of infertility.

The definition of self as fertile or infertile was as much a matter of perceived vulnerability as of medical probability or diagnosis. Perceived vulnerability was, in turn, related to the greater saliency of fertility for female, as opposed to male, identity and role enactment (Greil, Leitko, and Porter, 1988). For example, one woman conceived after only five months of trying, but recalled perceiving herself as vulnerable to infertility simply because she was thirty-four years old and because she had friends with fertility problems. Her perceived vulnerability to infertility demonstrates the important intersection between medical and cultural models of age and fecundity. Women have been made increasingly aware of the possible consequences of waiting too long before attempting conception and of when they are past the age when women are supposed both to be the most fecund and to have already had a child. Advancing age (over thirty) frequently sounds an alarm, even if most often a "false alarm," for women considered mature and attempting pregnancy for the first time (Bongaarts, 1982). One such mature woman pronounced herself "preinfertile" simply because she had not yet tried to have a child and contemplated asking her physician for a prophylactic prescription of a fertility drug.

In contrast to the heightened sense of vulnerability to infertility in the absence of any demonstrable factor indicating infertility was a decreased sense of vulnerability in the presence of a known impediment to reproduction. For example, one woman reveled in her image of herself as an excellent "breeder" and perceived herself as invulnerable to infertility despite the failure to reverse the effects of the tubal ligation she had undergone in a previous marriage. She recalled entering her present marriage certain that she could "whip out a baby" in the first in vitro fertilization cycle she attempted. Having already conceived two children easily (one while taking birth control pills), she felt she did not need intact tubes to conceive and that her chances of being among the small percentage of women who succeeded with in vitro fertilization were 100 percent. Because she had never had to "try" to have a child, her perception of herself as fertile began to falter only after her second in vitro fertilization failure. Both she and her husband managed to sustain a definition of themselves as a fertile couple despite her tubal impairment: she perceiving fertility as an essence (I am fertile even without functioning fallopian tubes) and he perceiving fertility as a mechanism subject to control, a "known resource [and] presence." As he remarked:

> I would categorize [my wife's fertility] as something you turn on and off, but the supply is constantly there. [It] is a known constant. Somebody turned the faucet off. We need to find the right person to turn it back on. [It is] interruptable, but [nothing] precludes its presence.

Importantly, confronting the assault that infertility typically poses for couples' assumptive, or taken-for-granted, worlds (Williams, 1984) often involved attempts to sustain multiple conflicting realities in an inherently precarious (Emerson, 1970) and even ironic situation. One woman recalled:

I was a virgin until I was nineteen because I was deathly afraid of getting pregnant and what the family would think. Now imagine my surprise when I get married and I can't get pregnant. That just blows me away. It's a laugh. It's a joke and I just crack up when I think about it because that's all you can do. It's just too funny. It's frustrating.

Another woman surmised:

You have to commit yourself to something that pretty much rules out a baby as the last thing in the world and that's when you'll get pregnant. One friend's doing an unofficial study of who gets pregnant and who doesn't. One friend quit his job and they went back to school and they bought a new car and they were deeply in debt. No chance of getting out unless he quit school and his job had been such that he really needed to go back to school. And she got pregnant. People who get into financial commitments, commit themselves to work on a project, that's pretty much been the case. When you say, "OK, it's not going to happen," that's when it happens.

Yet another woman noted that because they always thought they would get pregnant in an inopportune moment, she and her husband deliberately spent all their money on a sailboat. She explained, "figuring we were broke, now we'll get pregnant." They resorted to doing "dumb things like that" because they were always being confronted with the fact that people who did not try or want to get pregnant unaccountably did.

In the inside-out world of infertility, nothing seemed to make sense. As one woman summarized it:

You can do everything in your power to eat properly, take care of your body, not take any caffeine, anything that might possibly hurt that fetus. And whether it stays or goes is out of your hands. You can do things to harm it. You can have an abortion. People who take drugs and eat clay have normal babies. People who are careful don't. I think ultimately, it's out of your hands.

The Metaphysics of Infertility

Couples and individuals assumed over time a range of epistemic stances toward infertility, adopting combinations of scientific, historical, folk and/or metaphysical orientations to causation and proof in attempts to reduce the ambiguities of infertility. They sought to integrate the "I-knowledge" (Cassell, 1978, p. 59) of infertility with knowledge they obtained from physicians and others. Infertile couples lived out the longstanding philosophical tensions about the nature of truth and the meaning of misfortune.

Women tended to look for the origins of their infertility in their own and their partners' bodies and in their past lives and behavior. One woman thought a bicycle accident she had suffered as a child or the "stress" her parents had caused her may have caused her infertility. Another woman thought she might have "been born like this." Yet another woman wondered whether smoking was implicated in her infertility. A few women hinted that their inability to have a child constituted a punishment for past transgressions, including failed marriages and elective abortions.

Influenced by biomedical and other explanations of infertility, women identified a variety of both proximate (body dysfunction) and ultimate (divine punishment, past behavior) causes for their infertility, often juxtaposing science with religion, what they perceived as the rational with the irrational, and the temporal with the spiritual. Indeed, turning to explanations that were not wholly scientific seemed logical to these women; sometimes, such explanations seemed more rational than scientific explanations.

In contrast to women, men tended to identify luck and timing as key factors controlling fertility. As one man put it, it was just a matter of time and luck before he and his wife achieved pregnancy. While in the preadoption waiting period and after his wife had lost a second pregnancy, he still felt that their childlessness was "just bad luck other than anything weird." When confronted with the possibility of their infertility, this man said, "I don't want to believe that until I see or I'm told that." Men tended to demand more explicit proof that they would never have a child with their wives, especially in cases of unexplained infertility.

> I never liked the word infertile until they're proven—until somebody said that this is the reason why. I don't think we are infertile. I think we are unlucky. . . . You need to just get lucky, you need to find that perfect hour.

Childlessness was only circumstantial evidence of infertility, not proof of it. Also waiting to adopt a child, another man turned to the retrospection of historical explanation (Freeman, 1984) by asserting that infertility could only be diagnosed after the fact, ultimately proven only after a couple's childbearing years had passed.

DEFINITIONS OF SELF AND SITUATION

Couples had varying definitions of infertility that served either to distance themselves from or to lead them to accept an identity of self as infertile. They defined infertility (*a*) functionally, as the inability to reproduce without "extraordinary means" or "intervention," or ever; (*b*) behaviorally, as activities in the pursuit of a child; (*c*) empirically, as not yet having a desired child; and (*d*) phenomenologically, as characterizing the self, or "part of who I am." Functional, behavioral, and empirical definitions, emphasizing an incapacity of the body (what my body does not permit me to do), a set of activities (what I do to become a parent), and an incontrovertible fact (I do not yet have a child, I am not yet a parent), served to separate the self from the disease (Bury, 1982), or to localize it and put it in its place.

In contrast, phenomenological definitions (who I am) allowed infertility to engulf the whole person. Women especially often internalized images of themselves as incapable, abnormal, and defective. Not just an element of the body but the entire self was perceived as damaged. One woman, for example, admitted that the only place she felt "normal" was at the infertility clinic where everybody was like her, that is, everybody was infertile. Another woman recalled that she deliberately told everyone she could about her miscarriage so people would know she had been pregnant and a "normal . . . whole woman." Yet another woman felt that by not having a child she had not fulfilled her purpose as a woman:

> [Infertility] takes the whole person. I used to feel attractive; I used to feel like I had a wonderful personality; I used to feel like I was smart; I used to feel like I could have a child if I wanted a child. And now all those things are shattered.

The women who incorporated infertility into the self interpreted it as a state of being (an incomplete or diseased woman); infertility became something they were, something that had changed who they once were. For these women, infertility was an "I-am" disease (Estroff, 1989, p. 189). In contrast, men tended to encapsulate infertility, to halt its "spread," to keep it from assuming a "master status" or from "spoiling" their identities as intact males (Goffman, 1963; Schur, 1983; Wright, 1960). For them, infertility tended to be an I-have or I-had condition they shared with their wives.

The ambiguities of infertility diagnosis and prognosis permitted couples to disavow identities of themselves as infertile. For example, one woman never considered herself infertile and, at the most, only "subfertile," having conceived readily at an earlier time, before her current Pergonal/husband insemination–induced twin pregnancy. Her husband explained that they would have seen themselves as infertile if they had not already had a child and if they had been forced to undergo a great deal of testing and treatment; they achieved their second pregnancy after only two months of therapy. He defined their secondary infertility as an "obstacle," and one which they overcame, to their already established fertility. Interestingly, he suggested that if they had been expecting a single baby instead of twins, it might have been possible not to attribute this second pregnancy to the therapy at all.

This couple, like others with secondary infertility, had more difficulty defining their situation as one involving infertility because they viewed it largely in terms of the pregnancies they had achieved in the past (even if lost) or the biological children they already had. Because they perceived their fertility as already proven by having conceived quickly, by having conceived spontaneously, or by having successfully delivered a child, they had difficulty explaining their current failure to conceive as infertility; these couples believed that once fertile, always fertile.

Other couples and especially men disavowed infertility by defining it empirically; they were only infertile de facto by virtue of not yet conceiving a child. The identities of these individuals as fertile or infertile, like their fertility status itself, remained open, to be determined only after their reproductive years had passed. In the meantime, they were "infertile enough" to feel the pain of infertility, to be accepted by an adoption agency, to warrant medical services, and to do what infertile couples did to get a child, but they were not "proved" infertile. Continuing childlessness challenged but did not eliminate their faith in their reproductive capacity. In fact, one man was able to demonstrate the validity of this infertile-enough standpoint when he and his wife spontaneously conceived a child while waiting to adopt. One woman summarized the essentially precarious nature of such a standpoint.

> I think I accepted myself as an infertile couple when we had to prove it for adoption. We had to state that we had gone through all this stuff and everything. Yet our social worker said to us that if you become pregnant during your waiting period, just let me know and we won't take you off the list and you won't lose your place. I can consider us as an infertile couple because we haven't conceived yet and we've gone through the time period and we've gone through the testing and as far

as [the agency] is concerned, we're infertile enough to be adoptable parents. But in terms of having to stick myself in a slot and stay there for life, that is in God's hands. . . . When I go through menopause, then I can look back and say well, we did or didn't have them.

This woman's explanation underscores another key facet of the ambiguity of infertility: the part that conflicting messages about fertility status can play in the construction of infertility, such as when couples are advised that they might yet conceive a child.

EXPLANATIONS FOR INFERTILITY

Couples sought to explain or to explain away their encounters with infertility, attempting to move beyond what caused it to its greater meaning for their identities and lives. While women still in pursuit of a child and a few couples who achieved parenthood had difficulty finding meaning and purpose in their encounters with infertility, most couples who achieved parenthood came to view infertility as something that had to be to make them the people they became (understanding of and able to overcome adversity, and appreciative of the special nature of many taken-for-granted aspects of life) and to help them to get the child they now had (cf. Greil et al., 1989). There was a "meant-to-be-ness" about the egg and sperm that heroically "survived" to become their child or about the child who became theirs through adoption. The child they eventually got had made the struggle "worth it." One woman even asserted that she was "glad" she had been infertile because the infant she adopted was the baby she wanted. For her, infertility had served a purpose that she did not discern during her years of struggle to conceive a child; infertility served her as explanation (Engelhardt, 1982, p. 146).

A less cosmic but still prevalent "explanatory model" (Kleinman, 1980, 1988) of infertility was the chronicity model, which held as its organizing principle the notion that once a couple or individual was infertile, they would remain infertile. People in this category viewed infertility as akin to having either a chronic physical condition (a permanent impairment that either precluded conception or would always require medical help for conception to occur) or a chronic illness (a source of recurring suffering). Although the couples who had failed to have a child thought, at the very least, they might do so in the future with luck, time, and more advanced treatment, they typically viewed themselves as functionally incapable of having a child on their own. Even one woman who unexpectedly became pregnant on her own less than one year after delivering twins conceived with Pergonal and husband insemination believed that second spontaneous pregnancy to be a fluke. Similarly, another woman who became pregnant spontaneously while waiting to adopt a child continued to think of herself as infertile because she doubted she would ever again achieve pregnancy.

The chronicity model typically involved functional definitions of infertility that emphasized a physical incapacity, but it also included phenomenological definitions that emphasized the emotions and spirit. One woman observed, "even now being pregnant, I think I will never feel fertile. Even if I have a healthy child, I don't know if those scars will ever go away." After her child was born, she felt "intellectually" fertile, but "emotionally" infertile. Another woman illustrated the distinction between a functional and phenomenological view of infertility by noting that while she was no longer infertile "on a physical level," having delivered a child, she remained infertile "on an emotional level." For these women, their encounter with infertility was a landmark event that divided their lives into "before" and "after" and that they anticipated would continue to influence their worldview and behavior (Cochran and Claspell, 1987, p. 91).

A second explanatory model of infertility was an acuity model, in which couples perceived infertility as either a physical condition that had been cured by treatment or by the achievement of pregnancy, or as a past life event that was no longer relevant to them once they achieved biological or adoptive parenthood. One couple, three months after the birth of their son, surmised that their anxiety to have a baby had interfered with conception. Now that they had a child, they could be more "relaxed" when they tried to achieve pregnancy again. As the husband explained, they had each been "pressured" to conceive. By taking the pressure off, their successful pregnancy had likely provided them with a psychological cure for their infertility.

Even a pregnancy that was eventually lost could induce the belief that infertility was cured. One woman who lost her first pregnancy observed, "when I got pregnant the first time, I certainly felt, right, everything is working. I'm functioning and everything is all right now and I'm cured and I'm fertile." Some infertile couples described themselves as back on track with fertile couples as soon as they achieved pregnancy, their departure from normality confined only to the fact that they had required treatment to conceive. Once pregnancy was achieved, the infertile couple became like any other childbearing couple.

Despite a recognition of their probably permanent incapacity to procreate, some adopting couples described undergoing a "healing" process while working to be accepted by an adoption agency and then having a child placed with them. Achieving parenthood had cured them of infertility on an emotional level. Their fertility status was no longer relevant; they were now parents or parents-to-be, not infertile. Importantly, many infertile couples who recognized their impairments as chronic on a physical level were still able to conceptualize infertility as acute when considering its overall impact on their lives. The views of these couples contrasted sharply with those of the women who forecast that they would always remain scarred, despite having triumphed over infertility by achieving parenthood. These women appeared "psychologically imprinted" (Pellegrino, 1982, p. 159) with their infertility.

Interestingly, some couples who achieved viable pregnancies adopted explanations of infertility that infertile couples often find insulting, for example, the ideas that if couples will only relax or do it right, they will conceive. These couples considered whether their pregnancies and babies had not cured them of the anxiety or stress that they now believed had impeded conception. One couple remarked that if people had been more "positive" about their getting pregnant, they would have achieved this goal much sooner. After the birth of their child, one couple conceiving with fertility drugs and husband insemination in the first cycle wondered whether they had "timed it right," whether they had not felt too pressured to conceive, and, accordingly, whether they had not been fertile all along. As the husband recalled:

> I think that [his wife] put a lot of pressure on herself about the whole deal and, in turn, put pressure on me with getting up and taking the temperature and me laying down wondering what my fate is going to be this morning. Is it going to be the cold shower or is it going to be what everybody loves? And I think that to me it got to be almost clinical and it just—I just think that it would be so much different now that we've got a baby. . . . But I think [his wife] put more pressure on herself about it and worried about it and, if we went down there and inseminated one time, what's to say that if we hadn't made love that morning that it hadn't happened. You know, if we could have called them up and asked them what time to do it or whatever. We just weren't—all I can see is that we just weren't timing it right.

His wife affirmed his view by recalling that their infertility remained unexplained: no one had ever found anything wrong with either of them.

Importantly, the pregnancy/baby-as-cure explanation for infertility comprised common explanations of infertility that some couples had found "unscientific" and insensitive while they were still trying to conceive. After the birth of a child, such explanations reestablished for these same couples a sense of reproductive capability.

Living the Life

No matter how they interpreted their situations, couples initially acted to counter the threat infertility posed by doing "what infertile couples do," which included activities that any couple might engage in to have a child, such as taking daily temperatures, using over-the-counter ovulation test kits, and having intercourse at the times prescribed by these measures. Progressing to such distinctive activities as undergoing special test and treatment protocols, joining infertility support groups, and looking into adoption and actually going through the adoption process, however, required leaving the life of the presumed fertile. Couples who behaved infertile typically indicated some "basic acceptance" of infertility, admitting they had a problem by having tests done, or, when adoption was considered, that they could not or maybe never would have a biological child. But these activities were indicators not only of an acceptance by couples of themselves as infertile but also of their urgent desire not to waste any more time trying on their own to conceive, their impatience for a child, and their willingness to use medical and adoption services even before they were "pronounced infertile."

Significantly, couples may engage in the "round of life" (Greil, Leitko, and Porter, 1988, p. 184) associated with the infertile, but they may not necessarily share a common interpretation of that life. A couple might undergo diagnosis and/or treatment protocols explicitly for infertility, but they may also define their behavior not in terms of infertility but rather in terms of factors, such as age, stress, and the use of contraceptives, which have been associated with delayed conception. Couples' descriptions of living the infertile life reveal that simply doing what infertile couples do is not necessarily a sign of acceptance of self as being infertile. This is particularly well illustrated in two couples' explanations of their fertility problems.

Marisa and Evan (pseudonyms), currently expecting their second child, conceived each of their two children spontaneously, but only after two years of effort. For Evan, their first child was the "definition of being fertile," and a couple was "infertile . . . definitionally" if they had to use something like Clomid to conceive. Marisa, in turn, defined infertility functionally as "a very significant and relatively established situation that you couldn't get pregnant and you perhaps knew that you had . . . pin-pointed a reason." By virtue of this definition, she interpreted the fact that it took two years to achieve each of her two pregnancies as a factor of age, not of infertility. She described the diagnostic testing she had undergone to determine the reason for her not conceiving as "so preliminary and rudi-mentary," instigated because of her impatience and anxiety rather than incapacity. She designated the purpose of the hormonal therapy she had undergone as regulating her periods, not treating infertility. She was "ap-palled," "blown away," and "distraught" when a bill marked for "infertility" services arrived at her home. Concluding that the word infertility on the bill was probably not written by a physician and that they were "characterized [as infertile] for administrative purposes," and comparing the delay in their conceiving a child to "pump time" where there is a time lag between stopping one activity (oral contraception) and beginning another (concep-tion), Evan agreed with his wife that the label was "premature" and com-pletely at odds with their perception of their situation. By placing their activities in a *not*-infertility context, they had resisted the admittedly dis-comforting label of infertility.

Elaine and Steve had each achieved a pregnancy in their previous marriages that was electively terminated and a spontaneous pregnancy with each other that was lost. While in the first trimester of a second pregnancy induced by Pergonal and husband insemination, they recalled denying their infertility in the first two years of their marriage. Elaine remembered being "insulted" when a physician suggested she take Clomid after one year of failing to become pregnant. After receiving an initial diagnosis that she was "poison" to Steve's sperm, the couple felt better when a second physician decided their infertility was due to unexplained factors and especially when they achieved pregnancy spontaneously after two-and-one-half years of effort. Elaine recalled becoming "more and more infertile" as time passed, a reference to her increasingly negative concept of herself.

Several months after losing their first pregnancy and waiting for it to "happen again," Elaine and Steve achieved a second pregnancy after one cycle of therapy. Elaine observed that she never really knew what was wrong with her body and that, in any event, there was nothing wrong with her body anymore. By twenty-one weeks of pregnancy, she noted that they had only had "a little problem" requiring a "nudge," and Steve recalled his "battery being recharged" at the idea that their inability to conceive was un-explained. After the birth of their daughter, Elaine was still somewhat uncertain about her fertility status, while Steve concluded that they had really always been fertile. Elaine mused that because no one ever determined what was wrong, no one could be sure it was the therapy that had "fixed it." She assumed that her child was a "Pergonal baby" but recollected that she and her husband had once achieved pregnancy without any therapy.

Steve also recalled that spontaneous pregnancy and "resolved" for himself that the therapy had "simply stacked the deck" and that they had always had the "basic" ability to reproduce. In fact, he suggested that the therapy was not so much therapy as "insurance . . . added" to their basic fertility. Having previously characterized himself as fertile and himself-with-Elaine as an "infertile couple" with bad "chemistry" early in pregnancy, Steve stated, one week after the birth of his child, that he had generally perceived himself and Elaine as fertile. Invoking a behavioral definition of infertility and, like many men, attributing the failure to conceive to bad luck and timing, Steve now explained, "I more went through the motions of all that stuff for her. . . . In the back of my mind, [I] had the feeling that if we wanted to get pregnant, we could if we would just give it time."

Three months after the birth of their child, Steve reiterated his belief in their basic fertility, and Elaine felt more strongly than ever that her inability to relax (a common folk explanation of infertility that infertile couples often find annoying), rather than any body dysfunction, had contributed to her failure to get pregnant. This couple recast their situation over time, finally finding proof of their fertility in the birth of their baby.

A Crisis of Ambiguity

A crisis typically comprises opportunity and danger. Although the ambiguous nature of infertility was often a source of frustration for couples, this ambiguity was a source of hope for them also, hope that one day infertility would be successfully resolved. The very ambiguity of infertility served to widen the interpretive scope of the problem: couples could, for example, find ways to affirm the presumption of fertility or resist the infertility label; they could achieve some "interpretive control" of their situation (Rothbaum, Weisz, and Snyder, 1982). Beyond being a medical classification for infertile couples, *unexplained* infertility emerged in the descriptions of the women and couples interviewed as the paradigmatic experience of infertility as they searched for reasons for their infertility. In a most essential way, infertility was characterized by the lack of explanation for it, and it was made both tolerable and intolerable by its ambiguous nature. Uncertainty "haunted" (Mason, 1985) the lives of infertile couples and intensified their suffering, but it also permitted these couples to hope; the ambiguity of infertility was, accordingly, both enabling and disabling.

The responses of women and couples to the ambiguity of infertility reveal the complex and essentially different realities of situations defined as, as opposed to lived as, infertility. Significantly, the identification of self as infertile was not a necessary antecedent to effective action. Olshansky (1987) has argued that infertile couples have to take on an identity of self as infertile in order to rid themselves of it. Yet, among the participants in both studies there were those who only acted as if they were infertile without ever actually taking on that identity. The work of infertility was completed in the absence of an infertile self; some couples managed the threat of infertility by reinterpreting the work they had to do to overcome it. Accordingly, pursuing adoption can be an indicator of both acceptance of self as infertile and of a perceived need to move beyond medical routes to parenthood in the time available. Similarly, successfully delivering a child by circumventing fertility impairments was no insurance for women that they would circumvent an encompassing view of themselves as infertile.

The explanations women and couples gave of their situations helped them to resolve some of the paradoxes of infertility, to integrate the triumph (over) and the pain of infertility, and to manage the chaos of infertility while creating a "telos" (Williams, 1984, p. 179) for their disrupted lives and medically and socially liminal circumstances. By following couples prospectively over time, we were able to capture how they made and remade their encounters with infertility and how they reconstructed their encounters narratively (Williams, 1984) to fit changing circumstances and needs for self-preservation and harmonious closure. Their efforts illuminate the importance of this reconstructive work (Corbin and Strauss, 1987) in coming to terms with body and cultural failure (a subject to which I return later) and with the inadequacies of biomedical explanations. Most important, their responses reveal the gray zone and indeterminate world in which couples live the infertile life.

Note

1. All words and phrases in quotation marks in this and subsequent chapters without cited references belong to the women and men interviewed.

6. Alone in a Crowd

Four stages of a childless marriage. "Children?" (*Mild*) "Not yet." "Children?" (*Slightly rebuking*) "Give us time." "Children?" (*Gentle, sad*) "No." "Children?" (*Defiant, i.e. Should there be?*) "No." (Rudkin, 1974, p. 20).

Infertility is a most intrusive phenomenon. For couples who desire children and repeatedly fail in their efforts to have them, infertility is almost inescapable. As one infertile woman described it:

> You turned the TV on and it felt like everything is centered around the baby. Those commercials. And if you watch a movie, it's like the ultimate thing of love is if you have a baby. . . . You felt like that everywhere you turn.

Everyday events and interactions often serve to remind infertile couples of their failure. Even in circumstances where their fertility status ought not to matter, such as going to the supermarket and watching the news, infertile couples can feel virtually assaulted with their incapacity, caught off guard. I am thinking here of the recent tendency to advertise noninfant-related products (tires, credit cards) with infants and of several newswomen who have recently featured their pregnancies as news on their programs. Simply seeing a pregnant woman or infant or hearing an infant cry can engender a painful longing and despair. Holidays (especially Mother's Day, Thanksgiving, and Christmas) are symbols of the celebrations of family and fertility from which infertile couples feel excluded. Even such a mundane artifact of everyday life as garbage may intensify infertile couples' sense of being the Other in a world of fertile people. Kornheiser (1983) described the estrangement he felt in just seeing (and having to look at) the empty cartons of disposable diapers in his neighbor's trash. Mitchard (1985, p. 53) described her "orbit" around fertile people; "[I was] drawn and held by their force, but on my own, my separate path." Simply by virtue of the social isolation it often engenders, infertility can be a "social handicap" (Bury,

1988) that seriously undermines the affected persons' sense of self, belonging, and social competence.

The publication in 1977 of Barbara Menning's guide for infertile couples marked a watershed of sorts in understanding infertility as a social disability with important effects on couples' emotional well-being. Menning, a nurse and founder in 1973 of RESOLVE (the national lay information and support group for infertile couples) and herself infertile, emphasized the extent to which the psychological disturbances recurringly manifested by infertile couples were consequences, not causes of infertility. Drawing from her personal and professional experiences and the testimonials of "fellow infertiles" (p. xiii), Menning attempted to counter the often unflattering psychological characterizations of infertile couples by emphasizing the importance of the normative context in which couples struggled to conceive. Seeking to describe the "feeling aspects" (p. xiii) of infertility, Menning lamented the insensitivity shown to couples in a sociocultural milieu that emphasized the importance of having children to a couple's acceptance as normal, mature, and responsible adults. She also described the pervasive societal ignorance that existed about the causes of infertility, with friends and relatives often assuming that couples themselves were somehow to blame for their infertility. As she noted, the idea that many couples' infertility was itself "psychological" was "cruel beyond words" (p. 66). Infertile couples waged an "unceasing battle" (p. 67) not only against infertility but also against widespread ignorance concerning its personal meaning and impact.

Infertile couples still have to contend with rather negative characterizations of themselves and their plight. Infertility is too often dismissed as an unfortunate physical impairment, but one perfectly compatible with good health and life. As one infertile woman was told by members of her family, "You can always be dead. You could always have terminal cancer. . . . At least you've got a nice husband and a nice house and plenty of food. . . . At least you don't have cancer." Infertile people are still often viewed as somehow to blame for their infertility, as incompetent sexually or uptight psychologically (Miall, 1985; Simons, 1984). Alternatively, infertile couples are cast as selfish and materialistic people who only belatedly discover the importance of parenthood and family life (Schroeder, 1988). Infertile people supposedly typify and indict the self-indulgent and acquisitive baby-boom generation that "gleefully" separated sex from procreation and that prioritized getting "state-of-the-art stereos" over having children (Quindlen, 1987, p. 24). Apparently epitomizing the worst in capitalist consumption, infertile couples allegedly view children as consumer goods and are more than eager to buy them in adoption and surrogacy contracts, even if that means exploiting less socioeconomically privileged women and leaving less adoptable children behind (Chesler, 1988; Gibbs, 1989; Lacayo, 1989; Rothman, 1989).

Infertile couples have been accused of desiring children as objects to dominate and as "lifestyle commodit(ies) to be acquired" (Chesler, 1988, p. 124) and of a selfish "obsessive craving" born of the inability to accept the condition of " 'not having' " something that they want (Kamal, 1987, p. 153). Although Americans are generally taught to set goals and to work hard to achieve them, to want children, and to plan their reproductive lives responsibly around the goal of having children, infertile couples' persistence in the service of these goals has been viewed as a symptom of an illness, or of normal desire perverted into obsession. Infertile couples are cast as the compulsive gamblers who are willing to "play the odds" (Halpern, 1989) at any cost by undergoing expensive, risky, often ineffective, and, sometimes, controversial medical treatments. Women especially are characterized as "addicted" to treatment: like cancer patients, they are willing to subject themselves to round after round of painful medical procedures (Greil and Porter, 1988). Failing to recognize that their desire for children is socially constructed rather than authentic, women continue to submit to medical control (Arditti, Klein, and Minden, 1984; Corea, 1985; Rowland, 1987; Spallone and Steinberg, 1987; Stanworth, 1987).

Infertile people also appear as somewhat comical in their attempts to reverse the considerable reproductive "toll" (Kosterman, 1987, p. 6) taken by their sexually and otherwise promiscuous behavior. Women stand on their heads after intercourse and couples consult psychics and channelers in the anything goes, "try-everything world of baby craving" (Quindlen, 1987) and baby making (Elmer-Dewitt, 1991).

Although it is always dangerous and limiting to categorize people on the basis of a single attribute (merely by studying people with a certain attribute, researchers themselves serve to transform that attribute into a kind of master status), and although infertility is itself hardly a homogeneous condition or well-defined attribute, infertile couples may be usefully understood as involuntary members of a marginally deviant group. They are both inside and outside accepted society: they are normal by conforming to motivational cultural norms by wanting children and deviant by violating behavioral norms in not having them (Veevers, 1972).

Infertile couples are also "normal deviants" (Goffman, 1963, p. 131) because of the manner in which they choose to overcome their infertility. Infertile people are often cultural scouts and moral pioneers of sorts who, because of their social position on the boundary between normality and deviance, test the waters for normally fertile people and illuminate cultural norms. Infertile people are the ones currently attempting new and controversial reproductive and parenting partnerships, and their efforts reveal the cultural primacy of biological parenthood and prejudices against adoptive parenthood. Like other deviants who serve an important function in clarifying norms and maintaining the social order (Erikson, 1966), infertile people expose and are forced to contend with cultural failings that normally fertile people can afford to ignore. Normally fertile people never have to consider abandoned, relinquished, abused, and other children in need of parents, nor are they ever accused of being racist (if they are white) or prejudiced against the impaired and the disabled by not adopting or otherwise caring for children of another color or with disabilities. Only infertile people are viewed as having a special "obligation to adopt unparented" children "one did not beget" (Burtchaell, 1992, p. 106). No fertile woman has to regret or to explain not wanting any of these children, as one infertile woman wanting to adopt a healthy infant did when she observed:

> I really wish that I . . . was the type of person that could open my home to a cocaine-addicted child or an AIDS baby because I think that they are certainly deserving—but I'm not. I wish I was . . . and I don't think that it would be doing the child or us a favor by saying okay, well, we would like one. I just kind of regret . . . I don't dwell on it and I certainly admire people who can do that because that is great.

Whenever they expose cultural failures or make them their own, deviants bring normals face-to-face with uncomfortable truths. For this reason alone, the separation infertile couples feel and that exists between "us" and "them" is reinforced, making infertile couples members of a "neglected species" (Halverson, 1980) and "alone in a crowd" (Trepanier, 1985).

Us and Them

A recurring theme in the descriptions of the infertile women interviewed was the lack of understanding and sensitivity shown to them by their fertile counterparts who, having done "the American thing" by having children, ought to "understand" and "appreciate" their "struggle" to do the same.

The women, to a much greater extent than the men, experienced infertility as a social impediment preventing them from gaining admission into what one woman called "the special club of motherhood." Although women now have greater opportunities than ever before to pursue life goals other than motherhood, and despite the greater acceptance of a variety of alternative life-styles for women, biological maternity remains a critical factor in a woman's sense of herself as a normal woman. After the birth of her child, one woman recalled:

> When I miscarried [my first pregnancy], I actually went around and told people that I wasn't even that close to that I had a miscarriage. And after it was all over, I thought, "Why was it so important to me that these people knew that I had miscarried?" And then I thought, "Well, the reason was because I wanted them to know that I could get pregnant." The other day, when I didn't have [my baby with me], and I was walking somewhere, I passed some people and I thought, "I wonder if they know that I'm a mother?"

The very nature of pregnancy and of the vast majority of infertility diagnosis and treatment protocols make infertility a more salient and embodied feature of women's lives; it is in women's bodies that the success or failure to achieve a culturally prescribed goal will be manifested. Women with infertility are, accordingly, more likely to suffer "spoiled identities" (Goffman, 1963) and to define themselves wholly in terms of their inability to have a child.

Like chronically ill people who are deviant by virtue of their illness, the women had a rather truncated view of the world, tending to locate its inhabitants in one of two categories: infertile or fertile, not pregnant or pregnant, women "in the know" or women who "couldn't possibly know," and "just us" or "all of them." As one woman explained:

> There were two classes. There were those women who I was friends with who were all going through the same clinic and really understood. . . . There was another whole group of women who were the ones who would say, "I'm pregnant again and it was an accident," or who couldn't guess what you were going through. You really thought they were flaunting it, rubbing it in. They were just so insensitive. . . . There were all these other people who could understand and really empathize and then there was this other group who you didn't want to be around.

There were the women who conceive much too easily and then "abort and put 'em in plastic bags"; there were the women who would, if only effort, planning, goodness, and desire for children were rewarded with maternity, be "good mothers." There were the women who "take drugs and eat clay and have normal babies"; there were the women who do everything in their power to have a baby and still unaccountably fail.

One woman, who eventually gave up the pursuit of a child after nine years of effort, conveyed her sense of alienation and her anger at being unable to exchange in the "currency of women" (Pfeffer and Woollett, 1983, p. 127) when she observed:

> Before the children came, [my sisters-in-law and I] were real close. I felt that they were my sisters. Now I feel like there is a separation. In fact, I don't have a whole lot in common with them. Let's talk about what I have in common with my friends. I really feel left out.

The sense of otherness the women described included feelings of rage toward those women who, by the "twisted priorities of fate" (Mitchard, 1985, p. 119), were the least deserving of motherhood, and feelings of persecution, of being singled out for punishment. One woman stated:

> Just me, only me. The only person standing against the world to see people having children, and I'm not having any. Like all the people that I went to school with. Now all of them got kids and . . . I feel like I'm hurt.

Women identified with other persecuted groups, including Jews and blacks. Comparing the infertile to Jews, a woman observed:

> I think it's like the Jews used to feel in Europe when they had to wear the arm bands. You stuck out in a crowd. Someone would come up to you and say, "Do you have children?" "No." I felt like this sign would pop out in front of them. . . . I felt very set apart from everybody else.

Comparing the infertile to blacks, another woman observed:

> When you had someone like Jackie Robinson—maybe the best base-ball player that ever was—facing a very real possibility [of never playing ball]. Although he was lucky and he found a courageous club

that agreed to break the race barrier with him. It could have gone the other way for him. He could have been thwarted in achieving his life's ambition, his profession, for no good reason. For, in fact, a despicable reason. I guess in the old days that blacks were really helpless . . . nothing on their side. They were frustrated completely and there's nothing they could do about it. They were really just captives. Sometimes I feel . . . a little bit that way. It's like, why me? Why am I being singled out? I feel like I'm being punished for no good reason. I look around and I see people who are a lot less worthy being rewarded with kids. I know that's a terrible thing to say, but I do feel that way . . . Why me? I guess I've always thought that goodness was rewarded and hard work paid off and all the things you were taught and just, in this one particular area, it doesn't seem to be the case. . . . My husband and I would have great kids.

These women struggled with the ironies of life manifested in infertility. Moreover, their descriptions suggest that although infertility might be concealable in individuals as a potentially stigmatizing or discreditable condition (Goffman, 1963), childlessness in marriage was not.

Telling

A recurring theme in women's experiences with infertility and as Other was their being forced to talk about their childless state or to reveal their infertility. For example, one woman angrily described how hard it was when people came up to her at parties asking her whether she had any children yet or where her children were. As she recalled:

At first—it's changed over time—I kind of say, "No, we're trying," and that's how I'd leave it. And then I'd say to myself, the nerve that they should be asking me! Why do people ask me such personal questions? And then . . . some people come out and they'll say, "Well, why not? When are you going to?" I mean they push the subject. And, then one time, someone was really pushing me and . . . asking me one question after the other and finally I just turned around to her and I said, "because I can't have any children and we're trying to do something about it now. Just leave me alone." And I walked off. I was kind of rude but she pushed me to the limit.

This woman underscored the social visibility of conditions such as infertility that are not apparent to the eye. As a married and childless woman enjoined to adhere to a "cultural timetable" (Erikson, 1966) and a bio-cultural script (Kirk, 1964/1984) according to which children are expected after a certain number of years of marriage, she experienced an effect of a socially (if not physically) "visible stigma" (Goffman, 1963): tension in social interaction. Like pregnant women whose body and behavior become part of the public domain by virtue of their pregnancy (Balin, 1988), married women without children become subject to comment and scrutiny even by strangers. Even though it is now more acceptable, childlessness (if not infertility itself) still requires explanation.

The infertility of these women forced them to confront information management problems (whether, what, and who to tell) that have been associated with invisible stigmas, while their childlessness posed a social support problem (to reduce the tension in the give-and-take of social interactions) associated with visible stigmas (Goffman, 1963). Accordingly, infertile women often engaged in what they perceived to be both coercive and rejecting social exchanges (cf. Zabielski, 1984). Coercive exchanges were interactions in which the parties in the interaction felt forced to give or receive information or emotional support. Rejecting exchanges were interactions in which one party recognized that support was being offered but either wholly or partly rejected it because of the perceived nature of the support or because of who was offering it. Women described incidents where information was reluctantly shared, selectively imparted and with-held, or deliberately altered to protect self and others or to preserve valued relationships and emotional energy.

Some women told "the truth" about their infertility to forestall further questions, to avoid "remarks," and to prevent people from thinking that they "didn't want to have children." One woman recalled how reluctant she was to tell anyone that they were trying and not having any luck. Yet, relatives were "bugging" her, forcing her finally to share what she perceived as her failure. Another woman noted that although infertility was not something that she would bring up, she "felt the need" to inform her coworkers that she was being treated for endometriosis with Danocrine (a drug frequently causing moodiness and irritability) in order to preserve her relationship with them. Women also felt compelled to tell their coworkers about their infertility so that they would not think a more serious problem existed. As one woman remarked:

You have to tell some of the people at your job what's going on because you just can't be out from work. . . . As much as you have to go to the doctor for ultrasounds and blood tests and all of this, people are going to start to wonder, what's wrong with her, is she dying of cancer?

Women were often forced to talk about their infertility when their childlessness was socially remarkable and when the work absences mandated or the behavior changes induced by therapy warranted some explanation. One woman said that merely getting a prescription for a fertility drug filled at the neighborhood pharmacy had made it impossible for her to keep her infertility private. Women chose to share the "facts" of their situation with others, a kind of "deviance avowal" (cf. Miall, 1986; Schur, 1979), so that these others would not assume a condition existed that the women deemed even worse or potentially more discrediting than infertility: typically a mortal illness or voluntary childlessness. Some women felt obliged to talk about their situation to educate people about infertility and to prevent (cf. Miall, 1986) insensitive remarks.

I want people to know so they don't ask stupid questions. Or have crazy ideas about what we should do to get pregnant. I want people to see we are normal. That we are not horrible hunchbacks, the results of an incestuous relationship, or whatever stereotype.

In contrast, other women sought to cover their feelings of inadequacy, inferiority, and abnormality by attempting to pass (Goffman, 1963) as voluntarily and uncaringly childless. One woman, who eventually adopted a child, stated that whenever the subject of children arose, she acted negatively toward the idea. She said she would do anything to "kind of breeze it over" and make it easy for her to get out of the situation. One woman, who had been trying to get pregnant since she was fifteen years old, indicated that she would sometimes say she hated children because she could not get any. Because it was common for the young black women in her social network to have children in early adolescence, she said she used to act like she had "a mental problem behind having them." She recalled, "I just be saying it . . . deep inside my heart I don't mean it. But I say that around them 'cause I know I can't have none." Some women cited their lack of readiness for children or the poor economy as reasons for their childlessness so that people would not think there was something wrong with them just because they did not have children and so they could avoid the "shame."

Although women and couples might have initially found it comforting to share their struggles to have a child with others, they also found that having made one disclosure inevitably forced them to make others. One woman described how her friends now "followed [her menstrual] cycles" along with her, waiting to hear each month whether pregnancy was achieved. Other women were forced to reveal a miscarriage after sharing the news of a pregnancy, and adopting couples were repeatedly asked whether and when they would get their child. One man who was waiting to adopt a child felt as if he should have a taped response ready that he could play, repeating the same information he had already given many times before.

Infertile women and couples experienced the double bind of wanting to share information but also feeling that it might be better to withhold it. Although they derived some comfort or therapeutic effect (cf. Miall, 1986) from disclosure, they also sought to avoid some of the penalties of disclosure. Accordingly, women and couples were selective about what they told and to whom, especially concerning their efforts to conceive by in vitro fertilization and artificial insemination, techniques more likely to engender misunderstanding and insensitive remarks. Although women found it comforting and comfortable talking with other infertile women, they also, at times, felt compelled to reveal information they would have preferred to withhold. One woman recalled:

> And some of them, it's well, "what are you doing now? What are you into now? Have you done IVF?" Well, I'm not a good liar and so I couldn't say, when I was going through IVF, that no, I'm not doing IVF and I've never done IVF. I said, "Well, we're going to give it a try but we're really not that hopeful." And you tell those people and then two weeks later, they want to know. So, they mean well but it's been real difficult for me. I don't want to tell them.

Moreover, infertile couples who were more open about their infertility and open to information and support from others often suffered from overexposure to information. Hearing about other infertile couples' successes in treatment could cause either hope or despair; hearing about their failures could minimize a couple's own sense of failure or it could reinforce hopelessness.

Face-Work

Women with infertility also felt forced to put up a pleasant front in order to preserve their relationships or to protect other people from their negative moods. At the center of a typical infertility story was the baby shower that women were either forced to give or to attend for the sake of a pregnant relative or friend. The women uniformly felt much too "hurt" to participate in these affairs and that it was difficult to maintain a "seemingly normal friendship" between a pregnant woman and a woman trying and repeatedly failing to get pregnant: to pretend that the news of someone else's pregnancy was wonderful.

In one kind of "face-work," infertile couples, and women especially, sought to avoid such threatening situations (Goffman, 1969). Yet as one woman pointed out:

> You're always gonna face it. Whether it's my niece or my nephew or my friend's baby. You're gonna go to the shopping center, you're gonna go to the grocery store, you're gonna go on vacation, you're gonna see people with babies. You're gonna see things on the television. So what are you gonna do? You gonna go live on an island all by yourself and not see these things? So you have to learn to deal with it.

This woman understood that avoidance of situations that would remind her of her infertility was virtually impossible and would serve only to reinforce her sense of isolation. Another woman admitted that she sometimes wanted to close herself up in the house and not go out. As she observed:

> There was a time when all of my friends got together and we played cards during the day. They all talked about giving birth and about feeding and getting up and all this, and I just wanted not to go. But then, I said, "While they're all playing cards, where am I gonna be?" Because they're my friends, and I'll be stuck in the house by myself. So, I sort of resolved it.

Not avoiding situations but, instead, putting on a "happy face" made women and men disappointed with themselves for not feeling genuine happiness for another human being and angry with others for placing them in situations where they were forced to face it and to do face-work. One woman admitted how badly she had felt refusing to give a friend the baby shower she had promised to her.

> It's not nice. . . . I felt like I really dropped the ball on several accounts . . . [I] didn't like feeling like my childbearing years were over and here you have to be happy about somebody else's [pregnancy] and I really wasn't happy about it.

One man described his feelings for a coworker who constantly complained to him about her child.

> I finally told her I didn't want to be unfeeling, but I also didn't want to hear . . . about the problems she was having with her daughter who was two. She really made me angry one time. I didn't raise my voice or anything, but I just told her, "Stop telling me what a problem child your daughter is because she woke you up at five this morning. I can give you the names of a hundred couples right now that would trade you in an instant."

One woman captured the problem infertile women especially had in owning up to the true feelings behind the face. As she recalled:

> My sister-in-law found out that she was pregnant and I wasn't happy about it and everybody got upset and my reaction at that time was, "I'm entitled to be upset. I'm supposed to hold a happy face? I'm supposed to be strong through all of this all of the time?" That's ridiculous. I'm entitled to be angry. I'm entitled to be upset. After all, they're not going through what I'm going through. . . . Nobody has the right to tell me how I'm supposed to feel in that situation. . . . Just how strong am I supposed to be? There's a limit to the strength.

Women felt compelled to put up a facade, not only with pregnant women and, occasionally, women with small infants, but also with their spouses and close relatives. One woman had deliberately sought the assistance of a psychiatrist so she could cry. She explained, "I didn't want to put any more pressure on my husband. I didn't want to hear my mother—if I cry, she cries. I can go [to the psychiatrist] and cry and talk about it and not worry anybody else."

Women felt the need to protect their loved ones from their own sadness. Men, in turn, were distressed, less over the infertility itself than over what it was doing to their partners and to their lives together. As one man remarked:

> I don't think it affected me as badly as it did her. It began to bother me more and more and more the more I could see it in her. . . . I think I could have been happier, or less unhappy, childless than [she] would have been. . . . I don't think for any man it is as acute a loss or as severe a loss as it is for a woman.

One woman described how upset her husband was when she was upset. In order to keep him happy and to enlist his continued financial support for infertility treatments, she would have to put up a front. As she explained:

> I have to guard my emotions more than I used to. Because if I was to let it all hang out and let him know how depressed I get about this, or how upset I get about this all the time, he can't handle it. He keeps threatening me, "well, you're going to have to stop going to the fertility institute." . . . You have to keep up a facade.

The women expressed anger that they had to do the emotional work of infertility for themselves and their spouses. One woman remarked that she did not have the luxury of dealing with her own emotions, being forced "vicariously" to deal with those of her husband. Despite their love and need for their partners, women often cited men's overall inability to deal with feelings and emotions and admitted to suppressing their own feelings on behalf of their partners. Women also admitted sometimes mistaking their partners' seeming inability to cope with their feelings about infertility for lack of caring and for reluctance to have children. Men, in turn, described efforts to defer to the wishes of their wives, since they were the ones physically invested in treatment efforts, or to balance out the emotional tone in their marriages. Importantly, there was a certain gender incongruence in couples', or "his and her" (Greil, Leitko, and Porter, 1988), experiences of infertility, similar to the incongruent grieving found in couples after pregnancy and infant loss (Peppers and Knapp, 1980), that often affected partners' interactions with each other. (Such gender differences may also reflect differences in the way women and men cope with adversity in general or respond in research studies.)

Women also felt forced to "keep smiling" when friends and relatives gave them meaningless advice on how to get pregnant or made insensitive remarks. As one woman said, "What can you do?" Moreover, women had "to make a conscientious effort not to talk about [infertility] all the time." As one woman explained:

> If you talk about this all the time, people get tired of it. . . . I try not to dwell on the fact that I started my period and I'm all bummed out about that. . . . It's getting old. And they feel bad for me, but what can they do about it?

Another woman observed:

> I'd get so my friends didn't want to hear me talk about it—the ones that would listen, because I would just get into it. It was kind of a sickness. . . . I wouldn't talk to a lot of people about it because I'd know that they didn't want to hear about it. . . . And my husband would listen to me so much about it and finally I'd just shut up because I knew he'd heard everything he could.

The infertile women as well as those interacting with them felt constrained in their exchanges with each other and burdened by (cf. Charmaz, 1983) infertility. Relatives and friends deliberately withheld news of pregnancies from infertile women, fertile women stopped talking about pregnancy and children when they walked into the room, and husbands or boyfriends reluctantly went along with their partners' "passionate" pursuit of fertility. Demonstrating a kind of "aggressive" face-work (Goffman, 1969, p. 274), one woman recalled:

> Every time I'd walk in sometimes they'd stop talking . . . because they thought they were going to upset me . . . but I would push questions on her [pregnant friend] . . . "Well, how are you feeling? Do you feel the baby kicking?" and stuff like that because I didn't want to feel like I was left out. Just because I can't have one doesn't mean I don't want to take part in the joy of theirs.

Infertile women both wanted and did not want to be treated differently; identifying with other infertile people and with normally fertile people, they wavered in their alignments with both groups. One woman conveyed the constraint felt and "cooperation" (Goffman, 1969, p. 276) attempted by all parties involved in interactions with infertile couples in a story concerning her sister-in-law's pregnancy.

> They didn't want to tell us. And then they did and it turned out it was awful. And I'm real happy the way I dealt with their news and I told his mom that and his mom was crying and I was saying that she had just called and told us and she didn't say anything about it. And then [his] mother started crying and said, "Oh, you have no idea how much it hurt her to tell you and how hard it was." And I just wanted to say, "Oh, come on, it was harder for us." But then I thought, "Okay, just listen." And we had a really good talk. And she said that it was hard for [his] sister and that she postponed telling us because she kept hoping that we would get our baby. And I'm sure it was hard for them. Then I would go back to, "don't belittle her hardship just because it's not our hardship." And then I called his sister back and said, "I'm glad you told us. I'm sure it was hard." And she said that she knew it was hard and she was kicking at herself as soon as she hung the phone up because she hadn't said anything like, "I know this is hard for you and I know this stinks to you." She said she just didn't know what to say or what she felt. So I'm really glad that I called back.

This woman also described how she "gave people an out" when they asked her if she had children; she answered, "No, we can't have kids, but we are adopting." She wanted to help fertile people out since, "with one in six couples infertile, they are bound to hit someone who is having problems."

Infertile women recognized the interaction problems their infertility caused, not only for themselves, but also for those around them. As one woman noted, people felt "guilty" when they could not act "normally" around someone else and bad when they could not help. A woman who had suffered a miscarriage recalled feeling even worse when people avoided her because "they didn't know what to say":

> That made me feel more uncomfortable than if they would have said something to me. Because I wanted to talk about it. But nobody wanted to hear me talk about it. Everybody thought that I didn't want to talk about it. But I wanted to.

The infertile women understood that their friends and relatives meant well by their efforts and that it was difficult for them to know the right thing to do or to say. As two women admitted, "no matter what anybody did, it was gonna be hard," and "whatever they would say, something's wrong with it." Women acknowledged that if they had to put on a face and "put up with a lot" from other people, those people also had to put on a face and put up with a lot from them.

Between Worlds

As involuntary members of a deviant group, infertile women sought to concretize what they perceived as the amorphous boundary between normal and abnormal, them and us (Farrell and Swigert, 1982; Gove, 1980; Schur, 1983; Simmons, 1981). Being "us" but working hard to become one of "them," women with infertility compared themselves to each other and to fertile women. Such social comparisons permitted both self-evaluation and self-enhancement (Suls and Miller, 1977); they allowed women to determine where they "fit into the scheme of things" and to find the "slide rule" that would enable them to measure whether they were better or worse off, or "at least equal to everybody else."

For example, one woman compared herself to her fertile women relatives to try to assure herself that she too would eventually have children.

> I've had a few aunts that have always had bad menstrual cramps and some of them only have two children. My mother had five children, but it took her three years and she always had a lot of trouble with her menstrual cycles. Very heavy, just like I did. So I feel like once I get going. . . . Both of my grandparents had ten children. So I think it's just a matter of kicking my body in.

Another woman saw a great deal of similarity between her mother's fertility history and her own, and her mother was "real fertile." She also compared herself to the "type" of woman she had always thought would have trouble conceiving or bearing children, in order to determine why she was having a problem and to assure herself that her situation was not hopeless. Noting that other infertile women did the same thing, she described the social comparisons occurring in the physician's waiting room and her association of infertility with weakness and fragility.

> I think everybody that walks in [the waiting room], everybody checks them out. Like—she doesn't look like she'd have any problems. . . . I

would look at myself and say, "I don't look like the type that would be the type to have problems. . . . I look like I've got the good pelvis . . . I don't look like I should be having problems." And people say that to me, because I'm not one of these fragile little girls that need help. Miscarriages too. I had big misconceptions of people who have miscarriages and who have problems getting pregnant as being the type that are very puny and need help. I have a couple of friends that are like that, who just had babies so suddenly. So that was one thing, when I had the miscarriages, I kept saying, "This can't happen to me. I am not the type to lose a baby. I am not the type . . . I've never fainted, never." And so I equate that too as being a real frail little thing, and I'm not like that. So I don't think I should be having these problems, but I am.

Yet another woman thought infertility was related to a certain female "type." As she observed:

I'm tall and so many people look at me and say, "Oh, you'll be able to drop those babies like nothing." They think I have the shape to have babies, and I can't even conceive one, talk about delivering one. . . . My mother had no problems. My sister had no problems. . . . You'd just normally think it would just flow in line that I wouldn't. But everybody's different.

Infertility seemed to defy expectations of the kind of person most likely to have it; women had difficulty conceptually locating a health problem that had no distinctive phenotype.

Infertile women also worked to enhance their perceptions of their precarious situations and/or to separate themselves from other infertile women by thinking of themselves as better or worse off than other women. For example, one woman with a diagnosis of blocked tubes felt "luckier" than women with diagnoses of endometriosis because she perceived her problem as unambiguous and more easily treated. Moreover, having successfully conceived a child by in vitro fertilization, she also felt "luckier" than women who became pregnant naturally because she knew about her pregnancy earlier than they could and was, therefore, in a position to control her diet and other behavior earlier on behalf of her baby.

Even though she suffered a miscarriage, another woman felt herself to be much better off than women who could not conceive, because at least she became pregnant. She also emphasized the value of comparing stories, noting that more often than not, the other person had it worse. She felt lucky not to be living in a time when "there wasn't all these things you could do to try to get pregnant." Infertile women, in her mother's day, were less fortunate. Indeed, as another woman observed:

> It's easy to become a martyr. To have labeled myself as having a problem. But then when I think about what's happened to my neighbor next door, and her baby, I feel like I'm lucky because she had a perfect pregnancy until . . . the baby turned, wrapped the cord around her neck, tore the placenta away from the uterus, tore her up inside. She had to have an emergency hysterectomy cesarean section and the child is so retarded that she can barely hold her head up.

Having given up trying to have a child and contemplating sterilization, one woman came to the "95 percent conclusion" that she was really luckier than friends who had children because she had no worries: "all that vomiting, all that diarrhea, kids falling down, childhood diseases, all the shots." Yet another woman felt favored in relation to her fertile friends:

> I sat in the [high school] graduation line and I looked at all my friends that had babies. I mean really had the fast life. And they ended up hurt. While they ended up with kids, and I don't have any, but then I guess back then if I would have did some of the things [they did], I'd probably been dead now.

Although infertile women described the special "bond" they shared with each other and sought relationships with their "own," social comparisons sometimes acquired a hostile edge as a kind of competition occurred over who was really better or worse off and who was most deserving of support. As one man observed, in the world of infertile people, there were clearly "haves and have-nots." Infertile women who managed to have a baby were sometimes "resented": like "thin people going to Weight Watchers" and like "alcoholics who have it under control." Even women who miscarried were, at times, ostracized by women who had never achieved pregnancy; one of them demanded, "don't feel sorry for her, at least she got pregnant and lost it. I've never been pregnant in eight years."

This attempt to stratify one's "own" (Goffman, 1963, p. 107) caused resentment and division. One woman remarked, "I don't like it when people say, at least you—at least you can get pregnant or at least you can ovulate or at least you can father a child or at least you can get accepted at [adoption agency X]. It's like one-upmanship." For her, such remarks were no better than the ones she got from fertile people: "at least you don't have cancer." One woman described the dynamics in an infertility support group after she achieved pregnancy.

> When the group started, I had just found out I was pregnant. . . . I went and it was like apologizing, "I know that you're gonna notice that I'm already showing". . . . As I got more and more pregnant, and new people came in who didn't know me, it was like, "What is she doing here? She doesn't need this." . . . Then someone else got pregnant in the group, and then it was . . . "Can we let her come?"

This group eventually failed over differences. Another woman was told by her friends that they did not like "looking at [her] pregnant." Women who achieved pregnancy after infertility were sometimes denied and even felt the loss of their status as infertile women. Identifying with "both sides," they suffered a kind of identity deconstruction (cf. Lovell, 1983) in not being recognized as infertile.

Yet stratifying one's own also helped couples define the kinds of infertile people they were or did not want to become. Couples described themselves as different from other infertile couples in not being so desperate to get pregnant and in not being so devastated by infertility as other couples. One woman specifically sought not to become "a diehard infertile" who spent most of her life trying to get pregnant.

Infertility as Social Disability

Infertility clearly exerted a major influence on the everyday interactions of the women and couples interviewed. Although infertility may be a concealable stigma affecting only intimate relationships, childlessness was a socially visible handicap that often engendered complicated, strained, and painful interactions with family, friends, and even total strangers. Women especially viewed themselves as disadvantaged and disabled in relation to other women and this, in turn, made them feel personally and socially vulnerable.

Even though very few of the women described situations in which they perceived a deliberate intention to discredit or to degrade them (Garfinkel, 1967), it is wrong to dismiss infertility as a disability originating solely in the hearts and minds of infertile women. Rather, infertile women's

⟨perceived otherness testifies to the power of internalized cultural norms prescribing motherhood for women and to the social demands made on people who deviate from some norm, who have a condition that requires explanation.⟩Although the inability to have a child does not have to be perceived as disabling, these women felt disadvantaged by the biological impairment precluding conception, and they lived in a culture that views infertility as a disability. Infertility is a disability that is socially constructed from a biological reality (Wendell, 1989).

Infertile women's and couples' descriptions of their social exchanges illuminate the Janus-faced nature of social support. Although there is extensive literature on the positive features of social support in times of adversity and during life transitions, few studies have addressed the negative features of such support. In fact, negative social interactions or inequities in social exchanges may be more predictive of individual well-being than positive exchanges (Belle, 1982; Gottlieb, 1981; Rook, 1984; Rundall and Evashwick, 1982; Stack, 1974; Zabielski, 1984). Difficult social interactions, similar to those experienced by the infertile women interviewed, have been particularly associated with the physically and chronically ill (O'Brien, 1984; Peters-Golden, 1982; Slaby and Glicksman, 1985).

Infertile couples' descriptions of their social lives underscore the amorphous boundaries between them and us and the ambiguity of place that normal deviants must negotiate by virtue of their marginal social status. Their stories also reveal the everydayness of infertility that served to leave infertile people alone in a crowd.

7. The Quest

A quest is . . . a trip . . . that displays the logic of an encounter with wilderness. A quest must have a sacred goal. It must be fraught with peril. It must engage the whole being in a noble purpose combining determination, awe, and holy dread. No one may enter on a quest lightly, for solemn ritual is required, and the pilgrim must approach his goal as he would an altar: with ceremonial fear. (Churchill, 1982, p. 206)

As I have suggested previously, the quest of infertile couples for a child now involves more options than ever before, but not necessarily better chances of achieving the goal of parenthood. New technological developments such as in vitro fertilization and embryo transfer with a couple's own gametes or with donor eggs and sperm; the improvement, greater availability, and greater acceptability of old solutions such as corrective surgical techniques, fertility drugs, and artificial insemination; and the possibility of conventional and new adoptive parenting arrangements offer infertile couples hope. Yet the promise of becoming a parent through one of these means is undermined by the relatively high failure rates of biomedical techniques, the increasing complexity of adoption, and the increasing competition for a decreasing supply of infants to adopt.

Infertile couples who desire to become parents are forced to consider a maze of treatment and parenting options with no assurances that their goal of becoming parents will ever be reached. The women and couples participating in the Experiences of Infertility and Transition to Parenthood studies engaged in a recursive, iterative, and capital-intensive process of pursuit that demanded vast expenditures of personal and material resources. One man described the arduousness of the "medical and emotional journey" involved in the quest for a child:

The emotional journey was a lot larger stone to pull or push than the physical, because every time she would try something and it wouldn't work, the next step got her farther away from the basis in which she

started the whole thing and that was the most natural approach possible. . . . It compounded itself as you went forward. The best physical
image—if you ever see the tractor pull. . . . When the tractor pulls, the
further it pulls, the closer the weight gets to the tractor, therefore
applying more pressure on the tractor. Which is kind of a crazy thing.
That's the way this thing went for us. The more we tried, the harder we
pushed forward to get pregnant, the closer the weight got to our back
and the heavier the weight became on our back.

For this couple, the quest for a child involved not only negotiating Daeda-
lian mazes; it also entailed Sisyphean labors.

Couples described the fatigue involved in "trying" and "having to try"
to have a child. The amount of effort expended in negotiating the maze and
in managing its dead ends—treatment and adoption failures, and pregnancy losses—was staggering. The women and couples had been trying for
an average of five years to achieve pregnancy prior to their participation in
these studies. Of the forty-eight infertile women interviewed in the first
study, eleven women had been trying for five to ten years, one woman
thirteen years, and one woman seventeen years; sixteen of them had suffered one or more pregnancy losses prior to entering the study. Of seventy-
five infertile couples interviewed in the second study, twenty-eight couples
had been trying over a five to ten year period to achieve pregnancies and
two couples over an eleven to twelve year period; seventeen couples had
suffered one or more pregnancy losses or infant deaths prior to entering the
study and eight couples had suffered one or more adoption failures.

Women and couples thus entered the maze of options in the state of in-
betweenness that now typically defines infertility. The socioeconomically
advantaged couples typically sought medical assistance within an average of
one year of trying and failing on their own to have a child. In the first study,
among the twenty-one women in treatment with a private physician, and
for whom the time between trying on their own and seeking medical
assistance could be determined, only one woman waited nine years to get
help; the remaining twenty women sought medical help within two years
or less. In contrast, among the twenty women attending the infertility clinic
and from whom this information could be determined, nine women tried
on their own for three to six years before seeking medical assistance, and
eleven women sought help within two years or less.

By their own admission, the socioeconomically advantaged women
and couples were very "goal-oriented" and were used to "achieving" their

goals within the time limits they had set. These individuals expressed frustration with not doing what they had set out to do and concern with "wasting" time. One woman explained:

> You experience feelings of failure, especially if you've never encountered any before. . . . Never [had] any major failures. I had a divorce from my first marriage; that was a failure in its own way. But I was always into everything: very social, popular as a child and through school. I never had any trouble with grades and that sort of thing. I succeeded in college and in my career. I felt the only real failure I had in my life was my first divorce and then this infertility. And I really don't know if it is a failure. . . . Maybe it was just not meant to be.

Another woman recalled that the first feeling she had to deal with regarding her infertility was her frustration at not being able to achieve a goal.

These women were also accustomed to placing their faith in physicians to solve their problems. Although a few of the couples admitted to using a variety of natural remedies (herbs, relaxation techniques) to conceive a child, they generally sought medical assistance first. Even couples who placed a high premium on living self-reliant lives within a "natural" or "holistic" framework sought medical assistance within the conventional one-to-two-year-period allotted a couple to get pregnant on their own. As one woman put it, "When we started going to doctors, there I was encouraged again. Because I guess like most people, I thought well, they'll fix it. You know, the man in white will come to the rescue." Even when they were thoroughly "disgusted" with physicians or found them to be "opportunists" and their diagnoses to be "nonsense," they found it hard not to think of them as "God almighty . . . believing every word and hanging on to every piece of advice." In effect, these women sought a kind of "vicarious control" by associating themselves with the "powerful" physician (Rothbaum, Weisz, and Snyder, 1982).

In contrast, the less advantaged women were more likely to seek a vicarious control by believing that conception was in "God's hands." They were more willing to wait for the time when "God was ready" to give them a child. The treatment orientation of women attending the clinic was somewhat less persistent and more on-and-off than that of the women and couples under private physician care, a factor that may be related to the persistence and consistency of the physicians treating them and to their own beliefs concerning whether a physician or God was more likely to help them get pregnant. One woman said about going to the clinic, "I'll start and then I'll get disgusted and then I'll stop and come back again." Another woman noted, "I been trying but I stopped. 'Cause I am tired of going through all tests." One woman who had been trying to have a child for fourteen years said, "Maybe it ain't meant for me to have no children. That's all. . . . If it's for you to have, you gonna have it." Another woman attending the clinic on and off for eight years observed:

> If God is ready for 'em to have children, then He gives 'em to 'em. If he ain't ready for 'em to have none, then He won't give you none. . . . Maybe he just has His time set, when He wants me to have children. He ain't punishing me for nothing . . . He works in mysterious ways.

The more advantaged women appeared to have a more ambivalent and less tranquil relationship with God, praying to have a child but angry with God at the injustice of not having a child. When these women and couples took time off from the active pursuit of a child, they tended to do so because they had to move or because family circumstances made it difficult for them to pursue treatment for a time or because they lacked resources.

Women and couples usually began "doing infertility" when they felt they had passed the period of time during which most couples would have conceived, or when they had passed the time they had allotted themselves to conceive. Doing infertility involved getting physicians to look for "what was wrong" and to "make [pregnancy] happen," and it typically was initiated by the woman and enacted in a gynecological setting that utilized an investigative and treatment-oriented framework. Women with medical knowledge, or who were familiar with using ovulation detection methods, or who were otherwise anxious that they had not conceived within a few months believed that waiting even one year was too long. Physicians, in turn, tended to adhere to the one-year rule, after which they tended to start and often to keep looking for impediments to conception in the woman. The wife of a man who turned out to be sterile observed:

> After the first month, I was depressed. And after the second month it got worse and then by about the fourth month, I was in tears. I guess about the tenth month was when I mentioned something to the gynecologist that we weren't getting anywhere. She gave us two more months. She said traditionally the waiting period is a year and after a year you get referred on to infertility studies. So it was about a year

after we started trying when we were referred to a specialist. The workup initially focused on me.

Couples who were sterile (absolutely incapable of having a child), where the wives had undergone a hysterectomy (for endometriosis or cancer) or where the husband was quickly found to have no vas deferens, were spared much of the uncertainty of doing infertility. Although not spared the traumas of cancer, surgery, and sterility, they did not suffer a prolonged period of "wondering" why they were unable to conceive.

Couples usually embarked on "doing adoption" only after a period of time "doing infertility." Doing adoption was generally viewed as a "backup" measure, although there were a few couples who recalled being interested in adoption even before they discovered they could not have a child. One of these couples even felt that infertility had diverted them from, as opposed to forced them toward, adopting a child. Doing adoption entailed finding out about the many adoption routes available, including local and interstate private and public agencies handling domestic and foreign adoption, and private adoption; selecting an adoption route; and then meeting the requirements involved in traveling that route.

Once in the maze of treatment and adoption options, couples were confronted with a variety of paradoxical and frustrating situations. Couples doing infertility were often confronted with being infertile without definitive cause, with presumed causes for which treatments were unavailable or ineffective, and with treatments offered in the absence of any established causes. Similarly, couples doing adoption were confronted with available babies they could not get, bureaucratic policies they could not fathom, and varying criteria for acceptance as adopting parents they could not rationalize.

Calculus of Pursuit

Accordingly, couples engaged in as rational an accounting process as they could given the uncertainty and emotionality of their situation. They weighed the options known and accessible to them and then constructed their own calculus of pursuit, involving four domains of venture capital: time, money, and physical and psychic energy. Couples used this matrix of resources to determine which route in the maze of routes to parenthood to pursue. As one man remarked concerning in vitro fertilization, a couple had to consider the time it might take for it to work and what they could afford "financially and psychologically and physically."

Couples calculated the amount from each of these four categories of resources that was available to them, including what they could borrow. For example, couples considered the time available to them to pursue options such as adoption or in vitro fertilization given their ages and the age limits associated with these ventures. Couples approaching and in their forties found themselves literally at the "eleventh hour" for many options readily available to younger couples. Because of the great financial expenses involved in undergoing medical treatment that were frequently not covered by health insurance or in undertaking adoption, couples also had to determine what their budget would allow and whether it was wise to borrow money to pursue an option. Tables 7.1 and 7.2 show the costs of individual infertility services and the costs of services in four increasingly complex medical "scenarios" as estimated by the Office of Technology Assessment (U.S. Congress, 1988). Several of the couples interviewed estimated that they had spent $25,000 to achieve pregnancy. In addition, the Office of Technology estimated the average cost of adoption to be $3,000 to $10,000, although there were respondent couples who paid considerably more than $10,000 by the time they got a child.

Couples also determined the amount of resources any one option required for a reasonable probability of success. Because of the conflicting and confusing statistical odds based on varying group outcomes quoted to them, couples had to work to interpret these odds in a way that would provide direction for future action: to estimate what their very own chances were for having a baby, as opposed to some average (cf. Modell, 1989). For example, couples considering in vitro fertilization perceived the 15 to 20 percent chance they were typically offered of succeeding with this procedure as either improving or declining with each try and, therefore, as worth or not worth the high cost of repeated attempts. One couple calculated that the five percent chance they were given of conception after tubal surgery was not worth the necessary capital investments and decided to put their resources instead into two in vitro fertilization attempts. Another couple anticipated trying in vitro fertilization only one time, even though they were told that repeating the procedure would increase their chances of success. Couples understood that most medical treatments had to be repeated for any reasonable chance of pregnancy and that it typically took one to two years even to make an adoption agency's waiting list. By these calculations, couples attempted to achieve a kind of "predictive control" (Rothbaum, Weisz, and Snyder, 1982).

TABLE 7.1. Estimated costs of infertility services, 1986.

SERVICE	MEDIAN SURVEY COST	SURVEY RANGE OF COSTS	OTHER ESTIMATES
DIAGNOSTIC SERVICES:			
Patient history and full physical	$120	$50–415	$60
Infection screen	$40	$18–138	
Sonography (per exam)	$100	$40–186	
Hormone tests (per test)	$50	$25–85	
Pelvic exam	$40	$18–75	$40
Cervical mucus:			
Postcoital test	$40	$25–100	$25
Mucus penetration	$40	$25–200	
Hysterosalpingogram	$150	$50–1,500	$100–300
Endometrial biopsy	$85	$50–350	$100–300
Hysteroscopy	$400	$130–1,100	
Laparoscopy	$800	$400–2,500	$650–900
Semen analysis	$45	$15–108	$15–70
Sperm antibody test	$75	$35–300	$300
Hamster-oocyte test	$275	$35–390	$300
Infertility counseling	$75	$38–135	
TREATMENT SERVICES:			
Medical treatment:			
Clomiphene citrate	$30 per month	$16–75	$20/month
HMG	$28 per ampule	$24–38	$40–42
	$588 per month	$200–1,500	$420–504
HCG	$20 per 5,000 units	$10–45	
Danazol	$160 per month	$120–200	$120–135
Bromocriptine	$90 per Rx	$30–450	
Tubal reversals	$2,500	$1,300–5,000	
Reversal of vasectomies	$2,000	$1,000–2,500	
Tubal surgery for PID	$2,000	$750–3,800	$3,000–6,000
Repair of varicocele	N/A	N/A	$2,000–2,500
Laser laparoscopy	$1,200	$485–3,000	
Endometriosis-ablation	$1,200	$400–5,000	
In vitro fertilization	$4,688	$775–6,200	$4,000–6,000
Frozen embryo transfer	$500	$220–1,800	
Gamete intrafallopian transfer (GIFT)	$3,500	$2,500–6,000	
Artificial insemination			
Husband's sperm			$35–90
intracervical	$53	$30–105	
intrauterine, washed sperm	$85	$40–200	

TABLE 7.1.   *Continued*

SERVICE	MEDIAN SURVEY COST	SURVEY RANGE OF COSTS	OTHER ESTIMATES
Donor sperm			$25–90
fresh	$80	$35–150	
frozen	$100	$40–350	
donor fee			$50–100

Source: U.S. Congress, Office of Technology Assessment, *Infertility: Medical and social choices,* OTA-BA-358 (Springfield, VA: National Technical Information Service, May 1988), p. 141. Adapted by permission.

Yet because of the open-endedness of most infertility treatments and the difficulty of determining when the law of averages might work in their favor, couples found it harder to calculate the resources required of them by the various options than to calculate the resources available to them. Even when they could determine what resources they had, couples could not always reasonably determine what it would take and what they could take in pursuing an option. Couples were, sometimes, not prepared for (even if informed about) the physical and emotional hardships associated with any one treatment or adoption option. In addition, as other researchers have also found (DeZoeten, Tymstra, and Alberda, 1987; Johnston, Shaw, and Bird, 1987; Leiblum, Kemmann, and Lane, 1987; Modell, 1989), some couples tended to overestimate the likelihood of success in undergoing medical procedures. Women with previous biological children believed they would conceive easily by artificial insemination or in vitro fertilization. Although they knew the odds were only 15 to 20 percent that they would conceive by in vitro fertilization, some couples felt 100 percent certain they would be among that small group; one couple described themselves as the "perfect couple" for in vitro fertilization.

Couples also sought to determine the amount of resources they were willing to invest in pursuit of an option. For example, couples who perceived a 15 to 20 percent chance of having a child with treatment as "better than no chance" to conceive at all were willing to invest resources in therapy. Other couples had personal or moral objections to pursuing therapy. For example, one woman knew that because of her weight and other medical problems she was not a good candidate for any medical treatment.

TABLE 7.2. Scenarios of infertility diagnosis and treatment.

Infertility service		Cost

STAGE I SCENARIO—OLIGOMENORRHEA

DIAGNOSTICS

Patient history and physical	$120×2	$ 240
Hormone tests	$50 per test, battery of 3 run 3× in 1 month	$ 450
Pelvic exam		$ 40
Semen analysis		$ 45
Counseling		$ 75
	Total	$ 850

FERTILITY DRUG TREATMENT
Clomiphene citrate

Drug costs	5 days per month	$ 30
Blood tests	$40×3	$ 120
Ultrasound		$ 100
Physician visits	$40×2	$ 80
	Total	$ 330
	×4 months	$1,330

HMG (1 month)

Drug costs, 5–10 days	$28 per ampule × 3 per day × 7 days	$ 588
Blood test run each day		$ 350
Ultrasound		$ 250
HCG		$ 20
Physician visits	$40×7	$ 280
	Total	$1,488
	Drug treatment total	$2,818
	Total, Stage I Scenario (6–9 months)	$3,668

STAGE II SCENARIO—COMPLETE INFERTILITY EVALUATION

Screening for infections	$ 40
Sonography	$ 100
Cervical mucus	$ 80
Endometrial biopsy	$ 85
Hysterosalpingogram	$ 150
Hysteroscopy	$ 400

TABLE 7.2. *Continued*

Infertility service		Cost
Laparoscopy (outpatient) (including laser)		$1,200
	Total, Stage II Scenario (12 months)	$2,055

Stage III Scenario—Tubal Surgery

Tubal surgery (for PID)		
Physician costs		$2,000
Hospital charges (anesthesia, operating room, hospital stay)		$1,500
Laparoscopy		$ 800
Fertility drug treatment (see Stage I Scenario)		$2,818
	Total, Stage III Scenario (18 months)	$7,118

Stage IV Scenario—In Vitro Fertilization

History and physical, counseling		$ 150
Drugs (chemical stimulation)		$ 638
Clomiphene citrate		
HMG		
HCG		
Ultrasound assessment of follicular growth		$ 500
Hormone blood tests		$ 425
Laparoscopy		$1,500
Physician fees		
Anesthesia		
Operating Room		
Embryology and embryo transfer		$1,100
Laboratory		
Physician		
Hospital room		$ 250
Followup, routine tests		$ 125
		$4,688
	× 2.0 cycles	
	Total, Stage IV Scenario (6 months)	$9,376

Source: U.S. Congress, Office of Technology Assessment, *Infertility: Medical and social choices*, OTA-BA-338 (Springfield, VA: National Technical Information Service, May 1988), p. 142. Adapted by permission.

Some couples were not "comfortable . . . circumventing nature's course." As one man explained, perhaps there was some divine purpose in he and his wife not being able to conceive. He said, "Perhaps there would be more harm from our forcing the issue trying to reconstruct ourselves." Another man wondered whether, since he and his wife could not conceive "naturally," maybe they ought not to attempt assisted conception: "Maybe nature would like us not to." One woman believed that "you take the cards you're dealt. You don't try to alter your fate."

Couples were also unwilling to continue trying to achieve pregnancy when they perceived it as unduly risking their health and well-being or as adversely affecting their marriages or the entire tenor of their lives. Couples wanted to live normal lives again. Women expressed their ambivalence about "forcing" their bodies to reproduce by consuming powerful chemicals and undergoing painful surgical procedures. They described having "had" it with drugs and surgery. As one woman observed, infertility treatment was "like inflicting sickness upon yourself."

Time was a critical variable in couples' determination of the merits of investing in an option, with couples willing to invest in options they had once dismissed in the past as not worth it or too risky. In addition, couples considered their own and their partners' desires and preferences and the attributes they associated with the options themselves. Women described their husbands or husbands described themselves as willing or unwilling to invest further in treatments for the sake of their wives: willing because it was important to their wives or unwilling because it threatened the well-being of their wives. Although some women still in treatment described instances where their partners were reluctant to invest their resources in achieving pregnancy or adoption, the couples tended to agree that husbands deferred to their wives' wishes in the matter of pursuing treatment, because the wives were the ones whose bodies were directly involved in most treatments and because having a child was perceived as critically important for women. In only a few instances did wives indicate feeling compelled to undergo treatment because of their husbands' wishes. In the matter of adoption, husbands and wives were alternatively solicitous of one another's readiness for adoption.

Considering the attributes of options (cf. Shiloh, Larom, and Ben-Rafael, 1991), some women were unwilling to initiate or continue with drug therapy because of the short and potentially long-term side effects of these drugs. Women described the "craziness" and "off-the-wall . . . personality changes" induced by Danocrine, a drug used to treat endometriosis, and the pain of hyperstimulated ovaries induced by fertility drugs. One woman said, 'I don't like to lose control and I have a lot of trouble with drugs. Although I've tried marijuana and things, I always did not like to lose control of my body."

Some women perceived continuing with treatment as staying in control and as doing something about infertility. One woman remarked that for her, stopping treatment was not a solution. She said, ". . . then I feel like I'm losing even more control over my life. Because then you don't even have someone else trying to help." Other women viewed continuing with treatment as losing control and as possibly causing health consequences more serious than infertility.

> In the back of my mind, I worry that I don't want to die of cancer from all these ultrasounds or God knows what I'm screwing up with this constant fertility pills. You have to sign all these papers saying this is what could—that's what worries me.

While comparing adoption with donor insemination, couples drew different conclusions about the merits of options that involved entering into a reproductive partnership with a third party. One couple with male factor infertility considered donor insemination superior to adoption. As the husband explained:

> As long as donor insemination was an option, I wouldn't consider adoption. I mean as long as [it was] acceptable to [my wife]. Because they said that a baby is biologically fifty percent ours. . . . Short of producing the sperm, I mean the baby is entirely ours. I thought that was a lot, just superior to adoption. I hadn't even considered [adoption] as an option unless [my wife] said no way to insemination.

The wife then pregnant by donor insemination continued:

> We looked at a lot of things like, first of all, you cannot assure the health of the mother and, therefore, you cannot assure the health of the child in case of adoption. And certainly in terms of physical characteristics, this was the way that we were going to get the closest. And I think being pregnant was also a big piece of it. I see a lot of friends of mine becoming pregnant very quickly after they began trying and just wanting to be a part of that. It's like this woman's club . . . I just felt so left out and really. So I think that becoming pregnant was also a big part of it. But, also there is a lot of control. Like

I said, at least this way, I know that I'm not drinking during the pregnancy and I'm not taking illicit drugs and I'm eating well and I'm maintaining my health.

In contrast, another couple with male factor infertility decided against donor insemination and for adoption because they had heard how "dehumanizing" it was to undergo the procedure and that there were "no guarantees" of its success. A third couple with male factor infertility also favored adoption after the wife "completely rejected the idea" of insemination, having found doctors to be arrogant and "pushy." Also, this couple found the chances of success with donor insemination to be too low, and they had already considered adopting at least one of their children prior to learning of the husband's impairment.

Finally, as other researchers have also found (Tymstra, 1989), women and couples anticipated the amount of regret they would experience if they discontinued an option or if they did not pursue an option at all. If the immediate goal of the process of mazing was to have a child, the ultimate goal was to exit the maze with no regrets: an objective accounting for the high tolerance of infertile couples for suffering and failure and their low tolerance for the "should-haves" and "what-ifs" that threatened to shadow them in their later years. These women and couples were less "addicted" to treatment (Greil and Porter, 1988), or "driven" (Olshansky, 1988) to have a child, than they were intolerant of regret and of losing the control that doing something could afford them. They wanted a child, but, even more important, they wanted to feel that they had done what they could, within the parameters of technical and moral possibility they had set, to have a child. One woman recalled an infertile friend telling her that she would regret not trying everything possible and that she could deal with trying and failing easier than with not trying at all. Another woman asked, "How can I stop now if there's something else that might be done? . . . I couldn't accept it if I didn't try everything that there was." One woman wanted "to go all the way." She said, "I can have a clear conscience and say ten years from now, well, I did everything I could." Indeed, soon after the birth of her child, a woman recalled her decision to undergo in vitro fertilization:

> I didn't want to be seventy years old rocking in a rocking chair, thinking that "Well, I wonder what would happen if I had tried." I just, it was almost like a protection for myself to try it and go through it and make—yeah, make sure it didn't work. You know, that sounds kinda strange, but I didn't want to look back and say, "gosh, I should have, or what if I did?"

Couples attempted to "clear the slate" and "go the gamut" in order to avoid the "if-onlys." One couple described the one in vitro fertilization attempt they were willing to make (and which succeeded) as buying a "$7,000 peace of mind." In some cases, already regretting or, at the very least, reviewing fertility choices made in the past (such as delaying child-bearing, and elective pregnancy terminations and sterilizations), couples anticipated regret in their cost accounting of the benefits and liabilities of initiating or continuing an option. Before deciding to adopt their second child, for example, one woman went back on Clomid for six months to be certain that she had not "dropped" doing infertility "too abruptly." After this trial period and because she and her husband were so pleased with their first adopted child, they anticipated no regrets about stopping the pursuit of pregnancy.

Couples sometimes made mistakes in estimating regret. One couple decided to terminate the adoption process after years of waiting for and failing to get a child in order to get on with their lives. They anticipated they would be content as foster parents. Several months later they decided they could not be happy without children of their own to parent and decided to pursue a different adoption route. One couple waiting longer than they had anticipated to adopt a child reconsidered trying in vitro fertilization one more time, hoping that further refinements in the technique would permit them to conceive a child. As the woman observed, she thought that that "box" had been closed forever, that she had reached closure concerning her inability to get pregnant.

In summary, the calculus of pursuit for infertile couples helped them determine what part of the maze of options to parenthood they would enter. When a pregnancy was achieved, or when they made an agency's adoption list, a couple had the exit point in sight, the "light at the end of the tunnel." When another failure was incurred, couples repeated the process in order to determine whether doing infertility or doing adoption was the "surer thing," the path more likely to get them out of the maze. A few women and couples considered exiting the maze without any children at all.

In the Maze

Women and couples exhibited six patterns of pursuit: sequential tracking, backtracking, getting stuck, paralleling, taking a break, and drawing the line. The "sequential tracking" pattern was exhibited when couples elected to exhaust one route before they started another, such as trying a variety of treatment options in sequence for a limited number of cycles before selecting one of the adoption tracks available. In some cases, couples were forced into this pattern of pursuit. For example, there were couples who wanted to pursue several adoption routes simultaneously ("paralleling"), but adoption agencies would not permit this. In addition, although the typical sequence of diagnostic and treatment events moved couples from simpler, less intrusive, and less high-tech procedures to more technically complex ones, some couples moved to procedures like in vitro fertilization fairly quickly, depending on their diagnosis and the recommendations of their physicians.

In the sequence of treatment alternatives, then, in vitro fertilization was not solely considered an "end-stage treatment" (Plough, 1981); some couples contemplated undergoing other medical procedures only after in vitro fertilization failed. In vitro fertilization is increasingly being presented as a first-line as opposed to "last-ditch" (Johnston et al., 1985, p. 502) effort against infertility, as it is viewed as potentially more effective than more conventional therapies for a widening range of fertility impairments, including unexplained infertility (Lilford and Dalton, 1987; Oehninger et al., 1988; Seibel, Ranoux, and Kearnan, 1989). One man explained why he and his wife considered tubal surgery the last resort if their attempts to conceive by in vitro fertilization failed:

> [The choice was] either surgery, which was extensive and the yield might be low since you always get scar tissue after surgery anyway, or having the in vitro procedure which [the physician] thought would be less strenuous for [his wife] and with the same percentage of chance as the surgical/tubal reconstruction. And so we opted for in vitro. If in vitro doesn't work, we can always try and change the tubes.

Later, this man added that they planned to try in vitro fertilization four to five times until they were "bankrupt" and were forced to turn to "the only thing left," tubal surgery.

Importantly, there was no one sequential tracking scenario. Some couples found out quickly what their fertility problem was, some couples moved quickly to more complex diagnostic or therapeutic techniques, and other couples moved slowly as problems were found that turned out to be "minor," "insignificant," "borderline," or unresponsive to initial treatment efforts. What distinguished sequential tracking from other patterns of pursuit was not the orderly simple-to-complex or low-tech to high-tech scenarios depicted in textbooks, but rather the step-by-step move from one previously untried procedure to the next.

A second pattern of pursuit was "backtracking," in which couples restarted a diagnostic or treatment plan with a new physician or returned to a previously attempted treatment or adoption option. Advances in a therapy that had occurred since a couple had attempted it last was one reason why couples reconsidered treatment. Also, one couple returned to and was accepted by an adoption agency that had previously discouraged them from applying. Couples also backtracked when their physicians felt that a procedure had been improperly done or when their physicians did not have the results of a previously conducted test, or when a factor that can change over time, such as sperm quality and quantity, mandated that it be evaluated again. Finally, couples backtracked when they decided to seek medical assistance after failing to get pregnant and then failing to adopt, or when they sought medical treatment after successfully adopting a child. In all these variations of backtracking, couples moved over ground previously traveled.

A third pattern of pursuit was "getting stuck." Seeing, believing, or being encouraged by their physicians that persistence paid off, couples who got stuck in a treatment groove attempted the same regimen over and over and over again. One woman described having roughly two hundred injections of various fertility drugs before achieving conception. Couples told stories of other women who had attempted in vitro fertilization more than ten times. One couple tried in vitro fertilization four times before they achieved pregnancy. They admitted that they would have continued with this technique if they had not achieved pregnancy because they believed that their chances of success increased with every attempt. As they explained it, the technology was steadily improving, and doctors became more familiar with them and their bodies every time in vitro fertilization was tried. Moreover, the wife tended to blame herself for the three failures she had experienced before getting pregnant, a factor that encouraged her to stay in this treatment groove. Even though she knew that the odds were against her with in vitro fertilization, she wondered, "What did I not do that was right that would have made a difference?" She attributed the success of her fourth attempt to her having taken better care of herself. Similarly, another woman was encouraged to try in vitro fertilization a third time because she was told that persistence paid off and that she was a "good stimulator," that is, she was responsive to hormonal priming. Other couples felt proud that they were the "perfect couple" for in vitro fertiliza-tion, with sperm counts "off the chart" and with a high number and good quality of eggs.

As other researchers have found (Callan et al., 1988), continuing in a treatment groove was associated with optimism about succeeding the next time. In the couples we interviewed, it was also associated with a belief in persistence and in personal control over whether a treatment worked. Women who failed to become pregnant in treatment often blamed them-selves for treatment failures (cf. Milne, 1988), and they often assumed or were made to assume both the burden for being a good candidate for a procedure (a "good stimulator" as opposed to a "low responder") and the responsibility for making the procedure work. Soon after learning she had conceived by in vitro fertilization, one woman hinted at the "ambiguous responsibility" (Becker and Nachtigall, 1991) for treatment success that sometimes characterized the relationship between physician and infertility patient. As she recalled:

> We were in [the doctor's] office, and we were all congratulating each other. I was trying not to jump up and down and everybody was real happy and everything. And [the doctor] said to me, "Now just make sure that you hold on to it." And I remember thinking like, oh, that's just such a horrible thing to say to me. You know, it's like you're making me feel responsible for losing it or keeping, which I don't have that power. Obviously I would have ten children if wishes made it so.

One woman asserted that it was "up to the patient to get the ball rolling" in treatment and, later, after embryo transfer, that it was up to her body to make it succeed. One couple was unsure where the responsibility for success or failure lay, but believed that it was important to identify some cause even if that meant implicating themselves. As the wife explained:

> The first time we did [IVF], everything went well. They got seven eggs and all seven of them fertilized. And so I mean it was very exciting; we got four embryos put in and just around the time of implantation—that was upsetting—I took a bad fall. I was . . . trying to relax . . . I knew that was it. I mean, what do I know? Probably had nothing to do with it, but. . . .

Her husband added:

An awful lot of this as far as I'm concerned is the sense of helplessness that you have as to what's going on. You'd rather ascribe a cause to it, any cause at all, it doesn't matter as long as you feel like you have some control over what's going on.

The wife concluded, "Yeah. Rather than it just didn't work." By assuming responsibility for the outcome of a largely ineffective treatment, these individuals responded "as if a chance-determined situation were controllable" (Rothbaum, Weisz, and Snyder, 1982, p. 17). Attributing treatment failure to their own potentially modifiable behavior, couples thus maintained the possibility of changing their behavior to achieve success, thereby minimizing the apparent randomness of treatment outcomes (Janoff-Bulman, 1979).

Getting stuck was also associated with a low tolerance for regret and a perception that no infertility really existed. One woman tried donor insemination fifteen times before achieving success. Having easily conceived and borne a child in a previous marriage, she had difficulty accepting that she could not easily conceive again. She was, accordingly, willing "to play the odds" and would have continued to play them had she not achieved pregnancy.[1]

A fourth pattern of pursuit was "paralleling," or the attempt to pursue actively and simultaneously multiple tracks to parenthood, as opposed to simply "thinking about," "talking about," or "looking into" another track should the current track fail to lead to a child. Often exhibited by couples who felt "in a panic" and "desperate," paralleling was a means to "maximize the options" while minimizing the time wasted in pursuit. Feeling pushed to the wall, paralleling couples decided "not to close any doors," "to keep the options open," "to keep our irons in the fire," and, most significantly, "to never give up."

These couples thus attempted to navigate several paths at the same time, pursuing additional paths as they opened up. One couple, who had been trying to conceive for five years, decided after an initial period of doing infertility to "look into" adoption. They persisted in doing infertility because they felt they were finally making progress medically and had "something to shoot for." When that something was not reached, they moved along (in a sequential tracking pattern) to the next stages of doing infertility. Increasingly, though, they experienced "desperate feelings" as they lost "excess years," and they decided to "pursue both sides." Their physicians gave them hope, but they had not as yet succeeded in becoming pregnant. They felt compelled to get on an adoption waiting list, even though they had reservations about adopting, because they were "seeing time go by." As the wife explained:

> I'm having to decide now whether I'm going to go back and spend money that is not covered by insurance to go any further when we don't have to. [We are] kind of at a crossroads again since it hasn't worked so far. It seems like I would be better off psychologically if I'd been told that I can't get pregnant. Then I'd just forget that part and I could be all for the adoption with no reservations. But I just haven't got to that point yet.

Now at the end of the period after her tubal surgery when a pregnancy should have occurred if it were going to happen at all, this couple had to reconsider their options. The wife further observed, "If I could just . . . forget the adoption and know I'd get pregnant, or forget the pregnancy and go ahead and adopt." Four months later, after a chance to adopt fell through, she remembered that when they received the call about that baby, she forgot about getting pregnant: "forgot and didn't even care . . . a nice feeling." After the adoption failure, this couple was back to doing infertility (backtracking), undergoing repeated cycles of fertility drugs and husband inseminations (getting stuck), and waiting for another call that a baby was available for them to adopt.

Similarly, another couple maintained that you have to "seek all your outlets and investigate anything that you hear about." This couple's strategy illustrated the complete lack of closure, characteristic of paralleling, to any new option that might appear; they remained on an adoption agency's waiting list, continued to do infertility, and remained open to any chance for a private adoption. For paralleling couples, continuing to pursue treatment while pursuing adoption did not necessarily mean they were ambivalent about parenting an adopted child, but rather that they were eager to have a child by whatever means came through first. Paralleling couples paid a high psychic price by never letting go of the possibility of pursuing any available path to parenthood and by investing a tremendous amount of energy just staying on track with every option being pursued. The burdens of juggling too many options at the same time included marital tension, frustration, and, sometimes, even deception when adoption agency policy prohibited couples from simultaneously doing infertility and adoption.

A fifth pattern of pursuit was "taking a break." Women and couples had a variety of reasons for withdrawing from the pursuit of parenthood for a while, including geographic moves, family illnesses and deaths, financial constraints, the need to recover from failure and loss, and the fatigue and frustration of pursuit itself. While on break, one couple got pregnant. Other couples were able to recapitalize their waning financial, physical, and psychic reserves for the continued pursuit of a child or for some other goal. Taking a break was also a way that women delayed the "end" they knew was coming; by taking a break, they left themselves something else to try. As one woman explained:

> I've got three more months on Pergonal . . . I was supposed to go back . . . around Thanksgiving for my fourth . . . Pergonal episode. . . . I asked [the doctor] if I could go off of it for a month or two because of it being the holidays. I used that as an excuse, but I think what I was doing was prolonging my time. I was buying my time, so to speak. I don't want the end to come. I'm trying to prepare myself. But I don't know how I'm gonna handle it when the end does come—if I'm not pregnant.

Another woman found it "scary" to think she had reached the last thing she could try to have a baby. So she "put it off." She asked, "After I do this, this is serious. . . . What am I gonna do after this? I'm gonna have to throw in the towel."

Not taking a break had negative consequences for some couples. One woman moved directly from one treatment failure to the next without giving herself "time to grieve" the "babies" she had lost. Similarly, one couple decided only one hour after being informed that the wife could die having a child of her own to go to an orientation meeting for prospective adoptive parents. She recalled that her intensely negative feelings about pursuing adoption at that time had been a "reaction" to the stunning "blow" she had sustained and recognized that it had not been "good timing" on her part to think about adoption so soon afterward.

The sixth pattern of pursuit was "drawing the line." Couples drew the line on the pursuit of pregnancy at different points in time, depending on when they became "fed up" with, or were no longer willing to invest in, doing infertility. One couple decided to draw the line at doing infertility, finding "it wasn't worth the struggle or inconvenience."

> We have not proceeded with fertility studies and so forth. When I was in college, I had some—not fertility work done, obviously because I

wasn't ready to have children. But I was having some—not really, not medical problems—but just irregularities and I had a series of tests run then. And it was discovered that I had a few medical problems. Not to say that I couldn't ever have children, but I would obviously need probably a lot of help and might have difficulty with a pregnancy. So we—after having abstained from birth control for five or six years— have decided that we are not going to pursue the fertility route and that we know that even if I was able to get pregnant after several years of trying, I probably would have problems with that child. So we are just going to go ahead and adopt. So, it's not anything that—we didn't have the struggle of fertility or infertility, although we know we are infertile.

In addition, because of her bad experiences with birth control pills, the wife anticipated difficulty in treatment: "What of infertility when you get hormones and you get all the extra boost? I just couldn't lead a normal life. . . . So we're probably a little different than some of the people that you talk to."

Another couple decided to draw the line after two years, the wife finding the process of diagnosis and her one year on a fertility drug painful, degrading, and futile. Another couple also spent two years doing infertility before considering adoption. They were frustrated by the fact that before the wife's tuboplasty she was given a 30 to 50 percent chance of conceiving but after surgery was given almost no chance at all. She recalled thinking while she was being rolled into surgery, "Why am I doing this?" Having to undergo a second operation for an ovarian cyst that she had mistaken for a pregnancy, she decided she "had had it" with medical efforts. These couples reached a point fairly quickly where they no longer anticipated regrets for not doing infertility anymore.

In contrast, there were women and couples who had still not drawn the line after five, ten, and even seventeen years of pursuit. One couple spent seven years doing infertility, going to different physicians and trying Clomid, Pergonal, Danazol, cauterizations, inseminations, and varicocele repair to treat the irregular ovulation, endometriosis, and low sperm count believed to be contributing to their inability to conceive. The wife observed that there is a "little male factor, there's a little female factor . . . [but] there's no statement with all this evaluation that we will *never* be able to conceive a child." They finally decided that it was "very unlikely" they would achieve pregnancy, and they began to pursue adoption.

Couples who drew the line on doing infertility still harbored a "faint hope . . . like waiting for Publishers' Clearinghouse," that pregnancy might occur, but they no longer "actively," "seriously," or "aggressively" tried to make it happen. They had reached the "if it happens, it happens" stage. Couples who had difficulty drawing the line on either doing infertility or waiting for a child to adopt still anticipated regretting "quitting" too soon. A pregnancy could be achieved in the very next month; the call signifying that a child was available to adopt could come "theoretically" tomorrow.

One woman, describing herself as a "puzzle case" to her physician and at a point in doing infertility where she had tried everything save for in vitro fertilization, vowed to keep trying as long as she could, no matter what the odds. Even if her doctor told her there was no way she could become pregnant, she could not give up "100 percent: maybe 98 percent." As she further noted:

> Two percent will always nag me . . . I can't give up. Not unless that doctor looks at me and says there's no way under God's green earth that you are going to get pregnant. Sometimes they have told people that and they still have gotten pregnant. I just can't give up.

Her only impediment to continuing to do infertility was financial; she felt she could "deal with the physical anguish for now." What she could not deal with was regret; what if she gave up too soon? In contrast, another woman made sure that she would have to quit by having a hysterectomy after more than a decade of pursuit. Having also drawn the line at adoption, she decided to exit the maze without children.

Reframing Desire

At some point in their failed questing for a child, infertile couples had to confront what they really wanted. They had to distinguish between wanting to have and wanting to get a baby, between wanting fertility and wanting parenthood: distinctions that were at the most only theoretical for their "obliviously" fertile counterparts. Both medical and adoptive routes to parenthood forced couples to examine the differences among wanting a child at all, wanting a pregnancy, wanting a genetically related child, wanting a healthy baby or child, and wanting any child at all to parent. Adoption and conceptive techniques that separated genetic and gestational from social parenthood accentuated the complexity of having a baby. Women and couples were forced to determine what about having a baby they wanted and what they would be willing to forego.

The effort to clarify and, if necessary, to reframe desire was a refrain in infertile couples' efforts to "come through and come out the other end" of the maze with what they wanted. For those individuals who entered their marriage with little or no desire for children, the clarification and reframing of desire—the process couples used to examine, reconsider, refine, or alter their wants in relation to parenthood—began with resolving their ambivalence about becoming parents. One couple was unsure whether they wanted children of their own to the point of terminating a pregnancy in the early years of their marriage. For the wife, the hysterectomy she had later undergone for severe endometriosis came as a relief to her because she had felt a lot of peer pressure to have her own children. The hysterectomy "simplified" her situation and permitted her to pursue adoption (with which she recalled she had always been "fascinated") when she and her husband decided that something was "missing" from their lives by not having children.

Once the desire for a child was affirmed but still unfulfilled, the reframing of desire involved adjusting to the prospect of having a child with help as opposed to "naturally." One woman wanted to make pregnancy happen on her own but was forced to consider "unnatural" alternatives if she were going to satisfy her desire for a baby. She progressed from wanting to have a baby on her own and failing, to wanting a baby of her own with help and failing, to being unsure that adoption was what she wanted. The pregnancy she finally achieved made it unnecessary for her to consider seriously whether wanting to beget was more powerful than wanting to get and rear a child.

Couples succeeding with conventional (only in relation to treatments commonly considered more "high tech" and that are more sensationalized) therapies and with noncoital treatments that preserved their genetic and gestational connection to a child did not have to consider all of the varieties of meaning that having a child entailed. Couples undergoing donor insemination or in vitro fertilization with donor eggs, however, did have to consider whether their desire to have a baby could incorporate a child not genetically related to one partner. Couples choosing to undergo these therapies found ways to "own" the baby that would result. Both the husbands of wives conceiving by donor insemination and the wife pregnant by in vitro fertilization with a donor egg emphasized the importance of the biological link that still existed between the couple and fetus, the woman genetically linked and the couple sharing a pregnancy (like any other couple) in the case of donor insemination, and the woman gestationally linked in the case of egg donation. For the woman conceiving by in vitro fertilization of a donor egg, the reframing of desire was a fairly simple process. As this forty-one-year-old woman recalled:

> What we wanted was a child, a healthy child. And the doctor told us that he wouldn't even consider doing the regular in vitro on me just because of my age and the quality of my eggs. *And it was really just a short step to the donor . . . it just seemed a very normal step in the resolution of things* [emphasis added]. I had no question in my mind that I could love any child.

Using an analogy from the plant world, she explained that even though the seed did not come from her, the plant belonged to her and her husband and they "harvested" it.

Adopting couples appeared to undergo a more intensive and, at times, painful process of introspection, reconsideration, and revaluing than did couples conceiving with donor gametes. While these couples actually gave birth to a baby, adopting couples did not; it was harder for them to dismiss the complete lack of biological connection to a child. One woman explained that couples considering adoption had to ask themselves the right questions. "It's not, do you want to adopt? It's do you want children? You weigh the two things. Either have a child that's adopted or don't have children."

Asking the right questions, confronting self, having critical moments of revelation, and letting go were key components for adopting couples of the process of reframing desire. One woman recalled:

> It was very tragic that discovery that we would never have our own biological child. We went through a grieving period for the loss of that. . . . I have my whole life placed a high premium on being pregnant . . . I'd always wanted to be pregnant. I used to kid, "I'll get pregnant and give the baby to you." It fascinated me . . . It was very difficult for me to give that idea up.

She then recalled that her husband, who had no trouble with the idea of their adopting a child, had been shocked that she might not be able to love an adopted child as much as her own. She was forced to confront herself as she appeared in her husband's eyes. Grieving that she would never have her own child, she recalled, "It gelled in my mind that I want to be a parent rather than be pregnant. I did very much want to be pregnant, but if

I couldn't have that, I wanted to be a parent." Having admittedly focused for too long on what she wanted but could not have (indeed, one man described infertility as a state of "always wanting"), she gradually reframed her desire:

> I came to terms with what I really wanted, which was difficult for me. I fell in love with the idea of [adoption]. *That has become what I want* [emphasis added]. I want the child more than I want to be pregnant. . . . It didn't all of a sudden come to me in the middle of the night. Just through a lot of introspection and trying to figure out and talking to a therapist about what I really wanted.

This woman experienced a kind of epiphany while reading a story written by the grandparents of an adopted child; they had stated that love was not contingent on a blood relationship. She realized that there was no one she loved more than her husband who was also not her blood kin and said she started thinking in a whole new portion of her brain about relationships and the significance of a genetic tie. Her "awakening" led her comfortably to reframe her desire: to focus on the "idea" of a child rather than of pregnancy.

There were adopting couples, however, who had little difficulty reframing their desire to include wanting to adopt. One woman with a history of reproductive problems explained that her inability to get pregnant had not really bothered her. She said, "It doesn't eat at me. I would like to have children. . . . I don't necessarily have to be pregnant." Similarly, a man with deficient sperm explained:

> It was never what I have read that some people go through or people that I have known that have told me what they go through. Because I think before we ever got married, we kind of knew that there was a problem and it was kind of a given and it wasn't—it was a little upsetting—but it was never really the end of the world. It was never a really tragic type of thing . . . I don't think I've really had any kind of sense of grief over it really because to me the joy and the gift of parenting is giving to a child all that you have to give, and if it's an adopted child, it doesn't really matter. I don't actually have to have a genetic offspring [laughs lightly]. And I can say that with some confidence because I am really into genealogy and exploring my roots and all this kind of stuff. It never has bothered me to have a child that is not biologically my own.

For this man and his wife, adoption was an "adventure," an opportunity to have an "international family"; for the woman who did not care whether she got pregnant, doing adoption helped her avoid the misadventures of infertility treatment.

One consequence of the confrontation with self was a new appraisal of personal values and the discovery of certain prejudices. Adopting couples typically felt good about the fact that they could look positively on adoption and about the selves they had discovered while preparing the autobiographies and family histories required for adoption application. Although couples repeatedly stated that "adoption is not for everyone," they sometimes felt sorry for people who rejected adoption as a way to become a parent.

Yet confrontation with the self also included the discovery that the desire to parent could not as yet or might never include the desire for just any child. One woman waiting for an American child was upset "that she said no to a [Korean] child out there who needs a family," all the while professing to want a child. In addition, she was ambivalent about her ability to "handle such a child." Another woman still in treatment knew she was being "harsh" and "inhuman" in her judgment of adopted children as "bad seeds" and "rejects." Although these women had feelings that were very much in line with cultural prejudices about adoption, they, nevertheless, felt uncomfortable and even guilty for having them.

Mazing

The women's and couples' quest for a child was a deliberative process that helped them preserve mastery while coping with the in-betweenness and open-endedness of infertility. Although women and couples in search of a child appeared on the surface to be "wandering" (Daly, 1988, p. 52) in a maze of treatment and adoption options, their process of mazing seemed to be based on a rational, if idiosyncratic, accounting system: a system in which a 15 percent success rate viewed by one couple as worth a capital investment was viewed by another as not worth it, and in which an option that looked bad yesterday could look good today and tomorrow. The orientation of couples to available solutions to infertility and childlessness had few constants (cf. Frank, 1990a, 1990b); instead, it was characterized by renegotiation and change as time and circumstance demanded.

The descriptions given by couples of their pursuit of parenthood suggest the importance of action (doing either infertility or adoption)— and faith (belief in medicine or God) in the struggle for control. Couples' descriptions also suggest that researchers err when they oversimplify their condition as exclusively one of lack of control. Women and couples felt both empowered and disempowered in their quest for a child, more and less successfully achieving the various kinds of control they sought. In addition, couples' narratives suggest that a difference exists between struggling to maintain or regain control of a process and accepting responsibility for the occurrence of an outcome. A couple might fail to achieve personal control when they fail to get pregnant because they seek a kind of "illusory control" (Rothbaum, Weisz, and Snyder, 1982), namely, assuming responsibility to make a pregnancy happen. Conversely, a couple might achieve vicarious control by virtue of someone else—a physician—taking on this responsibility. Infertility is an event—often a "prolonged failure condition" (p. 28)—that engenders efforts to achieve control, with affected persons vacillating between or in various phases of encounter and retreat. Assisting infertile couples through the maze of options available to them means understanding the kinds of control they seek and that are possible for them to achieve and the adaptive functions this control serves in helping couples to cope with infertility.

Couples' descriptions also suggest the error in assuming that a positive relationship always exists among such factors as the number of years a couple has been trying to have a child, the level of desperation of a couple, and the degree of complexity of a medical regimen. For example, the couple who is somewhat ambivalent about having a child, suspects tubal obstruction as the cause of infertility, and then quickly obtains medical confirmation of the diagnosis may move directly to in vitro fertilization. This couple will likely be more inexperienced (cf. Shiloh, Larom, and Ben-Rafael, 1991, p. 859) as infertility patients than a couple who has been trying to conceive for years with less complex regimens, and less desperate than a couple trying for only a few months but clearly wanting to be parents. Such errors in assumptions about the so-called naïveté and desperation of infertile couples and about the so-called last-chance nature of high-tech therapies may serve to invalidate the conceptualization, design, and findings of studies of infertile people based on these assumptions.

Moreover, couples recognized persistence in the pursuit of fertility as both problem and solution. In the third trimester of a pregnancy achieved with Pergonal and husband insemination, one woman explained:

Persistence is what got me in trouble. . . . The persistence thing got in my way. Because rather than relaxing as I persisted and saying to myself, I'm doing all that I can, I just got more and more uptight about it and stressful about it and unhappy about it. And I think it really worked against me. But, yet, at the same time, we persisted, and here we are, so it worked for us as well.

Her husband described persistence as a "double-edged sword."

Couples also recognized the difference between persistence and obsession in the quest for a pregnancy. After achieving pregnancy by in vitro fertilization, one woman observed:

I considered myself infertile, but not a diehard infertile person. When I think of an infertile person, I think about somebody who has been in it for years and years and years. I sort of felt all along like we would be in this stage of life for a given period of time that would probably not exceed four or five years, if that. And that no longer would I consider myself after that an infertile person. I would consider myself childless.

This woman also told the story of a speaker at a RESOLVE meeting on the subject of "What If Never?" who had undergone in vitro fertilization ten times, who had had four additional surgeries, and who had received multiple inseminations. She recalled this woman saying that

she and her husband finally came to the agreement that they were going to set themselves some limits. I thought, "Well, that's encouraging, that's healthy, good to hear it." . . . And she said that she was thirty years old and she had decided that when she was forty, that that was it. So she was going to do this for ten more years. . . . And then she said, and this is verbatim . . . "If my husband can't support me through this, I'll find one that does." I said, then and there, "Life is now."

This woman illustrated the extent to which infertility has come to be defined by the actions taken and time spent to reverse it.

Finally, the process I have described here was observed in infertile couples wanting and choosing to get medical help or to pursue professionally assisted adoption. This public pursuit of a child necessarily excludes those individuals and couples unable but wanting to become parents who choose to wait for God to grant them a child, who cannot afford infertility and adoption services, who are reluctant to suffer the scrutiny of medical personnel and caseworkers and the indignities of professional help, who attempt folk and other extramedical remedies for infertility, or who arrange intrafamily and other nonprofessionally assisted adoptions. For example, best current estimates of the use of infertility services suggest that one-half to two-thirds of couples unable but wanting to have children do not seek medical services (Hirsch and Mosher, 1987). Whether their quest for a child is similar to the process described here is still unknown.

Note

1. As it turned out, she discovered after one year of trying that the sperm she had purchased were of poor quality. She conceived after the third cycle with sperm from a different donor.

8. With Child . . . at Last

> She had thought in the conception to have ended all things. She had
> only begun them. The conception meant the birth and the birth meant
> the death and in between was the important thing. . . . She was tired
> already. (Maitland, 1978/1980, p. 264)

When couples achieve pregnancy after an encounter with infertility, it is
frequently after having traveled a medical and emotional road of trials.
Although relatively little attention has been given to various components of
the aftermath of infertility, there are indications that couples who finally
achieve viable pregnancies may continue to travel a somewhat difficult road
(Dunnington and Glazer, 1991; Garner, 1985; Glazer, 1990; Gould, 1990;
Loftus, 1989). In this and the next chapter, I consider various components
of "life after infertility" (Leon, 1989, p. 3) for couples who manage to
achieve and sustain pregnancy.

Alienated Labor

For the infertile couples who had to struggle to achieve pregnancy, their
labor began before conception. These couples struggled an average of four
years before achieving their pregnancies; they were in preconceptional
labor to "make it happen." In contrast to their fertile counterparts who
conceived at the "drop of a hat" and within what one normally fertile
couple described as a romantic "cocoon," infertile couples had sex as a
"chore," lived their lives in menstrual time—"in thirty day segments"—and
encountered the goal of pregnancy as a "hurdle" to be overcome. Follicles
were stimulated, ovulation was induced, endogenous hormone levels were
raised or lowered, and/or fertilization was contrived in a laboratory. For
infertile couples, the essence of getting pregnant was "dreadful struggle" as
they fought body and nature to "force" a baby out.

Infertile women especially existed at the level of relation between self
and body that Gadow (1980) has described as "disrupted immediacy." At

this level, the body is experienced as Other, as separate from and antagonistic to the self and its projects.

> The immediacy of [the lived body] is ruptured by incapacity, the experience of being unable to act as desired or to escape being acted upon in ways that are not desired. Immediacy, in short, is shattered by constraint. The lived body becomes conscious of ineptness, weakness, pain. . . . The relation is one of implicit struggle. . . . Body and self are inevitably at odds with one another. (Gadow, 1980, pp. 174–75)

Commenting on his wife's inability to accept that she had finally achieved pregnancy, one man observed:

> Going through the infertility process for years distances you so far from the normal, natural and organic process of having a baby. But the whole thing becomes technological wizardry and no longer something where you can rely on your own wisdom, or the wisdom of your body *which has been proven over and over again to not be wise, in fact to be a traitor* [emphasis added].

The labor of infertile couples to conceive was also alienating in that it involved the estrangement of wife and husband as physicians, nurses, technicians, and/or donors, and bizarre techniques (from producing sperm on demand to lying on a table in the doctor's office to conceive) intruded into the act of getting pregnant. Conception was an intimate activity transformed into a public group affair. Couples had to be approved for various medical regimens; couples had to make appointments with each other and with their physicians to conceive; couples' activities were timed and carefully choreographed. Both metaphorically and literally, getting pregnant was something that happened in a glass and under glass, the contrived object of close technical scrutiny and manipulation. One man joked that the female physician who inseminated his wife with his sperm was the real father of his baby.

Infertility, like pregnancy, challenged the integrity of the body's boundaries by obscuring the line between what is inside—the self—and what is outside—separate (Young, 1984), and not the self. The removal of body fluids for laboratory inspection, the exchange of personal and donor eggs and sperm, and the externalization of fertilization itself served to create a kind of body boundary ambiguity (Burns, 1987).

For women, getting pregnant was often an experience involving considerable pain and discomfort. Within any menstrual cycle targeted for pregnancy, women experienced the pain of numerous injections to take blood and to receive the hormones, "thick like peanut butter," intended to induce conception and maintain pregnancy. They suffered from overfull bladders when diagnostic ultrasound examinations were required and when ovaries were hyperstimulated, and from the effects of anesthesia and surgery. Women felt "sick" and "tired" from their physical efforts to conceive; a few of them were literally sick with the flu while undergoing embryo transfer. The phenomenology of assisted conception involved pain, not pleasure; separation, not unity; public exposure, not intimacy; and artifice, not spontaneity.

Ambiguous Conception

Although conception is a biological process comprised of many sequential and interrelated events, the normally fertile couples were typically unaware of these events. For them, conception occurred accidentally, spontaneously, and, if planned, quickly (within an average of three months), and they were typically only aware that it had occurred after the fact. If they consciously experienced conception at all, it was as a unified process: a fluid but single moment in time. One normally fertile couple who conceived after only two months of effort intuited right after making love: "that felt like a baby."

In contrast, the experience of conception was fragmented for the couples struggling to conceive. The struggle itself and the medical protocols used to induce pregnancy tended to anatomize conception and to make couples very conscious of every step constituting this complex biological process. Infertile couples were more likely to think of themselves as in one or another phase of getting pregnant. They were, therefore, in a position to challenge the adequacy of a commonly accepted biocultural dichotomy—the either-or-ness of pregnancy—according to which a woman could either be pregnant or not pregnant, but could not be a little bit pregnant.

Infertile couples, especially women attempting and conceiving by in vitro fertilization, illustrated the new continuum principle that made getting pregnant a consciously lived experience. These women experienced conception while it was happening, as opposed to after the fact, and as more-or-less, rather than as either-or. One woman described her "non-growing pregnancy," while another woman concluded that a weakly positive pregnancy test indicated that she had been "pregnant on the lowest scale." Couples attempting in vitro fertilization were potentially pregnant so long as they were not "canceled" at any step in the process from the hormonal stimulation to develop eggs through the transfer of embryo(s) into the uterus, and so long as they had not obtained a negative pregnancy test. The externalization of biological events in the in vitro fertilization process, typically "hidden" and unconsciously experienced in "nature," permitted couples to live each step of getting pregnant: to think of themselves as conceiving over a prolonged period of time. Couples were aware of hormone levels, numbers and sizes of follicles, the grading or quality of eggs produced, the numbers of eggs fertilized, the numbers of egg cleavages, and the numbers of eggs transferred, frozen, and lost. One such couple lived a series of pregnant moments (cf. Seibel and Levin, 1987) until the one moment when they stopped getting pregnant. They experienced each "good blood test . . . each good ultrasound of the follicles," and the successful retrieval and transfer of eggs. This process ended abruptly with a negative pregnancy test: "all gone . . . in one instant."

While this couple lived conception as a series of successes that ended in instant failure, another couple experienced the process as a series of potential failures or "hurdles," becoming more anxious with the "gradual building" that defined getting pregnant by in vitro fertilization. Describing the process as playing Russian roulette, the wife kept asking herself, "Will my hormone level be high enough today? Will I be canceled today? Will I make it to tomorrow?" The continuum principle operated within a cycle of treatment but also between treatment cycles as couples electing to try in vitro fertilization again and again believed they were getting closer to pregnancy with each attempt (cf. Williams, 1988).

Conscious of the developmental phases of conception, women sought to differentiate getting pregnant from actually being pregnant. For one woman conceiving by in vitro fertilization, pregnancy did not begin with fertilization but rather later, at implantation. As she explained:

> You can't say pregnancy occurs when the eggs are fertilized because lots of people have fertilized eggs but don't have pregnancy. The pregnancy is actually when the embryo implants into the wall of the uterus because that's when actually something is going to happen. You can have fertilized eggs and nothing happens.

For this woman, conception was an in-body experience that began with implantation. In contrast, another woman who also conceived by in vitro fertilization believed her pregnancy began at the moment her husband's sperm fertilized her egg. For her, conception was an *out-of-body* experience and the beginning point of pregnancy.

Women also described pregnancies without babies and babies without pregnancies. One woman, who after losing her first pregnancy delivered a baby conceived with a combination of fertility drugs and husband insemination, explained that with her first pregnancy she was pregnant, but she did not have a baby. She said, "I had the sac and all the symptoms, but there was no baby." One couple observed that although most women thought if they achieved a positive pregnancy test they had a baby, "you don't have a baby, you've got a pregnancy." Alternatively, another woman who viewed her externally fertilized eggs as her babies suggested that a woman could have a baby, but not be pregnant. She described her embryos as being there, but not inside her yet.

Women also distinguished between being pregnant and having a pregnantlike body. One woman described how being on Pergonal was like being pregnant before you were pregnant: a kind of drug-induced pseudocyesis. Because of the abdominal bloating the drug caused, she began to wear her blouses hanging over open pants as a pregnant woman might. After the swelling in her ovaries subsided and she had actually conceived, her body became smaller. Her drugged body thought she was pregnant before she really was. Another woman explained how drugs had caused a positive pregnancy test in the absence of pregnancy, saying, "They put your body in a state of pregnancy and your breasts grow and they're real sore and tender. You're really pregnant, but you're not."

Conscious of conception as a process, couples were also more aware of stages of pregnancy that typically go unnoticed. Technical advancements in pregnancy diagnosis and the virtually routine use of home pregnancy tests permitted couples to learn of pregnancies in earlier stages of development, but they also caused more confusion about whether and what kind of pregnancy had been achieved. For infertile couples, there was more than one kind of pregnancy: there were false pregnancies induced by drugs and there were chemical pregnancies that might or might not become clinical pregnancies which, in turn, might or might not remain viable pregnancies. These newly discovered (but not new) physiological states served to impede infertile women's assumption of an identity of self as being really pregnant (Miller, 1978).

Because of the effects of infertility itself or of the treatments leading to pregnancy, infertile women were challenged to develop working interpretations of signs and symptoms (Patterson, Freese, and Goldenberg, 1986). Such factors as irregular ovulation and the side effects of drug therapies often caused the presumptive and probable signs of pregnancy to lose some of their "saliency" as indicators of pregnancy. Early pregnancy tests often captured the effects of therapy rather than the onset of pregnancy. Therapies aimed at inducing conception caused signs and symptoms, such as abdominal bloating, menstrual changes, nausea, and mood swings, that could be construed as indicative of pregnancy. In fact, women consciously conceiving with biomedical assistance were confronted with a variety of salient indicators typically invisible to other women. Such an information overload often caused for these women uncertainty about whether and what kind of pregnancy they had achieved. Although normally fertile women also have to work to acquire an identity of self as pregnant, to reconcile the physiological changes with the social, and to reduce the uncertainty associated with early pregnancy (Jordan, 1977; Miller, 1978; Patterson, Freese, and Goldenberg, 1986), infertile women had more information to reconcile. Adding to their confusion about where therapy ended and pregnancy began was the fact that women conceiving by in vitro fertilization had to take progesterone supplements in the early phases of pregnancy to maintain their pregnancy.

Moreover, in a position to know earlier than their fertile counterparts that conception had occurred, infertile couples had more difficulty believing that it had occurred. Infertile couples had more trouble conceiving of themselves as having conceived, not only because of the difficulty in separating pregnancy from therapy (or distinguishing pregnancy as a phase in therapy from pregnancy as an outcome of therapy), but also because they tended to anticipate failure with every attempt at pregnancy. Their anticipation of failure paradoxically coexisted with their more hopeful maybe-pregnant attitude. Women "trained [their] minds" that pregnancy was not going to occur or that a certain procedure was "not going to work anyway." Couples tried to maintain the attitude that they would not care when pregnancy failed to occur.

Infertile couples' self-protective waiting-to-fail standpoint, developed after years of failure, made success that much harder to accept. With so many negative pregnancy tests, it was hard to accept a positive test. One woman recalled having a hard time picturing herself pregnant. Both she and her husband required the first half of pregnancy to "change gears" from being not pregnant to pregnant. She had asked an ultrasound technician to convince her she was pregnant: "they are all saying that I'm pregnant, but I'm not convinced." By the second trimester, the "physical manifestations of pregnancy" were there, and everyone "acted" like a baby was there when she had her amniocentesis, but it was seeing the fetal spine on ultrasound—something "surefire"—that finally convinced her that she was having a baby.

Relinquishing Infertility

Taking on an identity of self as finally with child demanded letting go of the identity of self as still without child. Infertile couples who achieved pregnancy worked first to get pregnant and then to begin to relinquish aspects of their encounter with infertility. Relinquishing infertility was a special instance of the biographical comeback work (Corbin and Strauss, 1987; Strauss and Corbin, 1991) couples engaged in to let go of and leave behind the negative identity, feelings, and thought and behavior patterns developed in the course of their struggle to conceive.

The infertile and childbearing couples performed this comeback work in the context of pregnancies perceived as high-stakes and, sometimes, as high-risk pregnancies. High-stakes pregnancies were "premium" pregnancies that had been difficult to achieve and that, if lost, would be difficult to replace. Infertile couples indicated that the "stakes were higher" for them than for normally fertile couples because it took them so long to conceive, because they had invested so much of their material, physical, and psychic resources in the complex medical regimens required to induce conception, and because the treatments required to get pregnant often had low rates of success. Their struggle to achieve pregnancy had already included many treatment failures; thirteen of the couples interviewed had suffered one or more previous pregnancy and/or adoption failures.

One couple, conceiving in their second in vitro cycle, described the high-stakes nature of pregnancy achieved after an encounter with infertility. The wife observed:

> I think when I was going through the hard time—like ten to twelve weeks—it bothered me more because my friends, if they had a miscarriage, they could have another child. But if something happened to ours, we don't have the opportunities and other chances that other

people would have. And that was just real hard, because I knew if I lost it, I would just—it would be horrible. Because you know the chance for a second one is no better than it ever has been and we were just doggone lucky to have this one, for this to work. So that worried me alot. Like what was I going to do if it didn't work?

Her husband added:

> I think if you had a miscarriage, it's obviously a catastrophe and it would take a long time to get over it. But other couples would have more options later. I think they would be able to put it behind them quicker and move on because they would have other options where we couldn't. Because we know that we didn't have many options.

As shown in Table 8.1, more of the pregnancies among the infertile couples (as opposed to the fertile couples in the study) were complicated by medical and obstetric risk factors. Although not all obstetricians of the infertile couples treated their pregnancies as high risk, pregnancies achieved after infertility tend to be categorized as at risk because of the higher incidence of pregnancy loss and complications associated with the nature of a couple's fertility problem (narrowed fallopian tubes, for example, increase the risk of ectopic pregnancy) or with the treatment leading to the pregnancy (fertility drugs increase the incidence of multiple pregnancy). Also, factors related to the older age of women having their first baby and physicians' fears about losing a premium baby may contribute to the social construction of pregnancies achieved after infertility as at risk (Andrews et al., 1986; Australian In-Vitro Fertilization Collaborative Group, 1988; Behrman and Patton, 1988; Beral et al., 1990; Frydman et al., 1986; Howe et al., 1990; Jansen, 1982; Lancaster, 1985; Varma, Patel, and Bhathenia, 1988).

NORMALIZATION AND SPECIALIZATION

The most prominent manifestations of beginning attempts by infertile couples to relinquish their infertility were their efforts to locate themselves in the world of normally fertile and naturally conceiving couples. Infertile couples normalized and naturalized their pregnancies, describing them as just like or very similar to the pregnancies achieved by their fertile counterparts. One couple conceiving with fertility drugs, for example, believed that the odds for the successful resolution of their pregnancy were equal to those of other couples conceiving easily. In the third trimester of an in vitro

TABLE 8.1.   Risk factors and complications in sixty-three target pregnancies.

CONDITION	FERTILE (n = 19)	INFERTILE (n = 44)
Multiple gestation	2	5
Glucose intolerance	1	7
Preterm labor/contractions	1	9
Hypertension	0	3
Hyperemesis gravidarum	1	2
Carpal tunnel syndrome	0	2
Cholecystitis	0	1
Fetal heart block (diagnosed @ 34 weeks)	1	0
Pregnancy loss	0	3

Note: Eight of the women in the infertile group experienced two complications. One infertile woman experienced the same two complications in each of her two pregnancies.

fertilization pregnancy, one couple had come to the point where they felt like other couples. As the wife explained,

> I think we're starting to see ourselves more like other pregnant people. I don't think of myself as IVF so much nowadays. . . . [That] just seemed to go away. And watching other people that we know who are pregnant begin to really show and swapping the stories with them and that their pregnancy and my pregnancy seem very much alike. . . . It's not any less special to us, but it's—we're less—I'm less different.

Although couples in the process of normalizing their pregnancies recognized that they had achieved pregnancy in a manner substantively different from their fertile counterparts, they did not perceive the pregnancies resulting from medical intervention to be different from spontaneous ones or as more threatened by virtue of infertility. One woman who achieved pregnancy through her own self-help efforts (including herbs and meditation in combination with medically prescribed drug therapy) observed that she was high-risk for getting pregnant, but that her pregnancy was not high-risk.

Even some couples conceiving by in vitro fertilization were able to normalize their pregnancies by separating them from the special "high-tech" processes of conception that preceded them. For example, one man explained:

It's like there's a stack of dominoes. There are a million dominoes in a line and it's just that somewhere near the start of that line, there have been two or three dominoes that have been skipped, or were replaced by something else, something artificial. *Everything else is completely normal* [emphasis added], except for the fact that fertilization took place outside the body.

Although the infertility was "abnormal" and the manner of conception "special," the pregnancy that resulted was "normal," equal to anyone's pregnancy. As one man observed:

[We went] from abnormal fertility to normal pregnancy. Our fertility was very different from other people's in that we could not get pregnant at will and that she had to go through so much in the way of surgery and diagnostic tests and finally in vitro and I really didn't have to go through anything unusual other than being supportive for her and being there. Our fertility was abnormal but our pregnancy after about the first two to three months has really been normal and she has behaved just like anyone else would have if they had conceived normally.

Similarly, another couple viewed in vitro fertilization as "like nature" and as "just giving nature a helping hand." As the physician husband explained:

You just break a few days. You break a certain small anatomical barrier, but otherwise the whole sequence of events is not altered. You start with the same basic ingredients and apart from a two-day intervention, nothing really has changed.

He also normalized their situation by minimizing the abnormality of infertility and the artifice of assisted conception with a comparison to cesarean delivery.

Even though you don't feel fertile and you don't feel capable of—and you think, "Well, I didn't get pregnant naturally." Women who have babies by cesarean section don't give birth naturally either. And so, I think of it as the same sort of thing. So a cesarean is a little bit artificial and things are altered a little bit, but it's the same miracle and the same everything.

In the United States, where technological intervention in childbirth is routine, it was not always clear where the line between nature and artifice should be properly drawn.

Couples also specialized their pregnancies, describing them as more complicated or fragile than or superior to pregnancies achieved by naturally conceiving couples. For example, some couples viewed pregnancies achieved after in vitro fertilization as superior in terms of the health of the fetus. The embryo resulting from the in vitro union of egg and sperm was considered heartier, a "survivor" whose continued viability was likely. For one forty-one-year-old woman who became pregnant with an egg donated by a twenty-three-year-old woman, the fetus she carried was likely spared the risk of genetic malformations and other impairments associated with the fetuses who would be naturally conceived by older women. Also, this woman pointed out the advantages of knowing almost immediately that a pregnancy had begun; in contrast to other women who learned of their pregnancies well into their second or even third month, she was able to refrain right away from activities and habits that could jeopardize the fetus. In this case, technology was perceived as improving upon nature.

A man whose wife became pregnant by in vitro fertilization, however, noted the abnormal and disadvantageous aspect of knowing about a pregnancy very soon.

> The not knowing immediately is a blessing if you are going to lose the child. In a *normal* [emphasis added] population of getting pregnant and losing, you don't really pay that much attention to it. But when you are going through IVF, you know the second you've been blessed as being pregnant. Then you have to go through an entire worry process as we are going through now of, "Are we going to keep this child?" And so there is that kind of stress, whereas in a normal population. . . .

These two different judgments about one feature of a pregnancy achieved by in vitro fertilization illustrate that the effort to specialize was not confined to determining the advantages of pregnancy after infertility but also involved determining the liabilities and the disadvantages of assisted as opposed to natural conception.

Couples espousing a view of their pregnancies as normal or natural did the work of relinquishing infertility by separating the encounter with infertility that preceded their pregnancies from the pregnancies themselves.

Couples who viewed their assisted pregnancy as superior (one form of specialization) did the work of relinquishing infertility by emphasizing the benefits of biomedical over natural conception; these couples, in effect, transformed a loss into a gain.

In contrast, couples who perceived their pregnancies as more complicated or fragile than those of their fertile counterparts (the second form of specialization) had more difficulty relinquishing infertility. Contributing to this difficulty were the presence of one or more medical complications that prevented couples from thinking of their pregnancies as normal and the previous experiences of couples with pregnancy loss, adoption failure, and other kinds of adverse life events.[1] For these couples, pregnancy was a continuation of their encounter with infertility—neither a transition to normality nor an escape from infertility—in that they viewed their pregnancies or themselves as abnormal or lived their pregnancies "walking on eggshells," waiting for something to go wrong yet again. As one woman summarized it, infertility prepared couples—indeed, created the mindset—for loss and failure. One man whose wife conceived by donor insemination after more than fifteen attempts explained why he and his wife were not "terribly upset" when she was hospitalized for premature labor. As he observed:

> It's almost because we expect problems that maybe other people don't. That's terrible to say, but we always anticipate them and are almost more ready to deal with them in some respects. So we aren't shocked as to think, "you mean there could be something wrong with our baby?" I mean our viewpoint was always the other way around. "You mean we could have a healthy one—really?"

After his wife delivered their baby, another man admitted:

> We were just real cautious every time we did anything or when we thought about the pregnancy or whatever. We were always scared that something would happen. Everytime you go across a bump or slam on brakes real fast or something, you would think that you might lose this little thing.

Although infertile couples exhibited little difficulty in specializing their childbearing circumstances—in seeing how they diverged from the experiences of normally fertile couples—they had to work harder and, sometimes, did not succeed in normalizing these circumstances. For example, one couple described their pregnancy as "not a normal pregnancy" and later as "almost like a normal pregnancy." Another couple having a "sunset pregnancy" in their forties wished that they could just be like what they believed a normally pregnant couple would be like. One woman, who conceived spontaneously after an adoption loss, marveled that her alpha-fetoprotein test results were "incredibly normal," and she recalled her physician telling her that she had a wonderful medical history save for the fact that she could not get pregnant. One woman described how her physician had helped her feel normal by not assuming that because she had trouble conceiving and had complications in pregnancy, she would also have difficulty in labor.

> He said that I was the same risk as any other pregnancy. And he reassures me each time that even though I am thirty-seven and first baby, first pregnancy, everything else is normal and all my tests are normal and my blood pressure is good, my weight has been good . . . no reason for concern.

Infertile couples wanted to be just like other childbearing couples, but their infertility had taught them that, in certain respects, they were not like them. They also wanted to be recognized as special for their pioneering efforts in reproduction and, at times, were even defiant about their triumph over infertility and what they had endured to achieve pregnancy. One woman was disappointed that after eleven years of infertility, people did not make more of the pregnancy she had finally achieved. At the same time, she emphasized the normality of her pregnancy, and her husband acknowledged that all pregnancies were "all at once . . . miracles and yet mundane."

Veronica and Steven (pseudonyms) demonstrated the struggle that was, at times, involved in the attempt to leave infertility behind and the tension that sometimes existed between normalization and specialization. They had conceived their first baby by in vitro fertilization. In the ninth week of this pregnancy, Steven believed that they faced the same hurdles other childbearing couples faced. As he commented, "I don't feel like it's extra hurdles there now." Veronica was somewhat less certain about her status as just another pregnant woman but essentially agreed with her husband, adding, "It's like now we have an even chance. We're closer to normal now than we have been for a long time. . . . Not an infertile, not an IVF patient, we're just sort of even now." She acknowledged that the transition from the intensive care of an "IVF patient" to "just normal prenatal care" had been a hard one for her to make. Like other women who had gotten used to and were sometimes reassured by the constant medical scrutiny associated with medical therapy for infertility, Veronica felt somewhat awkward assuming the conventional role of obstetric patient who might go several weeks without seeing a physician. By the second trimester, Veronica's reluctance to assume a normal patient role was unfortunately affirmed when her pregnancy became, in her words, "high risk." She was encouraged to have an amniocentesis after her alpha-fetoprotein test indicated an abnormality; she underwent a cerclage for a threatened abortion; and she developed hypertension. At twenty-one weeks, she lost the pregnancy.

About one year later, this couple achieved a second pregnancy with an embryo frozen from the previous in vitro fertilization procedure. Neither they nor their doctors elected to treat this pregnancy normally, given past circumstances. By the eighth month of this second pregnancy, Steven had even come to believe that pregnancy was really like the in vitro process they had undergone in that they were taking the pregnancy one step at a time because there were so many points where failure could occur. This couple began with a view of pregnancy after infertility as high stakes but relatively normal. As a result of a pregnancy loss and a medically complicated second pregnancy course (which resulted in a healthy infant), they ended with a view of pregnancy after infertility as abnormal: as both high stakes and high risk.

IDENTITY AND EMOTION WORK

Another manifestation of the work of relinquishing infertility was the efforts by couples to abandon their identities of themselves as infertile and to assume the new identities of obstetric patient, expectant couple, and parents-to-be. As I described them previously, some of these couples, and more typically men, had never perceived themselves as infertile, while other couples, and more typically women, had permitted infertility to become central to their lives and the essence of who they believed themselves to be. Infertility was not something they could just set aside "over here," especially when, as one woman put it, it was their life for years. These couples had more difficulty making the transition from infertility to obstetric patient and from being couples waiting to get pregnant to couples who had achieved pregnancy. One woman in her second trimester recounted the difficulty she had in making the transition in patient status.

It was a different environment than being in an infertility clinic and they didn't quite—they don't treat you quite the same. Not that they don't care, but it's just a little less compassion. Because I think when you're going to an infertility clinic, they know that all you're doing is hurting. There are no—you never see a pregnant woman in an infertility clinic. It was really different and it took a little getting used to. Because I was just a normal patient and I hadn't been a normal patient in three-and-a-half years. . . . I felt like I had sort of been thrown to the wolves. . . . They've been wonderful. Once I kind of let my guard down. . . . But I felt really protected in the other clinics and I guess it was because I had seen those people so often for so long. It wasn't a monthly visit and it wasn't a yearly visit, it was weekly or daily or every other day for so long. That's sort of been the different experience. Being a regular patient.

This woman had "some anxiety" about not being seen by the doctor as often as she had been used to and asked for more frequent visits so she could hear the baby's heartbeat.

Infertility constituted a kind of "mental barrier" (as it had constituted a physical barrier) that impeded the transition of couples to pregnancy. Infertile couples often felt in a double bind, wanting to get excited about their pregnancies, but afraid of being "cut off at the knees" again. They wanted to look forward, to their pregnancies, instead of looking behind to where they had been. They wanted to enjoy pregnancy, but they often found themselves unable to "relax enough to enjoy it." One woman, who had conceived in her first in vitro cycle, still had the feeling that someone was going to "tap [her] on the shoulder and say—oh, there's been a big mistake," and that she was not "supposed to be sitting in these shoes." Other women suggested the "cameo appearances" (Glazer, 1990, p. ix) infertility could make in pregnancy. In the thirty-fourth week of her pregnancy, one woman recalled:

When I was doing that income tax stuff—I guess I was having to pull out all that in vitro stuff and kind of reconstruct all the expenses . . . and whew! I know pregnant women are supposed to cry a lot, but I really had a good cry. Looking back through all that stuff. And I really had forgotten how involved and how many hurdles we crossed. How unbelievable the amount of anxiety there is every day in that process as you wait to hear your blood sugar level, and look to see if there has been any follicles and just . . . unbelievably anxious process. . . . I was reminded what we had been through . . . I hadn't forgotten it, but I hadn't really . . . [crying here] It's just a relief that I've come so far.

Infertile couples typically spent the early weeks and, at times, the entire first half of pregnancy trying to "shift gears" and to "leave [infertility] behind." Women especially wanted to savor their pregnancies (possibly the only ones they would ever have) and to enter the world of motherhood denied them for so long, but they also found it somewhat uncomfortable to think and act pregnant and, more significantly, not to think and act infertile. One woman commented, "I sort of feel like [other infertile women] but the other side of me doesn't feel like—I don't—I can't relate really easily with my fertile friends that have children. So I still don't feel real connected to them." She later described her discomfort with people commenting on her pregnancy and with "maternity stores" and "baby showers," which she attributed to the "feelings . . . left over" from infertility.

> I think that it was unrealistic of me to think that all of a sudden I was going to get pregnant and I was going to feel miraculously better when I was in that mind set. Even before we got married, I wondered whether I could [have a baby]. I felt like that for so long that I don't think that the mere physical fact that you conceive and you carry a child changes patterns.

Another woman pregnant by in vitro fertilization described the "real air of unreality to" pregnancy after years of infertility. As she remarked:

> You think it's a dream. You think, this can't be happening. You think it's an evil trick. Somebody is setting you up. . . . If you make the mistake of really believing, it's taken away from you. You are almost always [with] superstitious feelings.

One woman explained that because getting pregnant had for so long been her only goal, having achieved it, she felt the "loss of not having something to do every month." She recalled, "That's all I did every month . . . there's a gap . . . glad it's all over, but I still feel that loss . . . missing something." One man in the third trimester of his wife's pregnancy achieved by in vitro fertilization described how difficult it was not to view the developmental milestones of pregnancy as "hurdles" of infertility still to be jumped. After his wife was hospitalized for premature contractions, he explained:

> I think we said from the very beginning that we had hurdles. We took it one step at a time. And that's because . . . we went through the infertility process, the conception, the in vitro and all that. I think that while the baby has become very real, and I sort of switch my thinking to this is a normal pregnancy now, we still—I still, I know I still see the hurdles . . . I guess she would really be heading toward the last hurdle and maybe we could say, "OK, now we're really in sort of a natural progression here and we don't have to worry about hurdles and it's just a goal."

Part of the discomfort women felt relinquishing the feelings and thought "patterns" developed while they were struggling to conceive derived from their guilt for having achieved pregnancy when other infertile women had not. One woman recalled wondering whether any of the women looking at her pregnant body were themselves infertile. As she observed:

> I think about what their situation in life is. . . . What is going through my mind is, are any of these women who are looking at me, are they infertile? And at times, I have felt like a Nazi survivor. That sort of guilt. Not often, but I have felt that on occasion. I'm the lucky one. We beat the odds by an incredible amount. . . . [Are] any of them . . . looking at my swollen tummy with a terrible longing like I used to do? . . . Sometimes, I want to pull my tummy in in case there is some poor woman who is looking at me who can't get pregnant.

Because her sister and three friends were infertile, this woman had no other woman with whom to share her joy.

Infertile women who achieved pregnancy often felt they had to keep their elation under wraps, and to refrain from complaining about pregnancy symptoms. These women wanted both to forget their infertility and never to forget it: like "Holocaust . . . survivors," they wanted to reestablish a normal life while retaining the wisdom and sensitivity to other peoples' suffering their encounter with adversity had given them.

Another way in which infertile couples demonstrated the difficulty of relinquishing infertility was by not permitting themselves to think too much about any particular baby they might have. Pregnancy was something they had achieved, but, as they well knew, there were pregnancies that were nothing more than "empty sacs," or nothing more than the hormonal effects of the therapy they had undergone to induce pregnancy, or that were just as likely as not to be lost. Although these couples had often "attached" themselves preconceptionally to the idea of a baby, "loved their [embryonic] sacs," or, in the case of couples conceiving by in vitro fertilization, felt a connection to their developing eggs and embryos, they sought more or less successfully to remain detached enough to protect themselves from further pain. As one woman observed in the second trimester of a pregnancy induced by fertility drugs and husband insemination, "I finally have let myself give in to the fact that there's really a baby there and everything is going to be all right. I was so skeptical in the beginning and too afraid to get excited." Another woman in the third trimester of an in vitro fertilization pregnancy attributed her moments of disbelief to her infertility:

> There are times when I can hardly believe that he's really there. I still have times when I vacillate back and think that there really *is* going to be a baby. Even though we're getting ready for him, and I think of him and read to him and talk to him. And it seems very real most of the time, but I still have times when it's just like, "Oh my gosh, there really is going to be a baby." That sounds so strange to me. . . . I guess maybe until I see him, I really won't believe it.

Another woman acknowledged after delivery:

> I didn't realize this until after she was born, but I didn't absolutely know the planning for a baby. Short of clothes and nursery and that sort of thing, I really didn't prepare myself emotionally by reading about infants and that sort of thing. . . . I dealt with [infertility] through my whole pregnancy. I would only accept to a certain point. I would only read to a certain point. . . . And I didn't realize that I was doing that, but it was like I almost wouldn't let myself go. Like when I was starting my eighth month, I wouldn't read past the end of the eighth month. When I started the ninth month, I would read about the ninth month. I realize now why I was doing that. And it goes back to the infertility and the feelings of loss that I had after the miscarriage. And I realize that now that I just wouldn't go ahead and let go and accept the fact that I was really going to have her in my arms. And

when I did, it felt sort of unprepared. . . . It's easy in the hospital. The routine is all set up and they bring her in and you feed her and they take her out and they change her and do all that . . . but then, when I got home, it was like wow, what is she doing? I would read and find out what was going on with this. Normally I would have done a lot of reading ahead of time. *I just wouldn't let go* [emphasis added].

This woman illustrated the critical difference between materially and emotionally preparing for a baby; for her, the material preparations had been more like going through the motions.

Pregnancy after Infertility

Pregnancy after infertility for the couples interviewed involved reversals in the normal transition to parenthood, with labor undergone before conception and with couples wavering back and forth between identities of selves as still infertile and as finally expectant. In an important sense, it was the labor of conception, not the labor and delivery of the child, that constituted the climactic event in childbearing.

While some infertile couples managed to relinquish much of their infertility in the early weeks of pregnancy, others struggled with elements of their infertility for a longer period or had still not, by the end of their pregnancies, relinquished the feelings of failure or impending loss so well developed during their struggle to conceive. One such couple described their pregnancy as nine months of worry and stress. Another couple admitted, after delivery of their baby, to being uneasy for the duration of their pregnancy. The husband observed, "We felt good about where we were but just . . . in the back of our mind, there was just this overwhelming feeling of something could go—" His wife completed his thought by saying, "It could happen. If it could happen it would happen." Other couples managed to experience a lull between worries about "getting it [a baby] in there [and] getting it out."

Most of these couples remained physically infertile even after achieving pregnancy because the treatments leading to their pregnancies typically only circumvented rather than cured infertility. Yet, even on an emotional and psychic level, couples were still not necessarily cured by the pregnancies they achieved or by the babies born to them. Many couples still felt the residual effects of the adversity they had experienced struggling to conceive a child.

The achievement of pregnancy by itself thus does not necessarily constitute the mythic happy ending associated with pregnancy nor a harmonious closure to infertility. As one woman remarked:

> I will always consider myself infertile because of the way you have to go to extraordinary means to get there. I mean I don't consider myself one of the masses. . . . If things are wonderful, things are beautiful and happy, it's like a dream.

Note

1. See Table A.4 in Appendix.

9. Machine in the Garden

The machine in the garden . . . [symbolizes] the root conflict of our culture. (Marx, 1964, p. 365)

The availability of medical technology to induce conception, monitor and maintain pregnancy, detect fetal impairments, and resolve complicated labors and births can be both boon and burden to infertile couples. Such technology permits couples who would never have been able to conceive or sustain a biological child to have one and allows couples at significant risk for transmitting a serious genetic disease to attempt to have a healthy baby. Yet, technological intervention may also reinforce suffering. For example, the use of fertility drugs and multiple embryos in in vitro fertilization procedures, which increase the risk of multiple pregnancies of three or more fetuses, may force couples to consider selective reduction: whether to abort one or more of these fetuses so that the remaining one or two can survive (Berkowitz et al., 1988). In these cases, couples, not free to choose not to be infertile, are also constrained to consider a solution to a "technological fix" (Overall, 1990, p. 7) gone awry.

Techniques such as ultrasonography, alpha-fetoprotein testing, amniocentesis, and cesarean delivery have become virtually routine events in childbearing in the United States. Childbearing, itself a process ambiguously located between nature and culture, is interpreted and treated alternatively as a natural biological process and as a pathogenic event frequently requiring medical/surgical intervention (Eakins, 1986; Oakley, 1980, 1986; Sargent & Stark, 1987). With the increasing availability and use of conceptive techniques, childbearing has become even more firmly entrenched in the domain of medicine, and childbearing couples are potentially even more technologically dependent. These couples trust technology to enhance the experience of childbearing, relying on it to reverse nature's deficits and to rescue them from the dangers of a *natural* process, but they are also constrained by this technology.

The infertile couples we interviewed who required assistance to conceive had come to depend on technology, but they also exhibited a range of responses to this kind of dependency. By virtue of their infertility, these couples had already resigned themselves to having something other than a wholly "natural childbirth," a term which they used to describe the entire maternity cycle from conception through delivery. While some couples embraced technology, even viewing it as a component of natural childbirth, other couples sought to resist its further encroachment on and even profanation of natural birth.

Infertile couples conceiving with biomedical assistance encountered the dilemma of deciding whether and when a "technological opportunity" furthered or subverted nature's designs. When couples contemplated whether to learn the sex of their child, whether to violate their baby's "space" by having amniocentesis, and whether to accept technical assistance to reproduce at all, they struggled to accommodate and not to contravene nature's intentions. One man confessed to having a "philosophical ambivalence" about in vitro fertilization. Having "lost faith in nature," he and his wife worried about disrupting nature's designs at the same time they had "mystical ideas about souls waiting to be born." They finally decided that helping them get born was right: that having a child "artificially" was "philosophically correct."

Assisted conception and childbearing was rejected as going against nature or, alternatively, accepted as helping, duplicating, or itself part of nature. One man described donor insemination as "seminatural." In having ultrasound examinations and amniocenteses, couples recognized that they were privy to information no one had ever known before—and perhaps, ought still not to know. Some couples in the in vitro process were excited by but also uncomfortable with "looking at [cells] that shouldn't be looked at."

Couples indicated the extent to which technology can make the mysterious mundane. An especially interesting finding in the Transition to Parenthood couples was that although the fertile couples were more likely to have personal images of a baby, both groups of couples found it hard to describe images of the fetus beyond the "generic baby" ones available to them from ultrasound or from fetal development books. Readily available technological and textbook images of the fetus appeared to impede the development of their own images. One fertile man stated, "I've seen too many of the books now . . . I've got some mental pictures, from pictures that I've seen in books of what a fetus looks like inside the womb." Whether fertile or infertile, childbearing couples in America now often share a "scientific" image of their baby.

Amniocentesis

The availability of amniocentesis posed a special dilemma for the infertile couples who finally conceived. They were forced to experience yet again the specter of despair and the "disturbing mix of uncertainty and hope" (Lappe, 1984, p. 20) associated with both the struggle to conceive and the ability to identify an impaired baby in advance of its birth.

Psychological studies of couples who undergo prenatal diagnostic procedures such as chorionic villus sampling, alpha-fetoprotein testing, and amniocentesis suggest the anxiety and ambivalence that couples experience toward prenatal testing (Beeson and Golbus, 1979; Evers-Kiebooms, Swerts, and Van Den Berghe, 1988; Fava et al., 1982; Robinson, Hibbard, and Laurence, 1984; Sjogren and Uddenberg, 1988; Tabor and Jonsson, 1987; Verjaal, Leschot, and Treffers, 1982), and the way it can alter the experiential milestones, rhythms, and social construction of pregnancy (Beeson, 1984; Rapp, 1988; Rothman, 1986). The prevailing concerns that women generally have about prenatal testing involve the risk of miscarrying a normal fetus in the course of testing and the very limited availability of therapeutic interventions to treat an impaired fetus. Tests such as amniocentesis have been called "search and destroy missions" (Drugan, Johnson, and Evans, 1990, p. 288), with abortion the only option typically available to women carrying an impaired fetus other than carrying the fetus to term.

For all of the advantages that prenatal diagnosis offers couples by reassuring most of them about the health of their babies and by giving couples with special reasons to fear fetal deformity an opportunity to determine whether they can have a healthy child, this technology has also increased the burden of choice and altered the notion of parental responsibility. Women have always exercised the option (whether legally sanctioned or not) not to have children by terminating pregnancies or by relinquishing their babies at birth. With the advent of more effective contraceptive technology, women have also acquired a greater ability to prevent conception and to choose whether and when to conceive a child.

But prenatal diagnostic technology has transformed the nature of choice in a way that makes women and couples even more vulnerable to guilt and regret. Women choosing not to get pregnant, not to maintain a pregnancy, or not to keep a baby are typically choosing against having or mothering any baby at that moment in their lives (Brodzinsky, 1990; Torres and Forrest, 1988); they are not choosing against a particular baby for reasons associated only with that baby. Moreover, they are deciding to

TABLE 9.1.   Amniocentesis by age and fertility status (N = 58).

| | AGE X FERTILITY STATUS | | | |
| | < 35 YEARS | | > 35 YEARS | |
AMNIOCENTESIS	FERTILE	INFERTILE	FERTILE	INFERTILE
Yes	3	1	2	13
No	12	22	2	3

Note: The number fifty-eight accounts for all of the fertile and infertile couples with opportunities to have an amniocentesis. Two infertile couples lost their pregnancies in the first trimester.

abort a fetus or to relinquish a child who is a consequence of a pregnancy that was typically accidental and unwanted; they are not choosing against a baby who was planned for and once desired. In contrast, prenatal diagnostic technology permits couples to get to know certain things about their baby before meeting it at birth and to reject it on the basis of that knowledge. In the context of infertility, conceptive techniques permit couples to achieve pregnancy, but prenatal diagnostic techniques offer and burden them with the opportunity to decide whether to keep it.

As shown in Table 9.1, nineteen couples (thirteen infertile and fifteen with the wife aged thirty-five or over) had an amniocentesis. As summarized in Table 9.2, both fertile and infertile childbearing couples considered a variety of factors in making the decision to accept or decline amniocentesis (cf. Pauker and Pauker, 1987). Very few of them were completely in favor of or opposed to amniocentesis, typically demonstrating some hesitancy or ambivalence toward the procedure and the information obtainable from it.

Whereas the fertile couples often cited the unlikelihood of their having an impaired child and their feelings that their babies would be healthy as reasons for declining the procedure, the infertile couples cited a greater variety of reasons, balancing the known "premium" value of their pregnancies with the putative value of information obtainable from amniocentesis and the risks of the procedure itself. As one woman, who had become pregnant spontaneously while waiting to adopt a child, explained:

> This may very well be our only shot at ever getting pregnant and the
> thought of losing a perfectly healthy, normal baby to find out that you

TABLE 9.2.   Factors involved in the decision to accept or decline amniocentesis.

To Decline	To Accept
Absence of fetal impairments, birth defects, or risks of defects in the family	Presence of risk factors (usually age) or impairments in the family
	Having worked with mentally retarded or disabled
Presence of other noninvasive and safer tests (AFP testing, ultrasound) perceived as giving equivalent or better information	
Perception that information obtained from amniocentesis is equivocal or incomplete	
Desire to avoid bad news	Desire to know status of fetus
Risk of the procedure to the pregnancy seen as too high	Risk of the procedure to the pregnancy seen as low
Increased value of a hard-to-achieve pregnancy	
Willingness/ability to care for an impaired child	Unwillingness/inability to care for an impaired child
Unwillingness to terminate pregnancy	Willingness to terminate pregnancy
Realness of the baby and advanced state of pregnancy by the time test results return	
Availability of good medical care at birth for an impaired baby	
Perception that an embryo conceived by IVF had to be hardy and resistant to defects	

might have some problems that you might choose to do something about just hasn't been worth it to me.

The efforts of some infertile couples to achieve a viable pregnancy had served to change their attitudes toward parenting an impaired child. As one expectant father observed:

Before all of . . . our infertility problems, if we had gotten pregnant and done amniocentesis and found out that we carried a child with Down's syndrome or with a severe chromosomal abnormality and severe birth defects, then I might have favored a termination in a situation like that. Thinking about how much the child would suffer and how much we would suffer and thinking selfishly in a lot of ways. But, now I honestly think I would take whatever happened. That it was just meant to be.

He further noted that what was really important was the child's ability to be happy and the parents' role in facilitating a happy life. One infertile woman observed that she felt confident in her ability to care for an impaired child, and described the two "exceptional Down's babies" in her own and her husband's family.

In contrast, couples who chose to have an amniocentesis balanced the value of pregnancy against the risk of having an impaired baby. Couples who stated they would consider aborting a fetus generally had in mind babies who were sure to die or who had severe anomalies. The factors contributing to the decision of couples to accept or decline amniocentesis reflected their appraisals of the burdens associated with serious fetal impairments and of their ability to cope with them (cf. Ekwo, Kim, and Gosselink, 1987).

When these couples contemplated whether to have an amniocentesis, they were clearly forced to consider the value of having foreknowledge— information about their babies prior to birth that used to be unavailable before the development and widespread use of prenatal tests. Such foreknowledge was viewed both as a miracle of science and as undermining the "mystery" and normal "suspense" of childbearing: in a sense, as profaning the sacredness of fetal existence. Couples weighed the advantages and disadvantages of knowing, both for the sake of knowing itself and for the sake of action, in an experiential vacuum. Several couples specifically commented on the difficulty of "premaking" decisions and of anticipating responses to so momentous an event as the diagnosis of a fetal defect. Couples cited the advantages of having the knowledge obtainable from amniocentesis, including (*a*) maintaining the option to abort an impaired fetus; (*b*) having the reassurance of normal test results; and (*c*) having the time to prepare medically and emotionally for the birth of an impaired child. The couples who wanted or were unable to resist knowing the sex of the fetus, an informational by-product of fetal diagnosis, remarked that knowing the sex allowed them to be better consumers, saved them time and effort in choosing a name, and promoted earlier attachment to the fetus by making it more of a person.

The disadvantages of having foreknowledge included (*a*) in the case of an abnormal test result, knowing about a defect for a longer period of time when abortion was not an option; (*b*) having to consider abortion at all; (*c*) having equivocal information on the severity of the defect; and (*d*) knowing something that ought not to be known. Couples struggled with the reality that much of the foreknowledge provided by prenatal tests has "nondecisional" value (Berwick and Weinstein, 1985, p. 883) for couples unwilling to abort any fetus; there was no action they or their physicians could take to reverse a disorder such as Down's syndrome nor was there any way to determine the degree to which a Down's syndrome fetus was affected. Couples describing the disadvantages of knowing the sex of the fetus remarked that it removed the surprise and wonder of birth. Some of these couples sought to avoid information about their babies by declining tests or by instructing their caregivers not to reveal the sex of their babies.

The husband in an infertile couple refusing amniocentesis observed that if the fetus is abnormal, "you're going to pay either way. You're going to have your disappointment and it's just a matter of when and what's best for you." Another expectant father wondered whether they perhaps knew too much. One woman, who had conceived by in vitro fertilization and whose husband insisted on her having an amniocentesis, remarked:

> I guess deep down inside, I almost wish [amniocentesis] didn't even exist. It's like medical science has allowed us to have this baby but then now, there's so much stuff you can do. It's almost not human. It really isn't normal to be able to tell in advance what the child's going to be. You just generally get pregnant, you take your chances. It's part of the . . . game. You run that risk.

While considering the value of foreknowledge, couples indicated the difficulty in confronting the imperatives of technology, often viewing the need to make choices about prenatal tests as an additional burden. Alternatively, couples laboring under a scientific and even moral mandate typical of Western culture to know what can be known (Rothman, 1988; Stewart and Bennett, 1991) have been found to be grateful for any technological innovation and reluctant to refuse it, despite its material and psychic costs. Such couples anticipate the regret they will suffer if they decline testing (Tymstra, 1989).

Some couples accepted alpha-fetoprotein (AFP) testing, used to detect neural tube defects and to determine the need for amniocentesis, almost by default, because for this test doctors "just drew a little bit of blood." One fertile woman, who eventually declined amniocentesis, recalled:

I think I was just panicky and . . . afraid of taking too many unnecessary things and at the same time worrying, "Well, you should find out
for the baby's sake if there is anything wrong." So before I left one visit
from the doctor's office, I told them no [to AFP testing], I don't want
it, and [the doctor] said, "You don't?" Then, by the time I left, I said,
"Well, no, okay, yes, I do."

Another fertile woman also viewed AFP testing as "a simple thing," even
though she knew that there was a chance that it would needlessly increase
her level of anxiety. For her, declining an ostensibly simple blood test
seemed harder to do, given the rather routine nature of having blood
drawn. An infertile woman whose first AFP test result indicated abnormality and who declined amniocentesis, however, eventually regretted
having had the test at all, worrying throughout the entire pregnancy that
her baby was impaired (cf. Burton, Dillard, and Clark, 1985; Fearn et al.,
1982). This woman suffered the "iatrogenic anxiety" (Rothenberg and Sills,
1968) that testing itself can engender apart from the normal anxiety associated with pregnancy.

Refusing a more complex procedure, such as amniocentesis, was also
difficult for couples, especially when physicians or friends encouraged such
a procedure. One fertile couple was forced to resist the encouragement of
physician and friends to have the procedure done. Expecting her first child
at age thirty-four, the wife admitted:

There's a part of me that feels like I'm going to be kind of haunted until
the baby is born. Wondering whether I made a mistake. . . . This is
probably the first time I've ever turned down a technological opportunity of that magnitude. . . . It's a bold kind of thing.

Describing the surprised reaction of her friends at not even having had an
ultrasound examination, she felt "negligent" for not having "demanded"
one. Another fertile woman in the first trimester of pregnancy described the
regret she anticipated feeling if she decided not to have an amniocentesis
done, a feeling that passed when she entered a phase of her pregnancy when
she could no longer have one. An infertile woman observed that she "would
never consider not knowing . . . the information there and available. [She]
couldn't tolerate it." Yet another infertile woman noted feeling that she
needed to have tests done "just to see if everything's okay."

Reprising Infertility

The infertile, as opposed to fertile, couples who made decisions about amniocentesis found themselves on familiar ground. Their encounters with amniocentesis continued essential components of their encounters with infertility by reprising their experiences with adversity, with the trauma of medical procedures, with the anxiety of waiting for good or bad news, with playing the odds, and with the burden of choice.

Having experienced the ironies and frustrations of repeatedly failing to do what most other people could do with hardly any effort at all, infertile couples were all too familiar with the fact that life was not a "perfect storybook once-upon-a-time" process. Suggesting the common ground of adversity that infertility and amniocentesis occupy, one woman who had a "Pergonal baby" observed that infertility had forced her to "give up . . . fairy tales," while amniocentesis had forced her to confront the possibility of having an impaired child, an eventuality her fertile friends avoided contemplating. Commenting on the negative responses of her friends to their knowledge that their baby was a girl, she and her husband explained that infertility had already interfered with the surprises of childbearing. As she remarked:

> Surprised at the pregnancy and then surprised at the sex. That's not the way things have gone for us, and we've accepted that. So, it's sort of funny to see the way other people feel about it, because they are in a totally different [situation]—they can live that way. Their kids came along that way.

Another woman who had conceived by in vitro fertilization suggested that infertile couples could never be as "flip" as fertile couples about pregnancy and children: "Our experiences . . . have made us not take two things for granted that I think 90 percent of the population take for granted: number one, even being able to have a child, and number two, that it will automatically be healthy." The infertile couples' pregnancies were encumbered by infertility even before conception. Couples worried whether they would ever conceive, fretted about holding on to the pregnancies they did achieve, and disbelieved their good fortune at achieving pregnancy at all. The personal acquaintance of these couples with loss and failure made additional adversity a more palpable eventuality for them and the loss of the surprises and mystery of childbearing more tolerable.

Integral to the painful struggle of infertile couples, and especially women, to conceive were their experiences of being "stuck, probed, and gouged" while undergoing medical regimens to diagnose and treat infertility. Fertile and infertile women who had undergone amniocentesis conveyed that they had "survived" a physically painful and/or emotionally "terrifying" ordeal. Yet infertile women and couples had become accustomed to incorporating medical technology into their lives. For some of these couples, amniocentesis was "just another shot," just another "part of the high-tech package," and part of having a "high-tech . . . eighties baby." Infertile couples were used to "invasions" into their personal "space," finding an additional incursion into their "baby's . . . space" frightening, but nothing out of the ordinary.

Moreover, waiting to undergo the amniocentesis and then waiting for the test results to come back echoed for infertile couples the seemingly endless waiting they had endured for other test results to determine the cause of their infertility, for treatment regimens to work, and, ultimately, for the longed-for missed menstrual period and positive pregnancy test. Couples who decided for and against the procedure commented on the anxiety and suppressed emotion attached to yet another period of anticipating either good or bad news. One man whose wife conceived by donor insemination described the "milestones in test," rather than in "development," which he and his wife had passed in their struggle to achieve pregnancy and then in their struggle to enjoy it. Concerned about the anxiety that testing alone was inducing in his wife, this man observed:

> [She] would come back from a test, we would be ecstatic, almost go out and celebrate because a test came back really well and then the next thing you think about is, "Well, four weeks from now, I've got to have that one done."

Amniocentesis also reprised infertile couples' encounters with playing the odds. Infertile couples had characteristically expended much effort in calculating the chances of success and risk associated with different medical therapies. Couples contemplating amniocentesis similarly considered the odds. One couple suggested the arbitrariness of advising amniocentesis for women over thirty-five years old by citing a thirty-year-old friend who had borne a Down's syndrome baby. One man, whose wife had already lost a pregnancy, contemplated the "risks of having one miscarriage plus having amniocentesis," noting that even though "there is a one in a million chance of having a plane crash, the anxiety about experiencing one is still there."

Because they were already a minority among couples owing to their difficulty conceiving a child, infertile couples understood, as few of their fertile
counterparts did, that the statistical odds against the occurrence of tragedy
are cruel, if not meaningless, to the one couple stricken by tragedy.

Finally, amniocentesis continued the experience of infertility in forcing
couples to make yet another difficult decision concerning an experience
that was supposed to be enjoyable. Although the question—should I or
shouldn't I—occurred to fertile couples, it was a question infertile couples
had become very accustomed to; infertile couples had to make and remake
decisions after each failure to conceive, choosing whether to continue
trying, which alternatives to parenthood to pursue next, and whether they
still wanted to have a child.

By reprising essential aspects of the struggles of infertile couples to
become pregnant, amniocentesis often disrupted their pregnancies; it
struck a discordant note by raising the specter of abnormality and loss and
by raising the stakes of an already high-stakes pregnancy. By its very
availability, amniocentesis undermined the joy and wonder of childbearing.
Infertile couples, especially, often perceived amniocentesis as a technique
that undermined ultrasonography, another technique that provided couples with pleasure and reassurance and that reinforced the viability of the
pregnancy and the babyhood of the fetus. One man described the powerful
ultrasound machine used with amniocentesis as bringing him face-to-face
with the fetus's humanity at the same time a potentially dangerous needle
was entering its space. Perceiving himself to be in a "strange situation," he
recalled almost fainting during the procedure. Amniocentesis, via ultrasound, validated the existence of a baby to disbelieving couples, but it also
placed that baby in jeopardy. For infertile couples, in particular, amniocentesis underscored the irony of having the technology to make babies, to
transform fetuses into babies, and to contribute to their deaths.

Couples alluded to an immorality of having foreknowledge about a
baby not yet born, of not playing "the game" with all of its attendant risks as
God or nature intended. Pregnancy was supposed to involve playing the
cards one was dealt. As one woman who had conceived by in vitro fertilization observed:

> It was like we had been through all this great ordeal to get pregnant,
> and we were going to turn around and consciously go and do some-
> thing that carried with it some risk of causing an abortion. And too, I
> think emotionally, I was just getting geared up to being happy, and
> believ[ing] that I was pregnant and it had worked out, and here

somebody told me to turn around and do something that might give me some information that would suggest that I abort. . . . Can't I enjoy this [pregnancy] for awhile, please?

Another infertile woman suggested that technology interrupted her sense of her own normality and that of her pregnancy and recalled resisting her doctor's attempts to persuade her to have an amniocentesis. She explained, "I feel like I'm normal now and I want to play it the old-fashioned way. I use technology when I have to, but I don't feel like I want to anymore."

The responses of infertile couples to amniocentesis, although similar in substance to those of the fertile couples, were clearly shaped by their encounter with infertility. By reprising negative aspects of their infertility experience, amniocentesis also contributed to the difficulty these couples had relinquishing infertility. Accustomed to failed effort and loss, these couples displayed a more finely honed sense of the value of pregnancy and of a baby and the special way that amniocentesis could enhance or depreciate it. Prenatal diagnosis is transforming the experience of childbearing for all American couples, but for infertile couples, childbearing as an idea and event had already been altered. As infertile couples repeatedly affirmed, infertility, by itself, changes things.

Getting It In, Getting There, and Getting It Out

While amniocentesis was a technique couples seemed to locate in the realm of choice (even if at times experienced as a forced choice), couples located cesarean delivery more easily in the realm of necessity. With amniocentesis, babies and couples' impending parenthood were jeopardized. With cesarean delivery, babies were rescued from trauma and death and women were rescued from the pain and futility of labor.

An important factor in their assessment of the value of technological dependency was the focus of infertile couples on one birth outcome— having a viable infant—rather than on the process of birth. Of the thirty-eight infertile couples delivering a baby in the course of the study, eighteen had cesarean births for such factors as failure to progress, breech presentation, previous abdominal surgery, and multiple pregnancy.[1] As they described it, they were concerned with the "end result, not the getting there." Indeed, being pregnant appeared considerably less important than getting pregnant and then having a baby to love.

Although there were exceptions, women tended to view pregnancy less as a process to be savored in its own right than as a stressful interlude or as a means to a goal. Some women admitted they could easily skip pregnancy to get to a baby; relying on technical advancements in the care of preterm infants, a few women acknowledged not minding an abbreviated pregnancy if they could have their baby sooner. Still, one woman described her pregnancy as "just heaven" and specifically stated that she wished her pregnancy could "go on forever."

These middle-class and white infertile women were similar to the lower income and predominantly black women of a previous study on cesarean delivery in their emphasis on the product as opposed to the process of birth (Sandelowski and Bustamante, 1986). Most psychological literature on women's responses to cesarean delivery has emphasized the greater distress of women highly invested in a natural childbirth who end up having to undergo a surgical birth (Affonso and Stichler, 1978; Cox and Smith, 1982; Cranley, Hedahl, and Pegg, 1983; Lipson and Tilden, 1980). Such women are typically middle class, have very defined expectations for their birth experiences, and, thus, tend to be more dissatisfied when their expectations are not achieved (Nelson, 1982, 1983, 1986; Sandelowski, 1984). Moreover, technology may itself alter expectations for childbirth, raising the expectations of couples for a risk-free birth and perfect baby and lowering them for a self-reliant birth and perfect birth experience.

Few of either the fertile or infertile couples in the Transition to Parenthood study articulated a perspective on childbearing at odds with mainstream obstetric practice that routinely incorporates drugs, technological surveillance, and surgical resolutions to birth. As one infertile woman put it, "It'd be nice to do it the regular way. I prefer it. But, if it can't be, it can't be." Instead of exhibiting conflict between what has often been described as the natural and medical model of childbirth (Nash and Nash, 1979; Rothman, 1982), couples tended to assimilate the one into the other, or, if they associated it with pain and danger, to resist the natural. Some women even scoffed at the idea of not embracing the technical assistance available or at the idea that anything about childbearing could be "natural" for them. Linking natural childbirth with pain and feminist masochism, one infertile woman remarked:

> I don't have this feministic goal that I'm going to have it natural. . . . I don't really admire women who go through all that pain that they don't have to [laughs]. . . . Even a C-section would be fine with me, because then I would be guaranteed my doctor.

For one couple conceiving by in vitro fertilization, nature was completely out of the norm for them. The wife recalled that everybody asked her if she was going to have her baby naturally. She remarked, "And I said, kind of always laughing and said, 'there's not a whole lot about me that's natural.' . . . When I'm not pregnant, my hair's colored. I have a perm, and I always had my makeup on." Having had to resort to in vitro fertilization this couple stated they would be surprised if they did not have to have a cesarean delivery. The wife acknowledged that she might regret not having a vaginal birth in the future, but that she was not "disturbed" thinking about a cesarean delivery now. In fact, it was only while she was in the final stages of pushing her baby out vaginally that she truly believed that she could avoid a cesarean. Even then, she and her husband believed it only because they thought it was "too late" to do a cesarean. In addition, the husband observed:

> [C-section] seems kind of natural . . . I waited in the hospital room [for conception]. It seems kind of natural that they wheel her back in and bring out the baby. . . . It's been so high tech all the way around, I don't know why you should do anything at this stage.

The wife also indicated the treachery of natural birth by telling a story of a woman whose baby died in the course of a vaginal delivery because of a cord wrapped around its neck. Cesarean birth seemed less dangerous to her and, describing herself as intolerant of pain, less painful.

In contrast, a few couples and women "agonized" over the birth experience they would have. One infertile couple described themselves as "fighting" what they perceived to be unwarranted technological incursions (from ultrasound examinations to electronic fetal monitoring) into their childbirth experience. This couple described successfully "battling" to prevent a "cascade" of interventions that they did not need. One infertile woman tried "fighting" having a cesarean delivery, but acknowledged that with her diabetes, age, and previous uterine surgery, and because she had required technical assistance to conceive at all, the odds were in favor of her having a cesarean delivery. Despite her husband's reassurances, she worried about "robbing" him of a natural childbirth. At the same time, she was very conscious of the fact that technology had permitted her to have a baby, something that would not have happened to her ten years ago.

Similarly, another infertile couple, although grateful for their child, was disappointed that their delivery had turned into "a surgical situation" and that very few of their birth plans had been realized. As the husband put it, they had already had to give up on conceiving a child naturally. He said about the delivery, "we relinquished all the ideals that we had had before about as natural as possible a childbirth." He recalled having "skimmed" over information they had received about cesarean deliveries in childbirth education classes, thinking that information would not apply to them. One couple, conceiving by in vitro fertilization, attributed the cesarean delivery they ended up having as being the result of "everyone being very nervous about this baby": physicians "jumping too soon" to intervene. Because they thought it would be the only birth experience they would ever have, they were disappointed that things did not "go their way."

Yet, for most couples who had struggled to have a child and who had endured the considerable anguish of that struggle, agonizing much over what kind of birth to have hardly seemed important. Having suffered failed expectations in the past, it hardly seemed logical to these couples to have too many and too high expectations about childbirth. What mattered to them was having a viable infant. Like the medically indigent women mentioned above who minimized the importance of the kind of delivery they had, these couples had more than a "handshaking acquaintance with doom and fate" (Mitchard, 1985, p. 97). One man observed:

> I feel like the getting pregnant was hard enough and it's kind of—I didn't expect it but I could—the difficulties that we had with delivering, you know, really was like water off a duck's back. It kind of—it didn't really soak in. It was just another thing we had to deal with and we dealt with it.

Failed expectations for conception in the past had tempered these couples' birth expectations for the future.

Still, cesarean delivery could represent one more failure in a series of failures in childbearing. As this man's wife, who had conceived by in vitro fertilization, observed:

> I'm a lot less [disappointed] now [eleven days after birth] because I can see what I have but I was real disappointed. I was real disappointed. I think I was relieved once they said that you haven't progressed, let's go ahead and do it. Because at that point, I was just—I had had it. But, you know, it would have been nice to have had one thing go right [laughs here]. You know, one thing that I could do that—that I couldn't—I mean I couldn't conceive by myself and I couldn't go into

labor by myself and then I couldn't deliver it. But, you know, I have a healthy baby and I keep trying to sort of tell myself that.

Later, commenting on the difficulty she had had when starting to breast-feed her baby, she observed, "It was one thing that I wanted to do. I mean one thing that I really felt like was, if I kept up with it, I could be successful at since I couldn't be successful with much of anything else."

Natural Birth

In their descriptions of natural childbirth, fertility drugs, artificial insemination, in vitro fertilization, amniocentesis, and cesarean delivery, most couples indicated a willingness to consider technology as part of nature's design, even if they also expressed some ambivalent feelings toward such a reconciliation. Their conflict reprised on a very personal level a larger Western and especially American dichotomy and "opposition of values" (Channell, 1991, p. 5) between the technological and the natural. Leo Marx (1964) described the "powerful metaphor of contradiction" (p. 4) revealed in Americans' historic embrace of and resistance to the "machine in the garden." Observers of childbirth in America have emphasized the conflicting sentimentalities and hard realities in both natural and technological approaches to pregnancy and birth. For many of the infertile couples, there was a special urgency about their efforts to separate sentiment from reality and to assimilate into nature what many in their culture still view as unnatural. Their sense of esteem and competence depended, in part, on the success of their efforts to see technological intervention in pregnancy and birth as part of the natural design and themselves as normal and moral people.

Note

1. Of the nineteen fertile couples, four had cesarean deliveries. In addition, two babies in the fertile group had complications: the one baby diagnosed prenatally with heart block required a pacemaker after birth and another baby had pyloric stenosis and periorbital cellulitis. In the infertile group, two babies had pyloric stenosis, two babies had inguinal hernias (one of whom had pyloric stenosis), and one baby had testicular torsion; these babies all had corrective surgery soon after birth. Another baby required hospitalization for jaundice. Among the women delivering in the infertile group, one woman had a placenta accreta and another woman, a postdelivery uterine perforation.

10. Tick . . . Tock

> We shall need many more fictional devices . . . to maintain within that interval following tick a lively expectation of tock, and a sense that however remote tock may be, all that happens happens as if tock were certainly following. All such plotting presupposes and requires that an end will bestow upon the whole duration and meaning. (Kermode, 1967, p. 46)

The infertile couples who had children through pregnancy had special work to do in making the transition to parenthood, but it was a transition that (even though initiated with biotechnical assistance) could still be and was construed as within the biological domain: as, in most ways and to anyone else, just like or just about like that of any other childbearing couple. In contrast, the infertile couples who had children through adoption had to work outside the biological domain to make a transition to parenthood that was in many ways unlike that of their childbearing counterparts. In this and the next chapters, I consider the special nature of expectant adoptive parenthood.

Adoption tends to be construed in relation to the biological standard, that is, as an "as if" (Kirk, 1985) relationship where a family is made as if the adopted child were born to a couple. In relation to this standard, adoption is conceived culturally (although not by adopting couples themselves) as second best and is typically the second choice of couples wanting children. The work of adoption, beginning when couples first contemplate it as a means to parenthood, is largely centered on its as-ifness in relation to biological parenthood.

Because of the prospective and longitudinal design of the Transition to Parenthood study, we were able to observe a critical and somewhat neglected (by researchers and clinicians) phase in the transition to adoptive parenthood: the preadoption waiting period. In this period, adopting couples, like their childbearing counterparts in pregnancy, worked to relinquish infertility and to prepare themselves to become parents. Like pregnancy, the preadoption waiting period is a liminal phase (Van Gennep 1909/1960) in the transition to parenthood in which couples are neither not-parents nor parents, but rather hoping-soon-to-be-parents.

Yet, the preadoption waiting period has neither the biotemporal order (Zerubavel, 1981) nor the sacred dimensions (Balin, 1988) of pregnancy that help childbearing couples internalize and celebrate their parent-to-be status. Child*waiting*, as opposed to childbearing, couples have no due date nor do they have any positive signs that they are in fact having a child. Moreover, there are no culturally familiar and acknowledged rituals, ceremonies, practices, or artifacts distinctively associated with childwaiting or that validate progress toward parenthood. Neither adopting couples nor the people they interact with have a biocultural script (Kirk 1964/1984) to follow to assist couples in making the transition to adoptive parenthood (Daly 1988, 1990), a journey that often occurs in the context of the deprivations and mythologies associated with both infertility and relinquishment (Berman and Bufferd, 1986; Blum, 1983; Brodzinsky and Schechter, 1990; Kirk, 1964/1984; Schechter, 1970).

In fact, couples often had to struggle to obtain recognition of their parent-to-be status. Two women, for example, were angry that they were denied or had to fight for the privileges—parental leave and unsolicited advice literature and coupons for baby items obtained in the mail—that society readily made available to conventionally expectant parents. One woman observed that people "look at you weirdly . . . [when] you're out looking for baby things and you're not visibly pregnant." Another woman mentioned that she was included as guest of honor in a baby shower only "as an afterthought." Her husband recalled feeling hurt at a party where he was not recognized as being an expectant father along with the men there whose wives were pregnant. Other women recalled with both amusement and anguish the downward gaze of confused friends and acquaintances to the belly when they presented themselves as "expecting" a child. One childwaiting woman who had been pregnant several times without giving birth suggested the importance of being acknowledged as an expectant parent, even if without-child. As she observed:

> I kind of feel like I'm pregnant again. And I tell everybody that we're expecting. And they say they're expecting and I say, "We're expecting too." "Well, when's your baby due?" "Anytime now. We're just waiting for the phone call."

Friends and acquaintances of adopting couples had to deal with the paradox of "they're having a baby, but they're not having a baby." One man summarized the problem that people encountered with an adopting couple when he observed, "You know how to react to a pregnant woman or a woman with a brand new baby. But how do you talk to a person about adopting a baby—that's in the process of adopting a baby?" A woman indicated that adopting couples constituted a separate culture. She maintained that adoption places the parents-to-be "into a whole new sector in society," with its own literature, support groups, and books. As an adopting parent, she said, "you are a subset of society."

Perhaps most significantly, unlike their childbearing counterparts who wait for their child with child (Bergum 1989), adopting couples wait for a child in absentia, without the reassurance that comes from an increasingly active physical presence. Although adopting couples experienced a range of physical and emotional symptoms, feelings, and moods in the waiting period, these did not in any way serve to validate their expectant status in the way that morning sickness and quickening functioned to affirm pregnancy and a fetal presence. In childwaiting, as one woman put it, there was no morning sickness, swollen ankles, or spreading hips to help her internalize her expectant status and "make it real." Adopting women had the "wait" without the benefits (and liabilities) of the "weight."

Most childbearing couples became increasingly confident that they would have a child by virtue of safely passing the various developmental milestones and "danger zones" of pregnancy. In contrast, adopting couples became less certain (and more despairing) that they would ever get a child the longer they were forced to wait for one, or the more time that passed beyond the date they had fixed in their minds as their "due date." Indeed, the temporally unmarked nature of childwaiting challenged the couples we interviewed to create the temporal ground (Zerubavel, 1981) that would permit them to regain some control over their lives and to maintain the hope that a child would eventually give their years of struggle and waiting meaning.

Childwaiting

Although childwaiting couples found the word "childbearing" inadequate to describe their circumstances, they nevertheless used the language or metaphor of pregnancy to convey the biotemporal deficits of the preadoption waiting period. Childwaiting women had, in the words of one woman, "not-pregnancy pregnanc[ies]"; they were not like the woman who announced her pregnancy after three months, had the baby six months later, and then returned from maternity leave two months after birth. As one woman noted, "It's not like that with me. I don't know when it's going to be." Another woman recalled a friend telling her that "theoretically," she was pregnant. She was not comfortable with that designation, however. She said, "Sure, it's a gestation period, but you don't know when it's gonna end." Her husband added that they could become parents "theoretically tomorrow." One woman envied her pregnant friends their due dates and described the "unended uncertainty, open-ended uncertainty" that characterized childwaiting. Another woman grieved "not being able to go through the ritual" of expecting a child, while other women felt somewhat uncomfortable having baby showers because it was a ceremony associated with the imminent end of pregnancy and arrival of a baby. One man summarized the temporal problem childwaiting couples faced when he observed:

> It's like when you get pregnant and have a child, it's nine months. You know the child's coming. You get it [the pregnancy] checked out. In the meantime, you find out—they give sonograms, everything to make sure it's gonna be a good pregnancy. They go through Lamaze classes, people in the same situation. And usually in Lamaze classes, everybody's having a baby about the same time. In adoption, it's real, real tough because there's a wait. Everybody's got a different wait. You don't know how long you're gonna wait.

Whereas pregnancy is by itself an event filled with biological milestones and a corresponding cultural script (Kirk, 1964/1984) for interpreting and experiencing them, childwaiting is experienced in a temporal vacuum (Glaser and Strauss, 1971), an eventless interval without a script, a "not really real" unplotted void filled paradoxically with absences—the absence of a child and of proof that there was or ever would be a child "somewhere out there." For childwaiting couples, time was a finite resource that became "nonusable . . . in waiting" (Schwartz, 1974, p. 844). Waiting to adopt a child could, accordingly, be even harder to bear for these couples than their time spent waiting to conceive a child every month had been. As one woman explained:

> At least with infertility, you knew on a month-to-month basis, well, this isn't going to be the month. You got some kind of feedback every month. But this—you don't get anything. . . . It's the hardest thing that I think I've ever had to do.

Childwaiting couples were forced to suffer the "torture" of waiting: to bear the burden of empty time and to wait and not know how to wait. Accordingly, they sought to create the temporal order missing from the preadoption waiting period that would provide them with the stability and normalcy of temporal regularity (Zerubavel, 1981). Feeling adrift in time and, at times, "cut loose" by their agencies, childwaiting couples sought to establish a chronology of waiting.

Because of their infertility, couples had typically spent years struggling and then waiting (from month to month) to conceive a child, and later, struggling and then waiting again to make an agency's waiting list. For the couples wanting to adopt locally, making a list typically meant that they had spent a one-to-two-year period finding an agency that would accept their application and that they had completed a comprehensive home study involving pictures, autobiography, and family history, medical reports documenting both their infertility and their good health, financial statements, and a caseworker's written evaluation of their suitability to adopt. Couples wanting to adopt a child outside the United States had the additional time-consuming tasks of submitting and having translated a variety of notarized documents demanded by this country and the country from which they hoped to get a child, including applications for visas from the Immigration and Naturalization service and fingerprint checks from the Federal Bureau of Investigation. Encounters of childwaiting couples with infertility and with the time-consuming bureaucracies of the adoption process had already made them reluctant players in a "waiting game." One woman captured the essence of infertile and adopting couples' experiences with time when she observed, "time . . . just gets eaten up . . . a little test here and a little test there. A little wait here and a little wait there."

For these couples, "wait [was] a four-letter word," something they no longer wanted to do. Childwaiting further reinforced their sense of power-lessness, failure, and, sometimes, anger that they should have to continue to wait to get a child (Schwartz, 1974). As one woman observed, "It's not that I have to have the baby soon. It's just that I want to have the waiting over with." Infertile couples were used to living their lives waiting; as one woman implied, how else was there to live?

Yet couples typically also felt relieved for having achieved some measure of success in even making a waiting list. They finally felt they were moving forward and making progress, instead of riding the infertility "roller coaster" going nowhere. One woman said, "[I] felt like I was in an action mode. I was doing what I could" to become a parent, instead of staying in "the same old rut" of trying and failing every month to conceive. Women felt as though they could finally relinquish aspects of their infertility. In the words of one woman, she could switch her mind off her menstrual cycles and stop taking her temperature every day of her life.

While in waiting for a child, couples continued the process of "healing" that began while working to get approval to adopt; couples continued to mourn the losses of infertility and to resolve any ambivalence they were still experiencing toward parenthood in general or toward adoptive parenthood itself. Women especially found they could attend baby showers again and comfortably be in the presence of pregnant women because they too were "expecting" a child. Certain episodes—scenes involving holidays and parents with children, seeing a baby, hearing it cry in a store—still triggered moments of acute yearning for a child. But couples typically experienced childwaiting initially as a peaceful interlude in their quest for a child where they felt they did not have to struggle or "push" anymore. Devastated by a recent private adoption failure, one man knew he could be riding a roller coaster back into depression again in his current pursuit of an Asian child. He said that for now, however, he was at least going to enjoy "the top" and "have a good look at the scenery nearby."

Although the desire to bear a child and the hope that a child might yet be conceived were not necessarily wholly "purged" by the adoption process, couples felt good about achieving some kind of closure to their infertility. They felt good about themselves for having been accepted as adopters and "special" among would-be parents because adoption "wasn't for everyone." Although there were a few couples who continued to pursue fertility concurrently with adoption, couples typically abandoned this pursuit once they made the decision to pursue adoption seriously (cf. Daly, 1990). Indeed, as one woman described it, the period after obtaining approval to adopt was a "sort of honeymoon period."

Establishing Timelines

Although waiting in the pursuit of a child had been inscribed into the text of their lives, couples typically did not feel comfortable saying that they were waiting to adopt and did not see themselves as "officially" waiting for a child until they had been formally sanctioned in some way as waiters, that is, until they had been "approved" to wait and had "all the paperwork together." One woman observed that only after they were approved and "actively waiting" did they tell their friends they were adopting a child. This woman suggested the importance of legitimators (caseworkers) in transitional states where there are few clear temporal expectations (Glaser and Strauss, 1971).

Couples distinguished among different kinds of waits in the process of determining when the clock started on the official waiting period. There was "preparing to wait," "prewaiting," "on a waiting list to get on a waiting list," and "on the waiting list that counts." One man waiting to adopt a Korean child explained:

> Purists say that you're not waiting until you have the picture [of the child]. When the picture comes, you're definitely waiting because you've had the referral and the child is assigned and you're actually waiting for that child to come to this country. . . . [But] we're waiting. We're not purists.

Although couples identified many kinds of waiting and intervals of waiting-to-wait, they typically marked a point where they were within a defined time frame for getting a child.

Couples had more difficulty determining the end point of their wait. A major component of the action of waiting was made up of attempts by couples to create some durational expectancies (Zerubavel, 1981) for their wait. Reasoning from information they obtained from caseworkers and other adopting couples, and also from the anecdotes, rumors, and intuitions of relatives and friends, childwaiting couples sought to create a temporal horizon. They tended initially to reason deductively that their agency's placement "track record" would indicate the duration of their wait. For example, if an agency had a track record of placing children within one to two years of approval and a couple had been approved by that agency, they concluded that they would probably be getting their child within two years.

On the basis of this kind of reasoning, couples then constructed a chronology of waiting, signifying could-be-time, anytime-now, and past-time. Could-be-time began with making an agency's waiting list and ended when that agency's earliest placement time had been reached. During could-be-time, no matter how long it was reasoned to last, couples believed that a child could be placed with them but did not really anticipate it. In fact, couples getting their child in could-be-time felt somewhat like couples having a premature birth; their child had come earlier than expected.

Couples began to anticipate the telephone call that a child was available for them when anytime-now was reached, a period beginning with their agency's earliest placement time and ending with its latest placement time. Past-time began after their agency's latest placement time, and it engendered the sense for couples that a child was "overdue" and that "time was running out" in their wait for a child from that agency. For example, one couple anticipated a one year waiting period for their child and set the beginning of their anytime-now marker at seven months because the wife had heard that many couples got their babies from their agency at that time. As she noted; "I think that it is reasonable then to start thinking and hoping." Another couple, who had to wait more than two years for their child, began several months after their anytime-now period had ended seriously to doubt that they would ever get a child, noting that no other couple had ever waited with their agency as long as they had.

Couples waiting for a foreign child constructed a timeline within a timeline. Unlike domestic adopters who typically got a call to get their child within a few days of assignment, these couples were "offered," "assigned" or "referred" to a child whose picture and brief history they got in the mail several months before the child became available to them. They set their first timeline to end with the referral and then set another to end when they believed they would be advised to pick up their child (at a designated American airport or in the country of origin).

As time in waiting passed and new information became available to them, couples were compelled to revise their timelines. They were, at times, forced to conclude that the premises on which they had originally based them were not necessarily true: that the past placement record of an agency did not always predict future placement and that neither their caseworkers nor anyone else could accurately estimate when a child would arrive. One couple had initially set their anytime-now period to begin one year after approval. Yet, when they heard that two couples, approved at the same time they were with the same agency, had gotten babies within only six weeks and three months of approval, they began to anticipate and prepare for the arrival of a child. They figured that "at that rate of speed," they would have their baby at anytime. Still waiting for a baby one year after approval, they had to conclude that those early placements were an "aberration" and, accordingly, reset their time markers again. Couples tended to attribute such aberrations to the higher income of a couple (who could make a larger "contribution" to the agency), to the specialness of the circumstances (older age of the adopting couple or their willingness to accept an impaired child), or to plain luck.[1]

The fact that couples were able to establish periods of time during which a child was not anticipated did not necessarily preclude their hoping for a child. As one woman admitted, "I wanted to believe that the day after we were approved, we were going to be *delivered*" (emphasis added). She and other women especially felt past-due in perspective, if not in clock time. In contrast, there were couples who were long-waiters in clock time who maintained a short-waiter's perspective. For example, because they had already adopted a child, one couple found it easier to accept waiting nearly three years for their second child. Another couple, who described themselves as less desperate for a child than other adopting couples, did not begin to feel overdue for a child until they had actually reached their past-time period, almost two years after approval.

Couples struggled to establish a "realistic" temporal framework for organizing their lives. As one man recalled:

> We were still thinking that, well, our two year mark, which they originally told us we would be up in March—would be—originally they had said up to two years. Well, up to two years was March [his wife corrects this to May]. And so, we're thinking, OK, we're coming up to the end of the year. But still, we're thinking, all right, well, you know, that was up to, and so let's say anytime, it could happen really anytime.

Like other couples who felt especially pressed to have a child when a relative or friend became pregnant or when Christmas was near, this couple sought to validate their timeline with their caseworker. The wife recalled a conversation she had with her caseworker in January, nineteen months after approval.

> I said, "Well, is March even a realistic possibility?" She said, "Well, when did you get approved?" I said, "We were approved in May. It'll be two years this May. She said . . . "I would say probably not for March." I said, "Well, what is a realistic possibility? What are we looking at here? Is six to eight months too soon?" And she said, "I would put it toward the outer end of the interval." I said, "Eight months?" And she said, "Yeah." She said, "You are not at the top of the list," which means that we're not in the top three, but she said, "You're close." And she said—I said, "Well, how have things been going with the agency?" And she said, "Well, it's been an extremely slow year." They just have not seen very many infants that have become available

for adoption this year. And she said right at that point, which was at the end of November, first of October they were wor—they had just received a phone call that day from a woman at the hospital who wanted to put her child into foster care prior to giving it up for adoption. And then she said that they were working with two other women. One of whom was due in January [the current month], and the other was due in March. But, she said, "You know, I can tell you this and this is unusual. We haven't had this many women in our program for the past six months." And she said, "But, you know, under these sorts of circumstances, that sounds—well, that's very hopeful, but you can't count on that because those three women could just as easily change their minds and decide that they don't want to go forth with it. So, under those circumstances . . . I really can't hold out any promises for you." She said, "I don't want you to get your hopes up." So. So, we figure, well—I said, "Well, if anything, it gives us more of a tight window now to look toward.". . . We were thinking, you know, at Christmas that we could possibly get a phone call and that we were living week to week and phone call to phone call. And that's no way to live. It's just crazy being that anxious all the time thinking, well, my life is going to get thrown into total chaos tomorrow. And at least now we know that the next six months, we don't have to worry about anything. We can go about our lives and we can do what we want to do. We can take care of business and not worry about getting this phone call. Which is fine. . . . When she said six to eight months and . . . the outer end of that eight months, I counted and it was August. So I figured, well, ok, I can deal with that. Now I can plan, you know, I can work toward August. And if it happens in June or July, great, you know, I can deal with that if it happens earlier. But at least I know August is my goal that I'm working for.

This woman's lengthy description indicates the problem both child-waiting couples and their caseworkers faced in maintaining an appropriate awareness context (Glaser and Strauss, 1971) in a temporally uncertain situation. Some couples wanted to operate in a completely open awareness context, knowing, for example, how many babies were potentially available to an agency at a given time even though none of those babies might ultimately be available to any couple. Caseworkers vacillated between forthrightness and concealment, wanting to provide their couples with as much information as they had, but also worrying that it would ultimately cause couples more anxiety. Couples also intimated that caseworkers might not want to be harassed by couples wanting information they neither had nor were allowed to give. In contrast, one waiting woman recalled specifically asking not to have any more information on available babies because it made her more anxious. She sought to close her awareness in the interests of preserving some emotional stability. Importantly, both an open and closed awareness context could maintain or reduce the ambiguity of the waiting period.

Adopting couples were also aware of the many factors that influenced the approval-to-placement record of an agency. They understood that they were only one among a cast of players; they typically felt "out of control" vis-à-vis these players, including caseworkers, government bureaucrats, birthmothers, other adopting couples, and just fate. One man described his frustration at being "like a worm on a fishing hook." He said, "You just sit in the water . . . you may get eaten. You may get tired."

Couples imaged scenarios in which one or more of these players acted to determine when the end would come. One woman described a group of "nameless and faceless" people sitting in a boardroom reviewing three or four couples' "portfolios" or "sales packages" to determine which of them would get an available child. At one point, she had also imagined that the birthparents of the child that would be hers had started dating during the past football season. By that accounting, the birthmother would conceive, deliver, and relinquish her child for adoption within the timeframe she and her husband had set. Another woman recalled her mother's friend locating the scene of her child's conception in a Portuguese fishing village during the summer tourist season. The birthmother would conceive in the summer and, unable to get an abortion for religious and financial reasons, would relinquish her child the following spring.

By far, the most prevalent component of these scenarios was the "matching" pretext. One man waiting to adopt his second child explained that caseworkers

> put down what you won't take and then, everytime a child comes through, they write up a background biographical sketch of the child and then, they hand it out to all the caseworkers and then, they go through all the cards and sorta read out and come up with their—each caseworker, with their best two or three matches and then, they present them and then, the board takes the two or three people from all the different caseworkers and like, start off with fifteen or twenty

couples that have the potential and then, they try to find the best match possible from that and then, if it comes down to a tie, so to speak, then I think the waiting period then comes into it as a factor, rather than you're the next one on the list, you're going to get the next child that comes in here.

Although caseworkers did the matching, the idea of matching itself allowed couples to feel more in control because it permitted them to reason that their selection criteria for a child could hasten or delay the end. Moreover, it made the adoption process seem less random and allowed couples to feel less directly "in competition" with other adopting couples for the same child, since no two couples could theoretically be the best match for any one child. For example, couples who wanted a girl did not see themselves as competing with couples who wanted a boy. One couple believed that they would probably not get their child until the end of their anytime-now period because they had stated more stringent criteria for the child they wanted than the other couples they knew who had entered the waiting pool at the same time they did.

Couples who expressed their willingness to wait for the "right" child, as opposed to "any" child or a "hurry-up" child, perceived themselves as potentially prolonging the waiting period. In contrast, other couples saw themselves as potentially shortening the waiting period by specifying few criteria for the child they wanted—by not being "too choosy."

Yet, knowing that there were a large number of couples waiting for a much smaller number of available babies, couples always suspected the credibility of the matching criterion. One woman believed in matching, but "logically" she knew there had to be some kind of ordering system that operated on the basis of time-in-waiting. One man wondered how one-to-one matching could occur when, as he surmised from information his caseworker had given him, there were two hundred couples waiting with his agency alone and thirty couples were referred for each available child. If a child was a "good match" for thirty couples, how could it be a good match for one couple?

Couples waiting to adopt locally cast birthmothers as ultimately the most important players in determining when and if they got a child. Some couples speculated that those agencies offering birthmothers the "best deal" were in a better position to accommodate the couples on their waiting lists. They worried that the brightest birthmothers were seeking more advantageous private arrangements in lieu of agency placements. Couples also worried about how they appeared, in their written autobiographies, to birthmothers who were permitted a role in choosing a couple to parent their child.

Couples adopting internationally perceived government officials and politics as playing key roles in the availability of children. One couple concluded that their wait would be prolonged despite their being "at the top of the list" because fewer babies were being released from their country of choice. One man imagined:

> Some horrible political thing going on and we won't be able to do anything down there either. And so a lot has to do with what the country thinks of the United States politically. Just in general, if they even want to cooperate.

Couples drew from a diverse and ever-changing information base to estimate the duration of the waiting period. But, they had difficulty determining "what's true." Couples revised their estimates the longer they waited and in response to new information; they agonized over what element or multiplication of differently weighted elements really prevailed at any moment in determining when a placement would occur. They found themselves "grubbing for [any] information" and even "making it up" to fill what they perceived to be a temporal void. As one woman observed:

> I found that I'll just try and latch onto any word [caseworkers] say and try to pick up any little subtle nuance and twist it however I can so it will be the best for us. But you can't. I mean there isn't anything to grasp onto really about it.

Couples tried to read between the lines and into the words of caseworkers, hoping they were right in taking what the caseworkers said "at face value" and that the caseworkers were not doing a "cover-up job." One woman highlighted the perils of trying to determine when a baby would arrive. She explained, "There are people who have decided where they are in the list, and by approval date, but what they don't know . . . are people . . . on the list . . . ahead or behind them." In the end, couples understood that when the end would actually come was anybody's guess.

WAITING TO LIVE

In addition to establishing a temporal order, childwaiting couples struggled to "survive" the waiting period. They sought to live while waiting and to avoid living only to wait for a child. One woman distinguished between these two states of existence when she observed, "We've just been sitting around, it feels like, for the most of this year—just waiting. And when [the social worker] said a year from now, that's it, I'm not waiting anymore. You've got to get on with your life." Similarly, a man explained:

> You still have a life that you have to live. . . . You can't make [waiting] your sole focal point . . . You'll drive yourself crazy. They said right up front that it's a long process and that most of it is doing nothing. It's just waiting and it's just time.

His wife added:

> It's like a holding pattern. It's like you're circling around the airport and you can't land yet. But you can't do anything else because you're stuck on the airplane. You're just sitting in the airplane, just circling around. I just have this feeling that when the child gets here, it'll be ok. I can finish the rest of my life.

Waiting couples had difficulty getting on with life when every life plan had a "footnote," namely, anticipation of a baby. For example, two men would not make career changes they desired because they would have to move from the geographical area handled by their agencies. One woman observed:

> I do everything in contingency plans. . . . I'm getting tired of that sort of thing. It just sort of gets to you because everything is still—we're making arrangements in such a way that I can either get out of it or make other arrangements, if we have the baby.

Living by contingency of adoption reprised for couples the life they had already lived as infertile couples trying to conceive—a life built around the possibility of a child.

Yet, some couples found advantages in the waiting period. One couple decided early in their waiting period that it was not a bad time for them. They said, "This is the time before the baby gets here that we have to spend together doing what we want to do." But they also described how hard it was not to make a life out of waiting for a child. As the wife remarked:

> Because we know other couples that are waiting, we try real hard not to do anything that causes a lot of extra stress. And that causes a lot of

extra stress. For them to think, "Oh, I want a baby by Chr"—that's like saying I want a baby by Christmas and, well, then if you don't have a baby by Christmas, then Christmas is depressing.

Her husband observed:

> I don't understand why . . . the people make it something that is so in the forefront of their consciousness because it's so stressful, and you really have so little control over the adoption process—so little—that why make that your constant thought? Because the fact that you have no control over it, the fact that it takes so long, the fact that it costs so much money, all of that combined. Man, you would spend your entire waiting period just completely stressed out.

Conveying how hard it was to temper waiting in mind and deed, the wife concluded:

> You're always thinking about it. . . . And that's what makes it so hard. It could be two or three years that you have to think about the baby is coming at some point in time. . . . People that get pregnant have nine months and then the baby is coming.

"Forced to wait" for an uncertain end, couples sought to make waiting not seem long and to protect themselves from the agonizingly familiar pitfall of "burning out" just waiting for a child. For example, two women worked overtime at their jobs to help pass the time. Six months into her anticipated two year wait, one woman explained:

> I get a lot of parallel activities that also come up in time frames. Like going through a graduate program time frame—three years, one semester, get that moving along simultaneously. I stay extremely busy at maximum level either reading or activities with the church, or activities involving education, and in that way, I pass the time off so fully that, yeah, it goes real fast. But it goes real slow at the same time. But it's not like I just voided everything out and I'm lingering in some sort of animated suspension until this thing comes to pass.

In contrast, two women made the mistake of leaving their jobs much too early in the waiting period and suffered empty time. Emphasizing increments of time rather than timed activities, another woman decided to wait in nine-month segments and speculated that after a year, she would start waiting in daily segments. Similarly, one woman recalled:

> I had things divided into months. Like, I decided that if nothing, if nothing happened by May, then I would be into the summer, and the summer I have a whole new ball game of athletic activities. . . . I had these little three-month intervals set up whereby I would be finished. Go to there and then stop. And then I had it from June to August, and then if nothing happened, then it would be August to Christmas. . . . I kind of blocked my activities.

Couples attempted with more or less success to pace their activities, especially those involving material preparations for a baby, and to script their thinking in the hopes that by the time anytime-now was over, their wait would be over. One couple had drawn a United Way–like indicator, charting the money saved to accomplish all the steps of international adoption. The wife commented, "It's funny. We said, ok, now this money brings us up to X on our trip [to get the child]. And then we finish the trip up, we say, well this money is—you know. It's the only way we've got anything concrete." Her husband added, "We are having to look at it like we're at this point along. It's a little game, but it helps. It's helping us keep things in perspective. . . . [We're] at the Bangkok airport now."

Pacing the wait involved for couples having "goals to string out to have something to do while waiting," goals related to careers, vacations, and home and self-improvements. Most important, couples pacing the wait had to schedule making purchases for a baby that would correspond well to their waiting timelines. For childwaiting couples, the empty nursery—the "shrine" to a baby with no baby in it—was the iconic representation of a poorly plotted wait. One man noted:

> One month, we'll buy one thing and just start building up and we'd set it up into a twelve-month cycle [equal to the longest projected waiting period]. We would kind of fill the room in twelve months thinking that the baby will go in twelve months. . . . Now [in past-time] we almost have to paint the walls again because it's just been kind of sitting there.

Another man, almost two years in waiting to adopt his second child, described how he and his wife deliberately delayed setting up the nursery to curb the impatience engendered by waiting.

I think if we would start working on the nursery, we would get more impatient than probably what we are. . . . You could look in there and you would say when? And I think that's one of the reasons, I think in the back of both our minds, that we really haven't started it yet because you can see it.

One woman had witnessed the psychological consequences of the empty nursery—of poor temporal articulation (Glaser and Strauss, 1971). She explained, "We have friends that have their nursery done and have had it done for a year and it's a constant source, a reminder to them that they don't have a child. . . . To me, that's just making agony for myself."

Couples thus sought to make good use of the time they had to "put in" waiting for a child, but they also struggled to create a comfortable rhythm for waiting. They attempted to "put the brakes on" and to regulate the impulse to behave like other couples who knew that they had a baby and when that baby was due. One couple, who had allowed themselves the joy of setting up a crib for their baby, nevertheless felt as if it had been "beamed down from outer space . . . like an alien living in [the] bedroom." The idea that a baby would be in it seemed "unreal," even "a joke." As the wife explained:

We are going through the motions of preparing. We bought this crib, we put the crib together, I've got some baby things upstairs. But I get deep joy out of messing with, touching—but then, I put them away because to me, that's not real world right now.

The encounters of couples with infertility—its losses and failed expectations—had made them wary of investing too much more of their psychic resources in the expectation of a child. One woman admitted to having "indulged in only one minor fit" of buying early in her waiting period and to "taking out of hiding in assorted intervals" the purchases she had made. One couple had "allowed" themselves the pleasure of buying a stuffed animal for their baby, even though they knew it could be a long time before they got her. One couple cited as a "good excuse" for buying things for their baby the fact that they were already in the infant department buying gifts for a friend's baby shower. In the waiting game of adoption, creating a comfortable rhythm gave couples something to do and stretched out their wait but did not prolong it; it helped couples regulate their activities, permitted them to recapitalize their waning personal resources, and enabled them to "think positively."

As time passed and moments occurred when not having a child became unbearable, the ability of couples to block out the reality that they
were "still waiting" for a child by mapping out time and activities in the
waiting period diminished. Couples recognized the Janus-faced character
of devices that allowed them to "set up goals to shoot for" at the same time
that they set themselves up for disappointment. In a manner evoking the
narrator in Dorothy Parker's short story "A Telephone Call," one woman
articulated the agony of reaching a point in her life where waiting for "the
call" had become the plot. As she observed:

> It's terrible to think that if you don't get a call today, how it just ruins
> your whole day and you cry. At four o'clock—I know [the caseworker]
> leaves at four and she doesn't work on Fridays and so Mondays to
> Fridays from eight to four you think, "She's going to call." And at four
> o'clock, you just kind of—she didn't call today. I told [my husband]
> Monday at lunch that I knew she was going to call. I just feel her and I
> know she's going to call. She didn't call at four. He said, "Well, the
> day's not over" and I said, "But she's gone home now."

Earlier she had recalled all of the time goals she had set and failed to meet.
She explained:

> You think on all the special occasions, "Wouldn't it be nice to have a
> baby for Thanksgiving?" I don't know if I can go through another
> Christmas without a baby. Then, March is my birthday and you think,
> "If I don't have a baby by March, I will be devastated. I'll be a year
> older. Will I be too old to be a mother?" Every special occasion, you
> think, "Well, we should already have a baby by now. I hope we have
> one by Christmas". . . . But I'm not really truly expecting one by then.

Having already suffered twelve pregnancy losses and one failed adoption,
she had even made a special occasion of the day on which, in three separate
years, she had lost pregnancies; she wanted a baby who had been born then
to "take the jinx off that day." Yet even while she was wishing for such a
child, she was calculating that the time had already passed for her to get a
baby with that birthdate this year.

The relatively peaceful interlude couples experienced toward the beginning of the waiting period ended as they approached past-time and was
rather short-lived for those women whose continued childlessness was
especially painful. These were the women whose lives and identities infer-

tility had "overtaken." One woman, who still grieved over her failure to get pregnant, reached the limit of her patience waiting for a child less than one year after approval. Nine months after approval, she began to feel that she would never get a baby. As she noted:

> I used to think if I could only be approved, I'd be happy. Well, I'm not happy. I was pretty happy for awhile and reasonably content with that, but now I think we'll be in this stage for a real long time. I guess I don't envision us getting that baby for a real long time. I don't know what a real long time is.

As their time in waiting progressed, women feeling especially deprived by their infertility and long-waiting couples became more and more despairing. They felt themselves either to be standing still again or as even sliding backward toward the ambivalence, isolation, and "always wanting" that had been such an integral component of their lives as infertile people, and from which they thought they had escaped. Couples started "running scenarios" on why they were still childless; in their descriptions, they were the protagonists who were yet again being thwarted from reaching their goal. Alternatively despondent and angry, couples questioned the credibility of their agency, the assumptions on which they had based their decision to adopt, their own fitness to be parents, and even the likelihood that they would ever have a child of their own to love. One man wondered whether he and his wife had been forgotten by their out-of-country agency. As he remarked:

> It's getting to the point where I'm beginning to wonder about this whole process. . . . Is it going to work and do these people even know that we're alive? Is our agency there? I'm sure there is, but we just haven't had any reassurance from anybody except the people that we talk to that say that this is the way that they work . . . I don't think that anyone that knows that you're adopting would intentionally hold on to something like this and say, "Ha, ha, I'm going to make them suffer." So I really think that if it wasn't going to work, and they know who we are, they would let us know that. So that's what I keep saying all along is that they wouldn't do that. So that's why I think that, yes, it's still going on. But it would also be nice to know that, yes, it is going on. It's a real Catch-22 right now. You're damned if you do and you're damned if you don't. You just sort of sit here and another day has gone by.

One woman, waiting to adopt for one-and-a-half years, began to question whether her becoming a parent was meant to be.

> Is this really what we're supposed to be doing with our lives? I mean, if it is really what we're supposed to be doing in our lives, then it should be going together easier than what it is. . . . If it just all came together in one nice lump sum, then you wouldn't have all these agonizing moments.

This woman found herself increasingly having to "push" herself to stay invested in her daily life. Until she fulfilled her need for a child, everything else was "just being done because it needs to be done." Comparing her situation to treading water near a whirlpool, she observed:

> The constant keeping our lives going, keeping meaning in our lives, not getting sucked into the negativism and the depression stuff. . . . I get tired physically and mentally about it the same way I would with being in water for a long time and not going anywhere.

The woman who had already suffered multiple pregnancy losses and an adoption failure expressed renewed feelings of failure when she remarked:

> It hurts to wait and think that something is wrong with you. When you knew something was wrong, physically wrong, with you before and that is why you didn't have a child. And you wonder, well, maybe God doesn't think I'm fit for a baby and He's just not going to give me one.

Attending a baby shower for the fifteen-year-old friend of her stepdaughter, she cried for the baby who should, she said, have been hers rather than a fifteen-year-old girl's and thought:

> What did I do wrong? What am I being punished for? . . . It's just like you keep losing. It's like you keep having miscarriages, because Christmas goes by and you don't have a baby. And people ask you and you said, "Well, we're still waiting," and they say, "Gosh, you've been waiting a long time." Every day somebody asks you. . . . [Every day you are] suffering the same loss.

Another woman remarked that she was

shying away from hanging around with anybody who is going to get pregnant within the next couple of months or is pregnant or has just been pregnant or has a baby or infant. It's just difficult. . . . If mother nature is going to make it so that you can't have children, she should at least cut off the emotion that makes you want to have children too. So that you don't have the urge.

After sixteen months in waiting, another woman also wished she could "purge" the need for a child from her brain, as one could, she said, "maybe on *Star Trek*." Questioning her fitness to be a mother, she explained that infertility had already destroyed, in her words, "the hope part" of her brain.

Knowing they had the "power" to end the waiting period, but feeling unable to use that power to end it without a child, long-waiting couples experienced again the deprivations of infertility and/or were forced to consider again alternatives with equally uncertain outcomes, such as whether to continue waiting with their agency or to start all over with a different agency, whether to begin medical therapy again, or whether just to abandon their quest for a child altogether. Thinking they had achieved some closure in their quest for a child by deciding to adopt at all, these couples found themselves reopening "boxes" they had assumed were closed forever. Waiting one year, one woman said, "things are coming up now that I don't think would have ever occurred to me to think about a year ago." She and her husband considered expanding their specifications for a child in the hopes of getting one sooner and returned for further medical testing. They also considered private adoption, an option they had previously dismissed as too emotionally and financially risky.

One woman recalled asking her husband whether they should "jump off the boat and get into another boat." Were they "chasing after something that is nebulous at this point?" Seventeen months in waiting, they looked at each other and said: "We don't think it's going to happen." After almost two and one-half years in waiting for a South American child, they decided to stop waiting to adopt and instead to foster children in their home. The wife explained:

> It's just something that I guess is closing a chapter that is not easy to close. I said to [my husband] the other day, I said, "I think I want to go back and do more infertility stuff." And he just said, "No, I don't think that we do."

He recalled how difficult that had been for both of them. She continued:

I think that being finished with adoption is easier again. [Doing infertility] is just such an unfinished chapter for me. And I don't know that it's ever going to be finished. . . . It's a hurt that there is no answer for. . . . When someone dies, you can't bring them back and you go on and you make the best of it and you make some other choices and that's pretty much how I feel where I'm at. It's a resignation and it certainly isn't with a lot of joy. But it's just the way that it needs to be for us for now. Foster care has been helpful for us. . . . [It] feels real good and that feels real positive. . . . I think it's a pretty remarkable choice that we've been able to make and I don't think that a lot of other people get to that point.

Although they still harbored hopes of adopting a child they fostered, they decided to quit the active pursuit of adopting. In fact, for this woman having a child of her own now seemed riskier than fostering children: what if, after all the efforts to have it, it got hit by a car? Her husband added that he had never been interested in "owning" anything. In the end, after ten years of trying and failing to get pregnant and after being on a list (for almost three years) waiting for "nothing to happen," this couple felt that their well-being and marriage were threatened. Six months later, though, they decided to pursue adoption again, but with a local agency.

Reaching an extremity of waiting, several women found themselves "beyond waiting," "in the ozone layer," and "lacking feeling"; they did not care whether a placement occurred and did not feel "terribly sad." These women articulated feelings of paralysis, a state of anesthesia that served only temporarily to block out the pain of waiting. One woman felt "numb" at a point in waiting when she "didn't think she'd be able to stand it another week." When her caseworker told her there were no babies then available to her agency, another woman recalled:

Something in my brain just kind of clicked over and now I'm sort of going off. I guess I look at it almost like a bell curve. And now I'm going down the other side. And it's not that I don't care about the baby. But I—maybe it comes in cycles and right now, I'm sort of—I don't think about it when the phone rings anymore. I've just sort of pushed it back into this indefinite someday and if and when we get this baby.

After twenty-one months in waiting, another woman said, "Either I want it to happen or I want it not to happen and not have the probability for it happening. I want it to be one or the other because I get tired of being always waiting." One month later, in a diary entry, she reassured herself that "it will happen." Acknowledging a fate more powerful than herself, she wrote, "This event is so big. I don't want to control it. When it happens, it happens. And that's the way it is."

The Unmoved Mover

The ticking biological clock is an image widely associated with infertility. Infertile people often suffer a kind of time sickness prevalent in American culture (Dossey, 1982), namely, an anxiety about time running out and time wasted in the pursuit of parenthood. Time is an antagonist to the accomplishment of the goals of infertile couples and an enemy to be vanquished. The adopting couples' descriptions of their experiences indicate that time continued to be problematic in the preadoption waiting period as it was for all infertile couples who worked against time to become parents. Time was the "unmoved mover" (Schechner, 1967, p. 186).

As they described it, the preadoption waiting period was an "irrational manifestation of the temporal organization of social life" (Zerubavel, 1981, p. xvi): a temporally unmarked stage in the passage to parenthood (Glaser and Strauss, 1971). For adopting couples, waiting was less a matter of time management (Calkins, 1970) than a state of dependency in a situation of scarcity and deficit (Schwartz, 1974). Struggling to free themselves of the burden of waiting, adopting couples lived in the state of "indeterminacy in which hope is not an emotion or state of mind but an absence of proof that one ought to despair" (Gilman, 1967, p. 72).

In describing the imaginative devices they used to create temporal order, couples affirmed the importance of time as a stabilizing dimension of the social world and of personal consciousness and the importance of "closure" in achieving psychological equilibrium. Albert (1984, p. 159) observed that it is the "sense of harmonious completion . . . that allows the pursuit of new challenges and activities." Yet, as he further remarked, merely reaching an end does not necessarily promise harmonious closure. By virtue of their infertility alone, couples understood the psychological value of setting time limits on their quest for a child, but they also worried about ending the quest too soon. Long-waiting couples had the power to end their waiting, but they felt incapable of doing it without a child; what if "the call" came tomorrow?

The experiences of adopting couples also reveal the taken-for-granted role that pregnancy plays in providing childbearing couples with a temporal framework for living and reducing the ambiguity associated with liminal stages in rites of passage (Van Gennep, 1909/1960). Although pregnancy is commonly construed as a time of quiet and uneventful waiting, it is a "temporality of movement, growth, and change" in which the "woman experiences herself as a source and participant in a creative process" (Young, 1984, p. 54). Pregnancy is a transformative kind of waiting that is wholly different from the means-ends kind of waiting characteristic of the world of the machine and of the preadoption period (Bergum, 1989). By not having a pregnancy, childwaiting women were deprived of the "participation mystique" of being with child (Bergum, 1989, p. 54) that makes pregnancy more than just passive waiting, and couples were deprived of being in time. Understanding this deficit and the need couples have to try to resolve it is especially important as an increasing number of couples wanting to adopt are likely to be facing longer waiting periods for a child. Of the thirty couples getting placements in the course of the Transition to Parenthood study, six couples got their child one to five months after approval; eight couples, seven to eleven months afterward; four couples, thirteen to nineteen months afterward; five couples, twenty to twenty-two months afterward; six couples, twenty-five to twenty-eight months after approval; and one couple, three and one-half years after initial approval. In addition, one couple waiting over four years for a second child had still not obtained a placement by the time this book was completed, and they terminated the adoption process.[2] The anguish of waiting and the value of time as a finite resource may, in part, explain the willingness of couples to try risky but perhaps less time-consuming options to parenthood, such as in vitro fertilization and surrogacy arrangements. What is rejected in adoption may not be adoption itself, but rather adoption waiting.

In a collection of essays on fiction, Frank Kermode (1967) suggested that by creating the fiction of "tick . . . tock," we make a clock speak our language. In order to maintain a sense of organization between tick and tock, we need many fictional devices to fill the interval. Childwaiting couples were like the fiction maker, creating and configuring the preadoption waiting period: converting *chronos* (passing time) into *kairos* (meaningful time) (Kermode, 1967, p. 50). Like other "heroes of stories," childwaiting couples "reckon[ed] with time" (Polkinghorne, 1988, p. 132), an old nemesis of the infertile on the "road of trials" (Campbell, 1986) to parenthood.

Notes

1. Although this belief suggests that in adoption, like other situations of waiting, the least-privileged are compelled to do the most waiting (Schwartz, 1974), the opposite is also true. Lower income and black couples, for example, can often get infants more quickly because of the readier availability of black infants.

2. Of the remaining five couples, one couple terminated the process after achieving pregnancy, three couples terminated the process after moving out of state, and one couple withdrew from the study in the waiting period.

11. Bone of My Bones, Flesh of My Flesh

> This at last is bone of my bones and flesh of my flesh. (Gen. II: 23)

While the temporal irregularities of the preadoption waiting period challenged adopting couples to create their own temporal order, the disembodied nature of childwaiting challenged them to negotiate a precarious situation where the culturally important "principle of biological filiation is violated" (Hoffmann-Reim, 1986, p. 167). Toward this end, adopting women worked to reconcile expectant motherhood with being without-child, and adopting couples struggled to create a flesh-and-blood presence for whom to wait, but to undermine the flesh-and-blood tie as the criterion for true parenthood.

Expecting Without Child

The disembodied nature of childwaiting had special significance for women who expected a child but who were not pregnant. One of the infertile and childbearing women I interviewed clarified an essential difference between childbearing and childwaiting when she observed:

> When you're pregnant, you have nine months to think about it and everything you do and every moment of the day on a daily basis is linked with . . . the health of this child and the well-being of this child. [With adoption] what I eat doesn't matter, where I go doesn't matter, and if I'm in a smoke-filled room, it doesn't matter. If I drink a coke with caffeine and sugar, it doesn't matter. And so you're thinking is not quite the same.

Although childwaiting women were freer to indulge in any habit they wanted without fear of hurting a child, they were not free "to matter" to a child in a way that could affirm the imminence and responsibility of motherhood. One childwaiting woman described how waiting for but not carrying a child caused her to feel more like an expectant father than an expectant mother: in her words, she was "reduced" to the same status as the father. Childwaiting implied a diminution of the female role while the male role remained, for all intents and purposes, the same in adoptive and biological fatherhood. As this woman explained:

> The father, of course, obviously is actively involved in the process of making the baby but at that point, he's just support. The mother raises the child in her womb and nurtures it and all that kind of stuff and feels it growing. Obviously, I'm in the same state as the father. . . . We're both fathers . . . I don't have the intimacy of being pregnant, so I don't think I really feel like an expect—like a mother would feel.

For this woman, expectant motherhood involved something much more than the disembodied waiting of fathers; it involved the intimacy of working to sustain and nurture a child within one's body—of mattering in a tangible way (Bergum, 1989). One waiting father, whose own fertility impairment precluded conception, explained that for him, not being able to conceive a child with his wife was a "psychological [and] sociological loss," but that for his wife it was a "biological" one. He remarked:

> I really can't imagine that it would be a great deal of difference from my perspective to be handed my own child or an adopted child. It's still going to be something that wasn't there, you know, fifteen minutes ago and now it is.

Similarly, another adopting man observed that whether a baby was adopted or biologically related, it was still someone he got to know only after it was "already born." In contrast, women's personal knowledge of their children typically began in pregnancy.

A child is thus biologically present for a woman from the moment of conception and experientially present for her when she becomes aware of its presence: when the fetus makes itself known to her. For a man, biological fatherhood is a "discontinuous experience," the inseminator role separated in time from the nurturer role. For both adopting men and women, and for fertile and infertile men with pregnant wives, waiting to parent a child was more remote than waiting to mother. The mothering role begins at conception, but the invisibility of men's biological link to a child serves to make expectant fatherhood feel the same to men with no such link.

Because paternity is an "abstract idea" and maternity is an "experience" providing women with "reproductive continuity" in gestating, birthing, and nursing/nurturing a child (Corea, 1985; O'Brien, 1981), the adopting men and the men whose wives conceived by donor insemination found it easier to think of themselves as being like any other expectant father. When adopting men felt like other expectant fathers, it was because they were doing everything with their wives that childbearing couples did except attending Lamaze classes, or experiencing everything that men with pregnant wives did except listening to the fetal heart and feeling the fetus kick. In contrast, when women did not feel like expectant mothers, it was because they had no morning sickness or other embodied manifestations of expectancy. The deprivation of being without-child was distinctively a woman's loss.

Expecting the Somewhere-Out-There Child

Because of the ambiguity of the expectant parent label in the situation of childwaiting and because of the discomfort some of them felt using it, adopting couples often referred to themselves instead as "prospective" parents, "approaching parenthood," "waiting to adopt," "in the process of adoption," "adopting," or "on stand-by." Some women were "expecting a child," rather than "expectant mothers." One woman recalled initially saying that she was "acquiring a child" and later, that she and her husband were going through the adoption process, which she compared to applying for citizenship. After this process, they were "accepted for parenthood." The linguistic choices of couples emphasized the waiting component of expectant parenthood; their language also evoked the scrutiny they had to undergo in getting approval to parent and the tentativeness of expectant parenthood without the legitimacy and security that comes from a fetal presence.

The fetal presence not only helped childbearing couples feel expectant; it also provided them with a tangible object of expectation. The childbearing couples knew of the existence and physical location of a particular child; they *had* it, they knew approximately when their child would arrive, and they knew that it would be newly born. They also knew that the history of their child's existence began with their pregnancy and that their baby would fall within a limited range of height and weight.

In contrast, the childwaiting couples knew only that their child would not be newly born when they got it, because it would not be available for adoption until a legally formalized waiting period had passed. (No adopting couple got a baby younger than four weeks old.) For couples adopting a foreign child, a baby could be what one woman described as an "arm baby" or already "running around." While one agency defined a baby as a child less than one year old, another defined it as any child up to four years old. A couple might begin the adoption process both wanting and waiting for a baby, but because of bureaucratic delays they might not get that child until it had passed infancy.

Moreover, the development of a pregnant woman's conceptions of the fetus appears to be a sequential process, with certain biological and technological events in pregnancy stimulating an increasingly differentiated and animated view of the fetus as a baby (Gloger-Tippelt 1988; Lumley 1980). Such events as quickening and seeing and hearing a beating heart during ultrasound examinations served to transform an abstract pregnancy and generic fetus into "my" baby. The childbearing couples had available to them several sources of information from which to formulate conceptions of their expected child, including ultrasound pictures of their own baby, photographs and artistic renderings of fetal development, photographs of themselves and other relatives as babies, the felt reality of fetal activity, family lore about themselves as babies, and folklore about fetal development. From these sources, couples could both image (conceive from a material, sensate reality) and imagine (conceive from a created reality) "our" child.

In contrast, adopting couples turned to other sources of knowledge to construct their child, including (*a*) their fantasies of the circumstances of their child's birth and its birthparents; (*b*) photographs and written histories of the child assigned to them; and (*c*) the criteria they had specified for the child they wanted.

THE MIND'S EYE
Adopting couples often had conceptions of what their child's birthparents might be like, which included scenarios of the circumstances in which they had conceived and carried a child and then were forced to relinquish it. One woman described the "bizarre" situation of "waiting for this sort of passionate event . . . for some couple to lose control [and] . . . to go over the

edge sexually." Her husband agreed that it was strange having to pin his hopes on the fact that "another couple is going to do something foolish."

The fantasies of these couples included culturally familiar scenes: the passionate affair, the one-night stand, the couple who had an ill-fated college romance, the lone young pregnant girl struggling against a society that stigmatized her. Women and men wondered, for example, whether their babies had already been conceived or whether the pregnant woman they had passed in a mall might be carrying their child. These romances concerning their child's origins were the means by which waiting couples could begin to create a biography of that child (Rosenberg and Horner, 1991).

THE PHOTOGRAPHIC EYE

Couples adopting domestic infants typically got their child one to two days after "the call" came informing them that it had been chosen for them. In contrast, couples adopting internationally typically received a photograph and brief history of the child selected for them several months before the child was placed with them. These artifacts provided couples with a new, material reality; like couples learning of a pregnancy, they now knew of the existence of a specific child "earmarked" for them.

Yet, because of the many pregnancy and adoption failures and losses they had already experienced, childwaiting couples understood that such a child might still not become theirs. As one woman described it, "you have [a child], but you don't have it." Moreover, like the ultrasound image of the fetus that captured it in a moment in time, the photograph of an assigned child at a certain stage of development was not likely to represent the child they would eventually get. One woman had to keep reminding herself that her baby was going to look different when they got him, "like himself but different." Like ultrasound pictures that couples found hard to interpret without assistance, these photographic images offered equivocal information at best. One woman described the "dot matrix picture" of her child that her agency had faxed to her: "one hundred black dots for a mouth and eighty-five dots for eyes." Another woman surmised that her child would be darker than the child imaged in the overexposed picture she had received. A man observed:

> You wouldn't believe how we've looked at these pictures to try to extract some information. . . . You can only extract so much information from a picture. The whole notion of a picture is worth a thousand

words is wrong. It's worth maybe a hundred words. . . . Face-to-face
contact is worth a thousand words. . . . A picture is . . . one dimen-
sional.

Despite the drawbacks of visual images, whether in photographs or
ultrasound pictures, both childbearing and adopting couples found them
to be key sources of information about the health and character of their
child, and of reassurance that they would have a child. Moreover, any visual
image that animated the child (showing it playing as opposed to posing, or
a video as opposed to a still shot) was especially prized. As one man
explained, these photos were unlike any other photos he had ever seen. He
did not look at the picture of his child with the "same feeling or concept or
eyes" as when he looked at other photos.

Like their childbearing counterparts with an ultrasound image of their
baby, adopting couples animated the photographic image they received,
seeking to interpret it and to claim the child imaged there as "our" child.
One pregnant woman, commenting on the ultrasound picture of the twins
she had conceived with fertility drugs and husband insemination, saw the
"family ears." Similarly, a man waiting to adopt an Asian child looked to
find a family resemblance, all the while knowing there could be none. Yet,
he felt that the baby looked like his uncle and had the family mouth. His
wife felt that the baby had her husband's "wiggly toes." She also heard the
baby say from the photo, "Pick me up." The man admitted to reading a lot
into the photo, deriving pleasure in this activity and finding gentleness,
delicacy, and finesse in the spread of his baby's fingers, the inquisitiveness in
his face, and the brightness in his eyes. After spending so much time with
the photo, he wondered what the "real" baby would be like. For these
couples, written histories and especially the photos were their only link
with a physical presence.

SELECTION CRITERIA
As part of the typical approval process for an agency adoption, couples were
asked to identify the criteria for the child they desired. Couples itemized
(often with the help of lists provided by caseworkers) the characteristics of
the child they wanted, including such factors as age, sex, health status,
background of birthparents, and circumstances of conception. Caseworkers then attempted to use these criteria to "match" a child with a couple.
Couples adopting foreign children had less opportunities to specify criteria,
but they too could ask for a child of a certain sex and within an age range

and health status. Choosing the country from which they would adopt also served to limit the possibilities of how their child would look.

Specifying these criteria permitted couples to "simulate an act of choice" (Hoffmann-Reim, 1990, p. 50) that provided them with the parameters within which they could imagine the child they would parent. Like childbearing couples who learned of the sex of the fetus, adopting couples knew what the sex of their child would be if they had requested either a boy or a girl. Like childbearing couples who were reassured from amniocentesis results that the fetus did not have certain genetic problems, adopting couples were reassured about certain features of the health of their child if they had specified the health conditions they would not accept. In fact, one woman perceived adoption as more certain than childbearing because with adoption, she did not have to fear for the health of her baby. Her baby would have been "through the medical ringer" before being offered to her. In addition, like childbearing couples who learned of a fetal impairment from amniocentesis, adopting couples had the option not to parent a particular child.

THE INTERPRETATIVE EYE

Couples also relied on other sources to imagine their babies. For example, one woman, waiting to adopt an Asian child, drew from a photograph of another couple's assigned baby a picture in her mind "of this little black-eyed, black-haired baby." The photo had offered her a more "concrete" source from which to fashion a baby; previously, she had thought of babies only "generically." Her husband drew his mental picture from a couple he had seen at a party who were from the country from which they were awaiting a child. He recalled saying to his wife that, in twenty-five years, their son or daughter would look like them. Another woman, who had experienced a "rush of all this imagery" early in the waiting period, saw the baby she wanted in a sketch of a dark and curly-haired child that she then bought for her baby's room. That picture and previous sensory experiences with infants allowed her to see, feel, and think about her baby girl. Yet another man imaged "little set pieces" at the beach where he was used to playing with children.

There was great variety in the imaging work of couples. Some individuals described themselves as having either very rich or rather underdeveloped imaginations. The intensity of their imaging work waxed and waned without any clear pattern over the waiting period. What is clear is that because of the uncertainties of adoption and the previous experiences of these couples with failure and loss, waiting couples, "right to the edge," did not really know if they would ever get a child. Accordingly, they sought to limit the emotional investment in a child that such imaging work implied. Like previously bereaved childbearing couples who try to suspend their commitment to a baby in the event of its loss (Phipps 1985/1986), childwaiting couples also experienced their impending parenthood as somewhat provisional. Childwaiting couples were reluctant even to think of themselves as "expectant" parents, not only because they had no physical relationship with a child and no due date, but also because to be expectant meant having hopes for a child that could still be dashed. *When* was always tinged with *if* and *maybe-never*. One man had learned from the previous disappointments of infertility to put a "governor" on his expectations. One woman, after waiting for what to her was a "nine-year pregnancy," was "excited" by the prospect of finally getting a child, but "not committed to the expectation yet," while another woman said that with adoption, "you don't let your excitement go full tilt." One woman described her situation as similar to having "first and second trimester bleeding" where there was a "great potential for loss." Another waiting woman who had suffered multiple pregnancy losses and two previous adoption failures admitted, "I put a shield up over the heart. . . . Just in case something goes wrong. . . . And I wait . . . for something to happen." Although their imaging work helped couples fashion a child for claiming, it was an activity in the service of concreting their situation that couples only cautiously permitted themselves. After all, in the end, they knew that what kind of child they got and whether they got one at all were really not in their control.

Staking a Claim

Adopting couples lacked the fetal presence to begin the work of parental claiming that has long been considered characteristic of and even vital to the establishment by childbearing couples of a loving relationship with their child (Rubin 1984). Although parental claiming in couples biologically related to their child has been described as occurring in the postdelivery period when an infant's characteristics are linked to those of other members of its family (Rubin, 1984), I use the term here to refer to the special kind of emotional and intellectual work that adopting couples did prior to and after placement to make someone else's child, "somewhere out there," their own child. Such claiming work is particularly important to individuals who aspire to social statuses to which they know they are not clearly entitled. Drawing from Schneider's work on American kinship, Miall (1987, p. 34) suggested that infertile and adopting couples have difficulty feeling entitled to their children because of the cultural "primacy of the blood tie."

Adopting couples waited for a child who belonged by nature, by blood, and by law (Schneider, 1980) to its birthparents, and who could become their baby only if its birthparents chose to relinquish it. Although adopting couples sometimes comforted themselves with the idea that no child was really "owned" by or "belonged" exclusively to anyone, they were, nevertheless, aware that they lived in a culture characterized by an exclusionary and proprietary model of parenthood in which parental ownership and child belongingness are based on the flesh and blood tie and on notions of property (Schneider, 1980; Smith, 1983). Unlike childbearing couples whose claim to a child is assumed by virtue of biology alone, adopting couples waited for a child for whom there would always be competing parental claims. In fact, the respondent couples typically chose agency over private adoption as a safeguard against potential future claims by birthparents.

UNBLOODING THE TIE

As part of a continuing process that began when they first considered adoption, couples worked to assure themselves that they could love a child not of their flesh and blood. Husbands and wives were comforted by the fact that they loved each other, although they were not blood kin, and by the fact that they loved their animals, who were of completely different species. These nonblood relationships provided the experiential framework and the "metaphor" affirming that biological ties were neither valid as criteria to determine a couple's status as real parents, nor necessary to establish and maintain a loving relationship with another being. As one adoptive mother observed:

> One thing you're missing as a nonbiological parent is a sustaining metaphor where a biological parent has just eons of the metaphors in our culture. Natural and kin, natural born, bone of my bone, flesh of my flesh. So many of our folk sayings . . . have to do with nature . . . are metaphors for what birth does to connect you. But, what's the opposite of all this? Well, there's unnatural. There's nothing for you to come up with a metaphor that explains. . . . The sustaining metaphor I

came up with is marriage. That a bonding with an adopted child is like a marriage.

Looking with affection at her dog, another woman observed:

> We realize how attached we've grown to just this animal. Because you do—you think to yourself, this is a totally different being. This isn't from our loins. It isn't something like we're making and there's an instant bonding or attachment to that sort of thing. And come to find out that that's not always true. That you can give birth to a child and you may not recognize it or know it as your own or bond with it right off. . . . We thought, well, we're not going to have that attachment. How can we adjust to something like that? But then we realized six months after having this dog and knowing how much he meant to us, we figured, yeah, a baby would be just that much more.

Her husband added, "imagine how much a kid would be."

The evolving faith of adopting couples in the insignificance of blood ties as the basis for the parent-child relationship was confirmed when they observed how well other adopting couples and their children had "bonded" to each other and how poorly bonded biological parents and children frequently were. In addition, one woman pointed to the fact that few of the biologically related members of her family even looked like each other. These observations served to accentuate the rightness of the adoptive relationship and the vagaries of genetic inheritance, and to separate the parent-child relationship from its conventional biological moorings.

RIGHTING THE CLAIM

By undermining the primacy of the blood tie, adopting couples could begin the deliberative process of making a biologically unrelated child into the right child for them: one biologically and biographically matched to them and/or one who was meant to be that couple's child. Couples, especially those adopting domestic infants, described how caseworkers tried to find the "most ideal parents" for a child and to find "which baby is right for which couple." One woman, who had just conceived by in vitro fertilization when she was offered a baby to adopt, felt compelled to take that child because he had been chosen for her and her husband. She explained, "I feel like if there were over five hundred applicants for that baby, and if we were narrowed down and we were chosen as that couple—I just feel like it's got to have meant to be." Having been among the "finalists" who were not selected for other babies, she felt confirmed in her belief that the baby for whom she and her husband were chosen was intended to be theirs. Her husband had wanted to "pass on this baby" because they had achieved pregnancy, but she maintained that that baby was meant to be theirs. She added, "I cannot honestly see myself walking away from a baby with somebody saying this is your baby if you want it."

A baby was also construed as the right baby if couples could see the hand of God or fate acting to bring them together with a particular baby. One woman, who had already suffered two previous adoption failures, concluded that the Hispanic baby offered to her and her husband was meant for them because he was born on the same day as her father-in-law and one day before her own birthday. One man found several factors significant about the Asian baby assigned to him; the baby was born on a holiday that was special to him and conceived in the very month he and his wife had begun the adoption process. In addition, certain career opportunities had all fallen into place to coincide with the adoption of this child. Although he did not look for such coincidences, this man said he found that they were there. In addition to these "providential occurrences," the man recalled feeling, in a dream, like the child was his. His wife found it significant that their chosen baby's foster mother's husband was in the same line of work as her own father. Moreover, she surmised that the caseworker had probably chosen this child for her because, like her, he had stomach problems. At this point, even if a mistake had been made and he was not the healthy child they had requested, his photo and history—the artifacts of a choice made—made him the right baby: "my baby."

Actively construing a baby as the right baby (by virtue of human and/or cosmic intervention) seemed essential to the claims by adopting couples of a baby as "ours," given the lack of control they admitted having over which baby they would be offered. Couples wanted to believe that when they saw their child for the first time, there would "be that recognition that [that baby] is the one—that the right choice has been made." Recalling a story she had heard about a couple who had returned a baby, one woman worried that she would look at her baby for the first time and feel that "a mistake" had been made. Other women also described the need to, and the worry that they would not, recognize the baby offered to them as their own, as the one they should have. About eight months after obtaining approval to adopt, a woman noted:

I feel she [the baby] is definitely out there somewhere in the grand scheme of things. Everything being put into motion, so that when all the elements come together at the proper time, when we get her, we'll be able to say, "She's the one."

The belief that they were waiting for the right child also served to rationalize a long waiting period (two to three years in some cases) for infertile couples for whom "wait" had become "a four-letter word." This belief also helped them to explain why other couples waiting as long as, or even less than, they had had secured placements before them. For example, seventeen months after approval, a woman observed, "I have a real strong feeling in . . . cosmic forces, God, whatever, that there is something out there that brings the right child to us. . . . I'm willing to wait for the right child." Almost two years after approval and still without a baby, she remarked, "It gets more and more appropriate that [the wait] has been that long. . . . Whatever forces are out there, that is all happening for the good." Commenting on the placement of a baby girl with another couple they knew, both this woman and her husband felt strongly that that baby was not meant to be theirs. As he explained, "it's not that we were rejected, it's that somebody else was chosen. So that baby was the right one" for that other couple. Waiting for the "next appropriate girl," he remarked:

I'm a big believer in the fact that when we get placed, it will be because it is the right baby. Because she is the right one for us. So from that perspective, it doesn't make any difference whether we wait one month or twenty-four months, or however long it takes, to make sure that they feel that the baby that has been placed with us is the right baby for us.

Adopting couples struggled to maintain the belief that the babies they would get were the ones they were supposed to get and that the right baby for them would be available through their adoption agencies. Even more important to their sense of well-being and esteem, couples wanted to believe that the babies who were placed elsewhere or who were otherwise lost to them were the "wrong" babies for them: like a miscarried fetus, a baby that was "not meant to be."

The concept of the right baby helped couples not only to claim a biologically unrelated baby but also to mourn the losses of the babies they could not have, who died, or whom they did not get, and to minimize the apparent fungibility of babies available for adoption. Couples struggled with themselves and with relatives, friends, and society as a whole not to commodify relinquished babies—not to see them as easily replaceable items that could be bought, sold, or returned at will. One adopting woman angrily observed that society did not see adopting couples as people who are becoming parents, but rather as consumers who are buying a commodity. One man, at times tearful over the insensitive responses he and his wife had gotten when they decided not to accept a severely handicapped child offered to them, insisted that babies available for adoption were not like "puppies in a litter," easily discarded or passed over. The child they had decided to "let go," whose picture they still kept months after making that decision, whose name they would not give to any other child, and over whom they still cried, would always be with them the rest of their lives. He explained, "He will always have a special place in our hearts, but we are also going on the feeling that he was not meant to be our child. We were just crossing paths."

The idea of the right baby helped adopting couples decommodify and renaturalize the adoption process: a somewhat ignominious process in which they were forced to put themselves on the market and to pay for a child. Yet, adopting couples also worried about being too choosy and, at times, reconsidered the characteristics that their right baby should have and even expanded their criteria. Couples took great pains to explain to their families and friends why getting a certain kind of child was so important to them, even if that meant delaying placement. After all, if they were deprived of pregnancy, they were entitled to take advantage of what adopting a child uniquely offered. As one woman asked, "Why not get what you want if you can?"

Adopting couples wanting young and healthy infants felt that by taking "just-any" or a "hurry-up" baby they were neither being true to themselves—admitting where their shortcomings lay—nor acknowledging the deprivations of infertility. Couples often felt that they deserved to do as well as they could and that they ought not to be made to feel like they were "discriminating" against certain children by wanting what any childbearing couple typically wanted and got, namely, a healthy infant and/or one who physically fit with them as parents. Couples remarked that it was very difficult for inexperienced parents, for example, to "start in the middle" with an older child; newly born infants and their parents had the advantage of growing and developing together. In addition, getting an infant minimized the "distance" between adoptive parent and child; as one man noted, "we'll know she was adopted, but it won't feel that way." Some couples felt they had to explain why, or were made to feel guilty because, they did not want to parent a just-any child. One woman specifically recalled how unmotherly she felt after a friend indicated her surprise that simply being any child's mother was not enough for her.

Faced with the decision to accept or decline a seriously impaired child, one couple illustrated the unique burden infertile and adopting couples carried for the children they did not adopt. The wife explained, "He will either be our child, somebody else's child, or no one's child. Our decision, whatever we say, that's what happens to him. Whether he ever knows about us or not, we will always know that." She observed that even the decision to abort an impaired fetus was easier than choosing to decline a child offered for adoption. At least, that fetus would be dead. As she put it:

> [There is] no "you're affecting their life forever." There is no life. [The baby offered] is not going to die. He's going to be there and something is going to happen to him. . . . [There is] no finality. . . . We're affecting him forever. He's not going to just go away.

This couple anticipated, if they chose against the baby boy offered them, seeing "their" baby become the "child of no one" and advertised for adoption in a newsletter proclaiming him to be retarded and disabled and, therefore, ultimately unadoptable. (They chose to accept him.)

Adopting couples knew better than any childbearing couple could the intrinsic value and uniqueness of every child; they, not their childbearing counterparts, worried and even felt guilty about all of the children who needed parents. They worked to reconcile for themselves and for others a "clash of principles": the intrinsic value of every child and their own estimation of the value of any one particular child as "a child for us" (Hoffmann-Reim, 1990, p. 50). Moreover, they understood that the only choice adopting couples really had was a choice against a child. In that sense, they were like any childbearing couple who encountered a fetus already chosen for them. Equating a chosen baby with the right baby made a decision not to accept that child all the more difficult. Turning such a child down was like going against nature and even tempting fate. After she and her husband had declined the offer of a severely impaired child, one woman explained:

> You feel guilty for not taking a child that is offered to you and you also feel a little panicky because you say, "I've waited this long. Here is my

chance." But you say, "I don't really want to deal with this." And you feel guilty about it. Even though you know it's not right for you.

In addition, the couples who declined children offered to them carried the burden of choice not carried by other adopting couples who suffered adoption failures because of someone else's choice. As one woman explained, while her friend had lost a child because the birthmother had changed her mind, she herself had been forced to "make a choice" not to accept the child offered to her.

The concept of the right baby served to minimize the randomness and to maximize the (humanly and/or cosmically) ordained nature of adoptive relationships. After all, adopting couples understood on a deeper level that the baby they got could just as well have been placed with another couple. They told stories of babies who were almost theirs or who might have been theirs, were it not for some fated contingency. The concept of the right child preserved couples' sense of purpose and order, and it imposed a certain natural and moral imperative on the adoption process as a whole. Perhaps infertility was something they had to endure to get the right child. Maybe the biological child they might have had would have been the wrong child.

Even more significantly, the concept of the right child served to reassure couples unable to conceive or carry a child that they were still meant to have a child. In their darkest and most anguished moments of trying to conceive, struggling to get "approved" as suitable parents and to make an adoption agency's waiting list, and then waiting for a child to become available for them to adopt, some women worried that perhaps their infertility was a sign that God or nature did not intend for them to have a child. By construing the existence of a right child somewhere out there, couples transformed infertility from an event signaling nature's deprivation or divine punishment to an event signaling nature's or God's purpose; maybe infertility had to happen in order for them to get the baby meant for them. In contrast, childbearing couples never described their awaited baby in terms of its being the right baby. The baby they expected was already right by virtue of their conceiving, bearing, and possessing it; their claim to it was already affirmed by both nature and culture. In fact, childbearing couples would have to work to disclaim it.

Although the concept of the right baby helped adopting couples preserve a sense of order, purpose, and self-worth, it also made them vulnerable to further losses. Once a baby of a certain kind or an offered baby was determined to be the right one in the waiting period, if they did not get that child, adopting couples had to grieve it or, at the very least, work to transform it into the wrong baby. One woman, who declined an offering after finding out about the baby's impairments, remarked, "We just had to believe that because we found out before he came and that he didn't come here right away that maybe that was meant to be and it was the way that it was supposed to work out."

Just being shown a photo of a particular child who might be available for adoption imposed on couples the burden of choosing for or against the child imaged there. According to one couple, their caseworker surmised that it might be unfair for her to show them a picture of an available child who was not the kind of child they had originally requested. Like the ultrasound picture of the fetus shown to a woman who must contemplate terminating her pregnancy, the photograph of a child could act subtly to coerce a couple to choose a child they might not really want to parent. These visual images created a real child who could not be disclaimed easily and without pain.

Different and the Same

Although drawn from a distinctive group among the varied individuals and couples involved in the adoption process, the respondents' descriptions suggest that the preadoption waiting period is potentially as rich a period of anticipation for a child as is pregnancy. Neither wholly nor even necessarily the "deprived, anxious time" (Marquis and Detweiler 1985, p. 1055) it is generally assumed to be, the preadoption waiting period for the respondent couples was a dynamic interlude in which they actively worked to get what was biologically and culturally denied them and to transform disadvantage into advantage.

The adopting couples worked to naturalize adoption, seeking to locate it in the more familiar framework of the conventional biological family (Hoffman-Reim, 1986). In doing so, however, they challenged some cherished cultural presumptions about biology and even exposed certain cultural failings. They resisted the "cultural story" of adoption by telling a new "collective story" of their own (Richardson, 1990). The cultural story, told from the point of view of the normative order in which couples conceive and bear their own children, emphasizes the indeterminacy of the adopted child, the principle of biological filiation, and the deprivations of adoption.

In contrast, the collective story, as told by a group of adopting couples occupying a marginalized place in the society of parents, emphasized the equal (in)determinacy of all children, the unimportance of biology to the parent-child bond, and the advantages of adoption. The adopting couples interviewed did not *deny the differences* between adoptive and biological parenthood so much as they emphasized the similarities and advantageous differences denied in the larger culture. In a sense, they turned the "acknowledgment/rejection-of-difference" discourse associated with adoption (Kaye, 1990; Kirk, 1964/1984) on its head by implying that it was not adopting couples who rejected difference, but rather the larger culture that had difficulty acknowledging the sameness and opportunity of adoptive parenthood.

Specifically, adopting couples raised the question of the importance of biology when a biologically unrelated child could "pass" as their own, or when a biologically related child neither looked like nor temperamentally fit in with any members of its family. Given the vagaries of genetic inheritance, was there any couple who could be confident about the makeup of their expected child? Although childwaiting couples had no pregnancy and no genetic parameters to limit the possibilities of the age and characteristics of the child they would get, they could still set some of their own limits by specifying criteria for the child they wanted. Indeed, an adopting couple could request features of a child that childbearing couples either could not dictate at all or could only partially control. Most important, by working to regain some of the esteem and control denied them by their infertility and the adoption process (Daly, 1989), childwaiting couples managed to confront the cultural prejudice and even biological hubris that having a child of one's own was better than adopting and that, only with an adopted child did they not know what they were getting.

Because of their social position on the boundary between normality and deviance, the childwaiting couples were forced to confront social issues that normally fertile and childbearing couples can afford to ignore. The normally fertile do not have to consider abandoned, relinquished, abused, and other children in need of parents, nor do they have to explain why they do not want to parent them. By contending with and even, at times, owning failures belonging to everyone in a society, infertile and childwaiting couples may permit their normally fertile counterparts to deny and divest themselves of any responsibility for such failures. In fact, these "deviant" couples are typically deemed the perfect match for these "deviant" children.

Finally, adopting couples now have at their disposal more than one model of biological parenthood from which to draw in staking their claims. With new technological advancements in reproduction permitting families to be "pieced" (Elmer-Dewitt, 1991) together with someone else's eggs, wombs, and sperm, there now exists more than one model of biogenetic kinship. As Schneider (1980) remarked, American kinship is construed as whatever contemporary science discovers it to be. The celebrated Baby M case and the equally celebrated cases of women carrying their daughters' children (and their grandchildren), for example, suggest that being with child is no longer necessarily a legitimate basis for the parental claim to a child. In contrast, childwaiting couples may also be with child when they engage in private adoption and surrogacy contracts in which the birth-mother is known to them. The question arises, in relation to what model of biological parenthood can conventional adoptive parenthood be accurately construed as different? The childwaiting couples interviewed are no longer the only ones enjoined to stake their claims to a child, somewhere out there and/or somebody else's.

12. Coming Home

She took all the mothers onto the plane. She walked us down into the plane and we got to the first class section. And there were some people trying to come off so she said we had to back up. And by that time, you could start to see them down the aisle. And all I could see was—I could see like these two men in the back and I could hear babies. I could hear one baby crying and I could see babies. And I kept thinking, I wonder if I was going to know what she looked like or if I would recognize her or how I was going to feel . . . how is it going to feel when I saw her? And so anyway, we got on the plane and I could see the babies and she started going down the aisle and I could feel myself getting really emotional and it was getting to be very tense for me. More excitement at that point. It was like too far in to it to get—to know that they weren't going to give you a baby. And she knew that we were really pressed to make our connections. So she rushed ahead of me and she started looking. At the first baby she came to see the wrist bracelet. And a woman was holding her and she had on a little pink outfit. So I figured it was a girl. And she said, "Whoever gets this baby is getting an angel." That's what the woman passenger said. And she looked at the wrist bracelet and she went, "Here's your baby."

*   *   *

And then we started pushing at about seven. . . . They had to feel my uterus and look at the monitor and tell me when I was having a contraction, so I could push. So I pushed and I pushed and I pushed and I pushed . . . for three hours . . . I didn't know what time it was. It didn't matter to me—I was doing something to get my baby out . . . Irv [her husband] brought him this way, and I remembered my vision of a big baby coming and he was coming this way. And I was so ecstatic and I could see the umbilicus and I thought, "There's alot of stuff on him, but he looks fine and everybody's cool, it must be okay." And he said, "It's a boy."

The homecoming theme is an important one in American dramatic literature, reflecting the aftermath of war and the return of the hero from a quest. The hero/homecomer (typically conceived as male) is a changed person as a consequence of his journey, often bearing scars from his encounters and having a new perception of life and of the society to which he returns (Counts, 1988).

In the "drama" and after the "trauma" of infertility, couples are similarly changed. Individuals writing of their experiences with infertility have described themselves as irrevocably altered by their encounter with it, having "lost [their] innocent belief that things always work the way they should" (Clapp, 1989, p. 5) but not the "feelings that come from infertility" (Loftus, 1989, p. 7). As "veterans" and "survivors" (Mason, 1987), infertile people may even suffer from the "posttraumatic stress disorder" associated with war (Hill, 1989). Similarly, the children of an encounter with infertility are "survivors" of the complex and seldom effective technical procedures that produced them, or of the processes of relinquishment and adoption. Both infertile couples and the children born to or placed with them are homecomers: the children (in their parents' words) "coming to be" and "coming home" under extraordinary circumstances and the couples coming back from the "long, strange trip" that was their encounter with infertility. In this chapter, I describe the homecomings of the infertile childbearing and adopting couples' children. In the next chapter, I describe the continuing comeback work these homecomings engendered.

Special Delivery

At the time this book was completed, thirty-eight of the infertile couples in which the wife was pregnant in the course of the Transition to Parenthood study had safely delivered infants (including four sets of twins and one set of triplets), and thirty of the adopting couples had had children delivered to them. Eighteen of these adopting couples had infants two months old or less placed with them; six couples, infants three to five months old; and two couples, infants thirteen and fourteen months old. In addition, four couples adopted children or sibling groups of two and three children between the ages of one and eight years old.

Adopting and childbearing couples shared the excitement, anxiety, letdowns, and sheer physical fatigue of the first days and weeks of having a new child (or children) in the home. Yet, as suggested by the adoptive mother speaking in the opening lines of this chapter, adopting couples also experienced these homecomings very differently from their childbearing counterparts.

The phenomenology of having a baby involved the embodied responsibility for the woman of bringing forth her baby. Whether fertile or infertile, childbearing couples' narratives of homecomings were the culturally familiar stories of labor and delivery set in the hospital. The events signaling the onset of these homecomings were the physical manifestations of labor; the action of these narratives involved determining that one's time had really come, getting to the hospital, and the easy or hard labors and births that progressed more or less "naturally" and painfully as expected.

In contrast, the phenomenology of getting a baby/child involved the culturally unfamiliar and disembodied task of picking a child up. Adopting couples told stories of meeting their children for the first time in "presentation rooms" in adoption agencies, in homes where their children had been fostered pending adoption, in airports and on airplanes, or in the country of their children's birth. The event signaling adoption homecomings was "the call" to either husband or wife that "this is it."

In contrast to childbirth, which couples anticipated would occur around a "due date" and which they experienced as a natural progression from the pregnancy that preceded it, couples experienced adoption homecomings as "sudden." Adopting couples typically felt in a "daze" and "disoriented," experiencing "sheer shock," and "shell shock" on receiving the call advising them that a child was available for them. No matter how long they had been waiting for a child, they perceived that call as coming out of the blue; with that call, they had achieved "instant parenthood"—as one man put it, they went from "zero to sixty in 1.8 seconds." Indeed, while the infertile and childbearing couples had taken "one year" to journey "from the depths to the heights," adopting couples felt as if they had become parents in an "instant." One adopting woman suggested that childbirth itself mitigated the "surprise" and "suddenness" of having a child. Another woman observed, "not having a nine-months pregnancy and waiting four-and-one-half years for an adoption . . . does not prepare you in any way, shape, or form for the arrival of a child." Conversely, one couple who got their baby within only one month of approval stated that getting a baby so soon was like having a "forty-eight-hour pregnancy," or like having a baby two weeks after discovering pregnancy.

Contributing to this feeling of abrupt change was not only the absence of a bioculturally circumscribed gestation period but also the relative lack of opportunities readily available to childbearing couples (such as Lamaze classes, videos of vaginal and cesarean births, television and movie depictions of labor and birth) for childwaiting couples to experience vicariously and to rehearse emotionally and physically their babies' arrivals. (One adoptive mother suggested an even more subtle advantage of pregnancy as preparation for motherhood; remarking on the backaches she had carrying her new baby around, she observed that she had not had a pregnancy to help prepare her for the physical weight of a child.)

Because of opportunities to experience birth vicariously, adopting couples who have never had children are better able to imagine childbirth than they can an adoption homecoming, which they have "never experienced anything even remotely similar to." One adoptive mother recalled, "I thought for so many years that you give birth and I had in mind these pictures of me huffing and puffing and sweating and me looking down between my legs and the doctor holding up a baby. Not walking into another room." Adopting couples knew something about adoption homecomings from other couples, however, and some couples had imagined the day of the call and the first meeting with their child: what it would feel like, what they would wear, what they would bring for their child to wear, and what they could do both to get the anxiety producing and too public "ritual" of the homecoming over with and to make it as sacred an event as childbirth. Yet, when the time came, couples often had difficulty believing it. This difficulty derived not only from having no due date and few opportunities for vicarious experience, but also from fear that they would never get a child; in the words of one woman, adopting mothers felt that they would "always be bridesmaids, but never brides." Another adoptive mother explained:

> It's kind of like being a hostage. And they have a hostage crisis, and you never really thought that would end, or you thought it would some day, but you didn't know when it's coming. Like, for as long as the [adoption] process went on, it's kind of like you were hostage to this dream almost. . . .

Couples told frequently comical stories of how they responded to the call and how they went about preparing for their child, which typically involved "dazed," frenzied, and frantic housecleanings, shopping sprees, and, in the case of foreign adoption, last-minute travel arrangements and paper chases. After waiting almost two years for her child, one woman described the call this way:

After all this time, it didn't—I've been dreaming about this call and I didn't—I mean I knew who [the caseworker] was, but it didn't hit me why she was calling. . . . She said, "This is [name]. This is your happy call." . . . It was like I was removed from myself. That it wasn't me on—that I could see myself. Sort of like an out-of-body experience where I could look down from the top of my office and see me on the phone with this woman, just sort of shaking my head and thinking that this is real weird.

After waiting so long for it, the call turned out to be "almost anticlimactic." Moreover, after hanging up, this woman was uncertain what to do next. She wondered, "What would Miss Manners say? What's the etiquette about what you do now? How do you tell . . . your husband that he's a father?" In addition, she wondered how to feel. She was "really struck" by the gap between her expressed emotion and that of the other people responding to the news that she was finally getting a baby. Like other couples, she was uncertain how to respond and both worried and regretted that she did not respond as she should have—as her caseworker, friends and acquaintances, and she herself expected. As this woman further explained:

> Even now, I mean I kept—looking back now, I kind of wished that I would have screamed or squealed or something, and I didn't. . . . That's something that really struck me is that throughout the next few days, everybody we told . . . just about everybody started to cry and we didn't. Again, I felt kind of like I wished that I was the burst-into-tears type, but I'm not. I'm very emotional about it, but these other people were just weeping all around us and that was real nice. But, it was just—it sort of punctuated how unreal it all was.

In the brief interval between getting the call and meeting her child for the first time, both she and her husband were "in limbo emotionally." He said, "The thing that I was surprised at was that there wasn't a lot of the joy of anticipation. My stomach was upset most of the time. We couldn't sleep." As she described it:

> I felt . . . like I wasn't waiting, but I wasn't expecting because we were afraid. We were so—not afraid—suspicious, afraid to let our guard down. And I think that's what created such a turmoil for us was that this appears to be happening, but there have been a lot of things that have appeared to be happening and they haven't, and so, what if this falls through?

Childbearing couples, by virtue of pregnancy, have "a sense of order" and, from the first signs of labor, an emotional script to go by, which typically includes an admixture of anxiety about childbirth, elation at the child's birth, relief at its good health, feelings of love for each other and for that child, and perhaps a little depression and some emotional lability associated with postpartum blues or failed expectations for the childbirth experience. Although they may experience discomfort and even guilt if they do not actually feel happy or love for their babies, childbearing couples have some "feeling rules" (Hochschild, 1979, p. 563) available. They know what they are expected to feel even if they do not actually feel it; in Hochschild's words, they know the direction their "emotion work" (p. 561) should take.

In contrast, adopting couples often experienced some degree of "emotive dissonance" (Hochschild, 1979, p. 565) among what they thought they should be feeling, what they wanted to feel, and what they actually felt. Should they behave like biological parents whose script they and everyone else knew (cf. Eheart and Power, 1988), or was there a special emotional script for adoptive parents? One adoptive father suggested the extent to which neither adopting couples nor people in their social network were sure of the feeling rules for adoption when he noted that he and his wife were repeatedly asked how they felt, a question childbearing couples were apparently not asked. He concluded that what they felt was "mostly relief" that the waiting was over and that they could now get on with their lives.

In contrast, one adoptive mother was angry at other people's assumption that adoptive parents did not feel the same things as biological parents felt for their child. As she explained:

> They'd assume that you'd worry—they assume that you'd be worried that an adopted child would not be your own. The most common comment I got was, "don't worry, she'll feel just like your own. You'll feel just like you've had her." Everybody said that and it was kind of— that made me the maddest because it was like assuming—I never assumed that I wouldn't anyway. . . . The normal process of bonding with a child, I don't think happens immediately anyway. Even if you give birth to it.

Although fertile and infertile and childbearing and adopting couples also reported a sense of emotive confusion in having to deal with "eight trillion emotions" simultaneously, the lack of clear feeling rules in the matter of adoption seemed to reinforce adoptive parents' sense of "unreality" and even inauthenticity as real parents beyond that commonly reported by childbearing couples in the early days and weeks of parenting.

In the Natural Way

While childbearing couples were already "in the natural way" by having a biologically related child, adopting couples continued the work they had begun in the preadoption waiting period of naturalizing the circumstances in which they became parents. These couples continued to discover signs indicating that, and reasons explaining why, a child biologically unrelated to them was meant to be their child and to emphasize the weaknesses in the cultural link between biology and nature. Significantly, adopting couples found more evidence that adoption "was almost like it was natural and it was supposed to be that way."

Now that they actually had their child, adopting couples identified the specific physical, temperamental, and/or biographical features that made that child the right child for them. One adoptive mother noted how her baby looked like her niece did when she was a baby. One mother explained that what had "swayed" the caseworkers toward placing her child with her was that she and that child's birthmother were "identical . . . enough . . . to be sisters." Another adoptive mother found it "eerie" how closely she herself resembled her baby's birthmother. Other couples mentioned the observations of family, friends, and strangers that their children "looked like" one or both of its adoptive parents. By noting these resemblances, adopting couples, in effect, suggested that nature was somehow in league with the making of a family through adoption (Hoffman-Riem, 1990, p. 237). Indeed, several couples implied that nature somehow corrected itself in adoption by remarking that their adopted babies were likely superior to any baby they might have had on their own.

In contrast, but also in the service of naturalizing adoption, there were individuals who minimized the significance of physical resemblance in biological families; they noted that biologically related family members often did not look like each other or denied that any resemblance could exist between babies and anyone else. One adoptive father explained:

> I have difficulty seeing resemblance in babies, I think, to parents. I mean you can look at hair color and eye color and a few things like

that, but, I mean, they all kind of have fat cheeks and jowls and stuff and I don't necessarily buy into it.

For this man, trying to determine who a baby resembled seemed somewhat silly and futile since babies looked more like each other than anyone else.

Couples adopting American infants remarked that their caseworkers had assured them that they were getting the "perfect" baby for them. For adopting couples, this factor served not only to accentuate the fated nature of the placement but also virtually to guarantee their acceptance of that child. Once an infant was ready to be picked up by a couple, and despite the fact that couples were supposed to decide at the first meeting with the child whether they wanted it, couples did not even consider not taking that child. The couples adopting foreign infants or children had generally made their decision on the basis of the photos and history of the specific children offered to them. Importantly, for the adopting couples interviewed, the first meeting was strictly "rubber stamping" a decision they had already made; as one mother put it, she and her husband went to pick up their child with the intent to take her and not to decide that they either wanted her or did not want her. As one adoptive mother observed, the characteristics of the baby became less significant when they heard that there really was a baby.

Couples also found signs in their children's behavior and in the workings of cosmic "forces in the universe" that the children they got were meant for them. One couple marveled at how soon their baby watched for and listened to them. One adoptive father observed that his Korean baby acted like he knew him right from the start, and an adoptive mother noted how both she and her South American child had tempers. Another adoptive mother was amazed at the behavior of the older siblings she and her husband had adopted. She noted that they "walked into this house like they had been here before. It was like, oh yeah, that's where the bedroom is and then just walked right on back there and went to their own bedroom." Her husband also remarked how uncanny it was that "they took over the bedroom as soon as they got here." Another couple noted that their baby had been born exactly one-half hour later than the time, and right on the day and date, of their marriage. One adoptive father managed to intertwine his own and his wife's fate with that of the birthmother of their child by remarking that they had had to wait for the birthmother, who was only fifteen years old five years ago when they started trying to have a child, "to go through a lot of major changes in her life before this ever happened." For virtually all of the adopting couples, the coda to the narratives of their children's homecomings was, "so she/he was meant for us," or she/he was the child "God meant us to have."

Although it was relatively easy for adopting couples to see in these homecomings the workings of "a hand . . . greater" than the merely human handiwork of their caseworkers, there were couples who attributed their good fortune more to "serendipity" than to fate. For example, one couple surmised that the only reason they got their baby was because the husband had called their caseworker while she was looking at the papers of a child just released for adoption. Since the baby had a defect the couple had not specifically mentioned would be acceptable to them, the caseworker would likely not have advised them of her availability. By calling, the husband had made the placement happen. Other couples also suggested that adopting couples had to be assertive in order to make things happen: that, even if not fully in control of the process, they still had "a hand" in shaping its course and outcome.

In addition, there were couples who allowed that the baby they got could have gone to another couple. As one adoptive father explained:

> I think that a different child could have been our child. That's not the case; this is our child. . . . Any number of things could have happened, any number of situations could have happened where we could have gotten a child six months earlier or a year earlier or six months later and it would have been a different child. But I don't feel like it would have been—she or he would have been any less our child.

His wife was less certain whether serendipity or fate was more important. As she explained:

> I have kind of mixed thoughts on that because I see the practical end side of it as far as, you know, there is a committee that votes on whether or not this is our child, as opposed to some other couple's. But, at the same time, what I think a lot of people feel—and I tend to have a feeling this way—that there's forces in the universe that brought all those—the meeting of the minds, the committee voting for us. That it was meant to be. And you know, to a certain extent, I think what they (other couples) are saying is that even when they were five years old, forces were in action that somehow brought them to this point. And so, you do—and I do think one reason why people feel that

way is because it is such a big thing, you almost don't want to accept responsibility. But, then, again, I could have applied to another agency and gotten a different child, you know. But then again, certain things happened that this is what fell into place.

She also remarked how uncanny it was how much she and the birthmother of her child had in common and the "little . . . strange . . . [and] coincidental . . . things" about her child's past that were similar to her own. For her, the very fact that the baby they got could have been someone else's, but was theirs, made the placement seem, in the end, even more fated. Another adoptive mother deduced, "Just all the sequence of events that occurred with her. We feel like *she almost wasn't, but was. Therefore, she was meant to be our baby*" (emphasis added).

Adopting couples continued to work to right their claims to be parents of a biologically unrelated child by challenging the cultural belief that what was biological was natural. Some noted that phenomena, such as attachment to a child, traditionally assumed to be natural (or instinctive) and, therefore, linked with biology were not. One adoptive mother observed that biological parents expect to feel love for their baby right from the very beginning. She maintained, "you still have to fall in love with your baby." There was no necessary biological component of love; both adoptive and childbearing parents often had to take the time to fall in love. Or, like childbearing couples who loved their babies before they were born, couples assigned to a foreign child loved them months before they got them. In this way, both the fetus and the assigned child were conceived as "the homecomers who [had] not been at home before" (Hoffmann-Reim, 1986, p. 169). One adoptive father felt as if his Asian child had been away from home visiting his grandparents. After his daughter's arrival, another adoptive father observed:

> We almost feel like she's always been here because we dealt with her pictures and everything. Just like she's been on vacation somewhere for a long time and just got home. . . . She seemed like ours a long time before she came. *She just wasn't here. I mean basically, we lived with her that whole last year before she came. She just wasn't here.* (Emphasis added)

(In other respects, though, the situation of the assigned child remained anomalous, unlike the fetus who was also owned and loved but simply occupying a different space: away at grandmother's house instead of in utero. The father just cited added, "We often said it felt like somebody being held hostage and you pay more money, but you never know if you're going to see them or not.")

Couples also indicated other ways in which they were able to locate adoption in the world of parents and children who came together "in the natural way." For example, couples described incidents where they completely forgot their child was adopted. Referring to her baby girl, one woman recalled:

> This is interesting to me—because I'm so aware of genetics in her [the baby]—that I said—she was pulling [her husband's] glasses off and I said, "You know, we're really gonna have to watch her vision as she gets school age." Because he always wore glasses his whole life. And, then I realized what I had said. I mean, I was saying it because he had always worn glasses, meaning we were gonna have to keep an eye on her vision. And then I realized . . . what I had said.

Another woman who adopted an infant and then delivered a baby conceived by in vitro fertilization told a similar story. As she recalled:

> I forget that [he] is adopted a lot of times. . . . [We] were talking about his teeth and I said—well, see [my husband] had problems with buckteeth and had to have braces and I never had braces and my teeth are pretty straight naturally, and I said that I hoped that [he] takes his teeth after me. Then I caught what I said and I started laughing so, you know, I'm constantly saying stuff like that. So I think that I forget that [he] is not ours at times.

For these parents, the adoptive status of their children soon became second nature; as Hoffmann-Reim suggested (1986, p. 169), they had developed a "new natural attitude."

Adopting couples indicated that nature resided not only in what was supposed to be, but also in what felt natural. Couples described knowing that their children were adopted, but not feeling that they were. While the childbearing couples had not anticipated how much they would love their babies, adopting couples could not "imagine" loving their children more if they had been their birthparents. Two couples were glad that they began their parenting with an older infant because they had trouble getting up in the middle of the night and because they felt themselves better suited to an older baby. Indeed, given their natures, it seemed more fitting for them to have missed the early infancy period.

Linking the natural with what is generally viewed as unfamiliar, the mother of an Asian baby remarked that Caucasian babies now seemed strange to her, and another adoptive mother concluded:

> In some ways, it's kind of strange that we weren't there for the first four weeks and that we missed that interval. In other ways, it's like it's perfectly natural. That this is okay. That her life is started with us just like this and it's just fine.

For some individuals, adoption also became natural when other people accepted it as natural. For example, for one adoptive father who did believe that "a natural mother and father" experienced an "automatic, physical, instinctive bonding" with their baby, the adoption of his baby became natural when "everybody was acting so naturally and normally, just like there wasn't any difference." He said, "To them, there wasn't any difference and that was when it became the same for me." Because he had no experience as a biological father, he seemed reluctant to assert the naturalness of his position as an adoptive father until he received validation from others.

In the end, most adoptive couples concluded that they had not really missed much or even anything that was really important by not achieving pregnancy and by not having their children right after birth. Meeting a baby for the first time in an airport or in a presentation room, as opposed to a delivery room, might be strange, but it was also more "special." Indeed, one father observed, "people who have children the natural way, I think they miss something." In a more polemical vein, an adoptive father of an Asian infant asserted:

> I just think our society has put so much emphasis on the genetic link and that because we've sort of been raised in that environment, we've short-changed the people that can't get pregnant by thinking that they're missing out on something or that they're not going to have the same kind of child. And when I look at [her], and I look at her personality and the way that she is physically and the way she acts, I could think, well, I couldn't have made a child anymore wonderful than that. And so, it's terrible that you could feel so trapped in wanting

to be pregnant for so long and that you can't make it past that stage more quickly to something that can be this rewarding.

This man admitted that infertile couples adopting children had to overcome in themselves and in others the ingrained prejudices against adoption; but, once they did, they could appreciate how constraining those prejudices had been.

Yet, although couples emphasized the similarities between adoption and childbearing, they knew these situations were also "miles and miles apart." There were couples who after placement still articulated feelings of regret for failing to achieve biological parenthood. One adoptive mother admitted that adopting a child did not "replace that urge" to have a child nor did it eliminate the feeling of "missing that experience." One adoptive father wondered what a child of his *genetic* own would have been like.

Moreover, as another adoptive father observed, although there were disadvantages to childbirth and too many advantages wrongfully attributed to biological parenthood, adoption was in many ways a harder "accomplishment" than "just having a child." Adopting couples could feel pride, but it was a pride characterized by what this man's wife described as a "defensive" posture; she felt she was always trying to get people to treat adoption properly and was always waiting for people to treat it lightly or insensitively. As she explained:

> What you [her husband] called pride, for me is a chip on my shoulder. . . . I feel like alot of people don't realize how hard adoption is. What you have to go through. When I find people treating it lightly, I get defensive. We waited a very long time. We really do want kids. Don't you dare take this lightly. Sometimes that's how I'm kind of defensive about still. Like I'm waiting for someone to intimate that [my baby] is not as good as. . . .

Familiar Strangers/Strange Familiars

Whether they had or got their children, both the fertile and the infertile couples worked to get to know them in the days and weeks after their homecomings, to develop that intimate knowledge of their children that made them their own. The adopted child is the one more likely to be viewed as a stranger to its adoptive parents (Hoffmann-Reim, 1986, 1990; Kirk,

1988), but the acquaintanceship process is one that all new parents experience. Both birthparents and adoptive parents encounter the paradox expressed by one adoptive father in describing the Asian child whom he knew from photos and a brief written history: "I know you, but I don't know you."

Although knowledge of one's own child, like love for it, is culturally presumed to be naturally derived from the blood tie between parent and child, the childbearing couples actually knew as much and as little about their newly born babies as the adopting couples knew about their newly arrived children. Couples may know of and something about their children before birth and placement, but they can only get to know them as persons afterward. Fertile and infertile, and adopting and childbearing couples described the trials and triumphs of learning to respond appropriately to the children they had only recently met, of learning to understand how their infants and young children (including those few older adopted children whose primary language was not English) communicated their needs and to anticipate and then satisfy those needs. All of the couples described the knowledge they had acquired, and the sense of comfort based on that knowledge they had developed, in the first three months after their children's "debuts" and their own debuts as parents to these children. In an important sense, their feeling fully like parents depended on the development of knowledge about their children that only they possessed.

Both adopting and childbearing couples described incidents of parental gazing: of admiring and inspecting their children. Couples looked at their new-to-them children, taking in the whole of them, feeling awe at what they had produced or had been chosen to get, and validating to themselves the actual presence of a child. While normally fertile couples were awed by what they had produced, the infertile adopting and childbearing couples were awed by what had not once more eluded them or again been lost. They found it "awesome" that they had a normal vaginal or uneventful cesarean delivery, had a healthy child, and/or that they had a child who was so beautiful. Most important, they found it awesome that they had a child at all. As one adoptive mother observed, "We just laid her there and looked at her for awhile and just couldn't get over it."

In a more anatomizing and scrutinizing vein, both adopting and childbearing couples also looked for signs of their child's health status and parental or family fit, counting fingers and toes, searching for signs of birth defects they especially feared, searching for physical and temperamental resemblances, and, in the special case of couples with babies conceived with donor sperm who feared the wrong sperm might have been used, ascertaining that their babies were, for example, wholly white. One adoptive mother commented on distinctions among different types of parental gazing (and between the gazing of adoptive parents and birthparents) by describing how she was informed by her caseworker that "natural mothers" first inspected their babies' fingers and toes to make sure they had everything. She recalled, "because of what we had been told about her already, I knew that eventually I would get around looking at them but that wasn't the first thing that I looked at. I looked at her—not for things."

Moreover, like childbearing couples who worried about getting the wrong baby from the nursery (implying that they would not necessarily recognize their own child), adopting couples, especially those couples adopting foreign children, wanted to ensure that the child they got was the child to whom they had been assigned and whom they were supposed to get. They looked for features that made the child released to them recognizable as their child; the child described in the histories and imaged in the photos they had received was their point of comparison. For example, an adoptive mother of a Korean baby explained:

> The first time I really had a chance to look at her. I mean I started looking for things that I recognized. And I recognized the inside of her eyebrows because they kind of turn up right at the inside. I recognized that. I recognized she had a little birthmark on the back of her neck that they told us about. And the more I looked at her, the more she looked familiar to me. But, of course, she didn't look anything like her picture. She didn't have nearly as much hair as I thought she was going to have.

Although the acquaintanceship process was in many respects similar for both adopting and childbearing couples since both groups of couples had to get to know a being they had only recently met, the acquaintanceship process for adopting couples also involved learning as much as they could of the history they did not share with their child. Adopting couples were typically pleased with what they learned of their children's backgrounds but often wished they had more information to, for example, establish proper medical records, to prepare them to tell their children the story of their beginnings, and to answer any questions their children might have. In addition, some couples implied that having more information would allow them to determine what about their child they could then claim as coming from them as opposed to its birthparents or foster parents. One adoptive mother explained, "I know as time goes on, I'll probably wonder less and less because as time goes on, she'll become less her birthparents' child and more mine because what will happen is, she'll start to take on our mannerisms." Noting that he and his wife had "reached the point" where their child had been with them "as long as she had been with . . . the other significant people . . . in her life and that being the foster parents," one adoptive father observed:

> Up until that point . . . we didn't know what all groundwork had been laid for some of her behaviors and her responses to certain stimuli. Whereas now we're right about that point where we're the ones who are going to have had the major contributions toward her behavior and toward her routine and her responses. . . . We're going to know why certain behaviors are exhibited. And, therefore, it's going to be more comfortable.

Some women were especially interested in learning more of the story behind their children's birthparents. One mother wondered, "How did they meet? Where did they meet? How long did they date? What did they look like? What kind of goals did they have? Was the birthmother . . . an early starter? Did she get her first teeth early?" Another adoptive mother explained that because she lacked complete information, she "just made . . . up" a story from the information she had about her baby's birthparents. As she observed:

> I kind of constructed the scenario around her and about how her parents met and in my mind, I've decided that her birthfather was a married college professor and the birthmother was this beautiful young thing and was one of his students. And intellectually, I know that may not be true but with some things that we know, that gives it credence.

This woman continued the work she and other adopting couples had begun in the waiting period of constructing a unique family "romance" (Rosenberg and Horner, 1991) of and for their child. Couples were very concerned to create a "time capsule" for their children so they would not suffer "lost time." They described the bits of information they received—photos, medical reports, letters, listings of milestones reached—that chronicled their children's existence before their homecomings. Commenting on the information that came with her child, one mother remarked, "Everything that has happened to her in her first two weeks is symbolized in that little box."

Making a history for their children inevitably involved for couples a mental encounter with the birthparents, especially with the birthmothers, of their children. Couples adopting American infants, who typically received more specific information about the birthparents than couples adopting foreign children, tended to cast birthmothers as heroines in their children's and their own stories. They lauded the birthmothers as having given them the "greatest gift" and as having made the "ultimate sacrifice." Some couples expressed a fellow-feeling for the losses they had experienced and intimated that as adoptive and birthparents, they both shared a love for their child. One mother felt an "ethical or moral obligation to remember" the birthmother. One adoptive father suggested that now it was the birthparents, as opposed to the adoptive parents, for whom their baby was "somewhere out there." Another father admitted:

> When I was going to sleep . . . last night . . . I thought about the birthparents. I was thinking about, you know, I was thinking about how happy—I was thinking about how much I love her and how happy I was, and then I started thinking, wow! That means that the parents may be feeling that bad about this situation. I just thought about it, saying, wow! That's terrible. . . . I hope they're doing okay, and I hope they don't think it's—don't have negative thoughts in the sense like, worried about her safety and well-being and stuff like that. It's just, I know they're going to have their thoughts about "did I do the right thing?" Forever, probably. That made me kind of sad.

Recalling a baby they had who had died soon after birth, his wife observed:

> But you know, I often think of what [that baby] would be like, if she were here today and what age she would be and what she would be like. And I wonder if they'll [the birthparents] do the same thing, since it's a child that they don't have.

Both she and her husband worried that sending to the birthparents pictures they had requested of their baby would "cause them more pain."

At the same time, adopting couples righted their claims to what the birthparents had lost by praising them for the correct and "courageous" decision they had made in relinquishing, as opposed to aborting or keeping, their child. One mother described the relinquishment process as a loving way to give a baby up. These couples did not right their claims by typifying birthparents, and mothers especially, as bad or unfit; rather they noted the goodness of the birthparents and their mutual participation in a process that was inherently right (cf. Hoffmann-Reim, 1990, p. 224–25).

One factor that appeared to be related to the casting of birthmothers as heroines was the wish of adopting couples to believe that their children were loved by their birthparents—that they had been "products of love . . . not bitterness." Couples often remarked on some kindness a birthparent or other member of the birth family had shown their child; they also frequently commented on how well cared for and loved their children had been by their foster families. The fact that birthparents had relinquished their children out of love and/or with courage and that foster parents had found it difficult to hand their children over to them made those children all the more desirable and lovable. As one mother put it, the fact that her foster parents were so attached to her "means she's a neat baby."

Couples felt comfort (and also anxiety) in knowing their children's birthparents had loved them; in some cases, the birthparents loved their children enough to want pictures and news of them. This fact served to undermine the common assumption that children relinquished for adoption were somehow less desirable than other children. One adoptive mother commented on her friends' beliefs that only unhealthy babies were available for adoption, and other mothers reported reacting negatively to their friends' surprise that any birthmother could give up such appealing babies. Yet, at the same time, adoptive mothers, in particular, often marveled at the beauty of their babies. One mother commented, "they gave me a pretty baby." Their wonderment seemed to suggest that they too had not expected to get beautiful babies.

Although adopting couples typically acknowledged thinking more or less about their children's birthparents, there were couples who felt more emotionally distant from them or who expected to think about them more in the future, especially when the time came to begin telling their children about being adopted. One woman, for example, had difficulty developing empathy for her child's birthparents because she viewed their goals as unlike her own. As she explained:

> I think of them as more like a piece of paper in a box rather than real
> people. [We] realize that there are two people out there that we are

very thankful to. . . . But, at the same time, I could never relate to that person because our goals are obviously as opposite as could be. But, if it weren't for something like that, then we wouldn't be so happy right now.

One couple adopting an Asian child felt as if the birthparents of their child were more fictitious than real; they wondered whether the information they received about them was only a variant of the "generic stories" told to other couples adopting Asian children. Remarking on the similarity in the stories behind the first child offered them (whom they decided not to adopt) and the child they did adopt, the mother remarked:

> The birthparents . . . don't seem very real to me. I know they're two real people, but it's sort of like the picture where you know their names and you know their ages and you know they went to school and you know how they met and how they got pregnant and how they split up. But, beyond that, it's sort of a little story. And actually, between the two offerings, the stories were kind of similar. So you have to wonder.

Another mother had "fleeting moments" of thought for the birthmother of her child. As she explained:

> It's usually just fleeting and it's usually not any extensive thing at this point. Now it may be later on, but at this point, it's not more than a fleeting and it's nothing negative. I think about, you know, wonder what she is thinking and wonder what she felt when she decided to place [the baby]. At times, I wonder—and I don't pick out any specific person—but just wonder, could she be where I am? And if she was, it wouldn't make any difference and none of us would even know at this point, but sometimes that crosses my mind.

The thoughts of this woman portrayed an anxiety about both knowing too much and knowing too little about the birthmother. What if she were, for example, in the same grocery store as the adoptive mother? Although couples quickly dismissed as of little concern the fact that their children were not legally theirs until about one year after placement, they nonetheless conveyed some anxiety about the entitlement to their children they still shared with birthparents who were somewhere out there.

Passing and Passing It Over

Both fertile and infertile as well as adopting and childbearing couples worked to overcome the "unreality" and inauthenticity of the early parenting period—the feeling that they were only playing at being parents. They worked to align appearances, emotions, expectations, and performance, or to reach that stage where they felt fully parents in identity, feeling, and deed.

Yet, infertile as opposed to fertile couples, and adoptive as opposed to birthparents encountered distinctive dilemmas involving ownership and authenticity in their transition to parenthood, which were manifested, in part, in their special efforts to naturalize adoption and right the claims to children not genetically theirs. Adopting couples in particular expressed their sense of tentative ownership. For example, after meeting his child for the first time, one adoptive father recalled:

> I didn't feel like her parent or not, but I didn't feel alienated either. I didn't feel not like her parent, but I didn't feel like her parent either. It was just sort of an experience seeing her there and seeing how beautiful she was. Sort of thinking that she would be ours.

While describing what she would write in a letter to her child's birthmother, one adoptive mother observed:

> I think of her as my daughter, but I can't call this woman *her* mother more or less. It's like, well, I'll say that *your* child is doing well. Your little girl—baby girl is doing well. But I can't say that it is her daughter because to me that takes on a different connotation than she's *my* daughter. So, she really has become a part of us. (Emphases added)

Whether adoptive parents or birthparents, infertile couples often expressed their disbelief that the baby they had was theirs to keep. One week after the delivery of her baby conceived by in vitro fertilization, one mother said, "I feel like a parent, but I think I feel like that this is not really my baby and somebody is going to come and take it. This is my sister's baby, and I'm just keeping it for awhile." After delivery of the son she conceived by in vitro fertilization, another woman observed:

> I just can't believe that somebody is not going to take him. I don't have to give him back to anybody. When I go to the pediatrician . . . I can walk out of the office and take him home again. I don't have to give

him away. I mean, every baby that I have ever held . . . I had to give
back and this one I can keep.

One adoptive father remarked, "I felt like I had somebody else's child . . .
like we're going to wake up in the morning and somebody's going to come
and pick her up and take her away and our life is going to be like it was." No
fertile couple expressed such "keeper" sentiments, that is, feelings that they
might have to give their child back to some other rightful owner.

An additional issue for adoptive mothers was that while no man,
whether an adoptive or biological father, ever "goes through the process of
childbearing anyway," most women who become mothers do. As one
adoptive father explained:

> I don't think it would be any different if she were our biological child. I
> think it would be *just as strange* for me—I mean, there would be this
> day when my wife, who had been gradually getting larger and larger
> and larger, went to the hospital and then we had this baby. It would
> still be *just as alien*. (Emphasis added)

I suggested in an earlier chapter that a woman's embodied pregnancy
makes her transition to motherhood different from a man's to fatherhood
and that the transition to adoptive motherhood is thus different from that
to biological motherhood. One mark of this difference was that some
adoptive mothers, as opposed to adoptive fathers, described feeling illegiti-
mate in the role of mother. These women felt as though they were passing
for, as opposed to passing as, their child's mother. For example, one
adoptive mother felt "weird" when her friends began to treat her like a
legitimate mother, asking her about how old her baby was and how she was
eating and sleeping. This woman felt that the answers she gave were not
hers to give, that her baby was not really hers. But the "double-edged
sword" for her was that she also felt "real awkward" being left out of
conversations about childbirth and postpartal recovery; that also made her
feel as though her baby was not really hers.

Similarly, another adoptive mother felt as if she were "using" her baby
to get the attention denied her by not achieving pregnancy. Describing
her responses to comments from people on the beauty of her baby, she
explained:

> Because I had nothing to do with her, I just say, "She sure is . . . cute . . .
> isn't she?" . . . People think that I'm her birthmother. Somehow I feel

like it might not be quite seemly if I were saying, "Yes, she is really cute, isn't she?" Like somehow, I did have something to do with it.

Three months after her child's homecoming, this woman was still reluctant to take any credit for her baby's characteristics, believing that she had not had her daughter long enough to have made her own mark on her.

Adopting couples were typically concerned that they pass as, or be considered and accepted as their children's true parents, as opposed to passing for, or misrepresenting themselves as, their child's birthparents. Yet these couples also believed that passing for the birthparents of their children was warranted in certain situations. For example, couples gradually felt less of a "compulsion" to correct strangers' assumptions that they were the birthparents of their child. As they conveyed it, if a person commented in passing on how well a woman looked so soon after having her baby or how much a baby looked like one of its parents, it was acceptable just to say "thank you."

Couples sought not to make an issue of adoption unnecessarily and to respond in socially and morally comfortable ways that affirmed both adoption and their child. The efforts of adopting couples to pass as their child's parents (and when warranted, to pass for its birthparents) were oriented not toward denying that they did not have the child biologically nor toward deceiving that child or anyone else about adoption, but rather were oriented toward their desire to make adoption no bigger or smaller an issue than was beneficial for their child. One woman summarized the dilemma adoptive parents faced in experiencing adoption as a natural but variant form of parenthood. She said, "There's sort of a fine line there, I think, between not wanting to make an issue of the whole adoption, but yet accepting it as something that's real natural." In a similar vein, one adoptive father observed:

I don't think it's an issue for us, [but] it's definitely an issue. It's something that has to be dealt with. I mean, that's part of the adoption process, dealing with the fact that the baby isn't really related to you. That she or he is from a whole different line of people altogether. But that's a physical level. Now my emotional level, that's our baby. There's no—there's no question in our minds. It's only been three or four months, but, you know, we might just as well have had her biologically because the bond, the attraction is there. It's like a physical thing. But other people will say things. Whether tactful or not, they will say things and that's one of the things that we and she, when she grows up to cognizance, will have to deal with. And if we—if we handle the situation right, up to that point, then she won't have a problem dealing with it. She'll feel comfortable with the situation.

Owning an adopted child and feeling authentic as an adoptive parent thus involved not only a process of encountering one's own attitudes toward and feelings about adoption, but also of engaging—in an appropriate and timely manner—larger cultural views and social practices that emphasized adoptive parents' nonexclusive claim to their child and inauthenticity as parents (cf. Miall, 1989). One father suggested the critical intersection of timing (Kaye, 1990) and cultural prejudice in the proper acknowledgment of the difference of adoption by noting:

> She's my daughter . . . I know we'll have to distinguish that for her. And [the caseworkers] suggested that at the earliest age that she starts to question it, go ahead and make it clear. But, you know, I don't consider her adopted. . . . It's a social thing that we'll have to make her aware of. I guess there's good and bad stigma involved with it that we'll have to prepare her for.

Even if couples themselves found it easy to forget their children were adopted, they were reminded of it in their interactions with other people. Couples adopting foreign children who clearly looked nothing like them lived in a "fishbowl," unable to make a simple trip to the supermarket without encountering the stares and questions that marked their difference. Although their visibility as adopting parents was not wholly unwelcome and could even be pleasant, some felt they could never just be themselves or be in a bad mood or, most important, that they could never think of themselves as parents just like other parents. As one father observed, couples adopting foreign children were "ambassadors for adoption" everytime they walked out of their front doors.

In a related vein, one adoptive mother recalled feeling an initial pang of discomfort in the pediatrician's office as the word *adopted* was written in bold letters on her baby's chart, as if there were "a mark on this child." As she continued:

> I just kind of felt like—it didn't really bother me one way or the other—it's just that I thought there's almost like there is just a stigma

attached to her already and it will always be there that she's slightly different from other people.

Because their family and friends knew they had adopted their children, and especially in cases of foreign adoption, couples could not always pass as simply parents. In fact, couples found themselves taking on or, alternatively, "passing over" or "letting pass" comments about adoption that accentuated their children's difference in hurtful ways. For example, as I mentioned above, adoptive mothers told stories of friends expressing their amazement that any mother could give up a child who was both beautiful and healthy. One adoptive mother angrily explained this response by noting the general assumption that only "a little sick child nobody wanted" would be relinquished.

Similarly, an adoptive mother of a five-month-old Asian child remarked:

> In talking to other women who have had children, they look at me and they're like, "You are so lucky. Here you are with this very young baby and you didn't have to go through all that bother and all that trouble." The first time around, that used to bother me. That bothered me emotionally because I'd think about how hard I tried to get pregnant. Don't tell me that; that's all I wanted. The second time around, it hasn't bothered me. You know, it's like, well, I guess I knew that they were going to say that to me. But I wasn't expecting it the first time. But so many women have said, "You don't have to . . . worry about that pouch." You know, have to lose it, and make your skin go back together again and just things like that, that at first, I think, I thought were insensitive and how can you say that to me. But this time, I just sort of laugh with them and say, "You're right, you know."

For this woman, passing it over involved altering her emotional response to a recurring remark and, perhaps, even discovering another way that adopting a child was more advantageous than bearing one. For another adoptive mother, passing it over also meant protecting well-meaning but insensitive people from rebuke. Telling a similar story of being advised how "lucky" she was not to have endured the trials of childbirth, she observed:

> I just sort of pass it off and say, "Yeah, but you don't realize what all we have gone through either." You know, they don't know that side of it

and they can't know and they don't—I have to remind myself that they mean well. They mean well and there is no way that anybody can know what you've gone through unless you've been there . . . I just pass it off. And maybe that's just my personality but . . . I mean I always want to be real tactful with everything I say. And maybe it's just because I don't know how to be tactful with that. But when I think about explaining, I would feel like they might feel like I was slapping their hands or something.

Interestingly, while adopting couples typically sought to pass as—to be accepted as—their children's real if not biological parents, couples with babies conceived with donor sperm were more likely to want to pass the father off as the biological father. The medicalized anonymity of sperm donation, as opposed to the storied anonymity of birthparents relinquishing a child for adoption, and the experience of a pregnancy-like-any-other-pregnancy made it easier for these couples to think of their babies as naturally their own. One father of a baby conceived by donor insemination, who never indicated any difficulty with fathering a child biologically unrelated to him, stated that having a baby this way became "natural" when people kept commenting on his baby's physical resemblance to him. He remarked, "It's natural. He's mine. He's always going to be mine. I'm putting all that behind me." Pleased that others thought he resembled his baby, he also marveled at the degree of resemblance between the baby and other members of his family.

In contrast, two couples with babies conceived with donor sperm believed in the possibility that their babies were genetically entirely their own. One of these fathers remarked:

There's a possibility that—we haven't had another sample for about a year . . . I mean there's always a chance that she is mine. I hope that we never take the trouble to find out. We don't have any reasons to find out one way or the other, but that is a possibility.

Another couple admitted having two opposing thoughts concerning the pregnancy they had achieved with donor sperm, namely, a concern that the baby would be biracial (because of a mistake in selection of sperm) or would inherit from that donor a genetic disease that was not detected and, alternatively, the idea that the baby was genetically the husband's baby. Once the child was born white and healthy, the second idea gained prominence. The father, with his wife's agreement, observed:

We had the same thought that it could easily have been my baby. You know, what happens if one little sperm happen to—got lucky? . . . We've always had that feeling. And I still today have that feeling. . . . And the more that we know him, the more I have that feeling.

His wife continued:

It's real—it's real uncanny because his parents and . . . my mother know the whole story. They're the only ones that know. . . . And they've brought pictures from home of [her husband] when he was that age and [the baby] has a cowlick just like [he] had a cowlick when he was a baby. And their ears have this funny looking thing on them. And, I mean, it's just, you know, it's real hard not to let yourself entertain those ideas. . . . When I first saw [the baby] . . . it just overwhelmed me how much he looked like [her husband]. It was just—I don't know if I just let myself do that or what, but I kept—he's just—he's got the same wrinkled forehead. And it wasn't like I was going, oh, let me hurry up and find something here so that I can feel like he's going to look like his father. It was more like, how could this be? You know, it was a real strange feeling like this—I mean this is real crazy, but look at that and how do you explain that? . . . And, I don't think I ever want to know. I think I always want to entertain that thought. You know, I think I'll deal with it a little better for one thing. And for another thing, I think that you can't ever say never. You know, you never know exactly what happened.

Both agreed that in all the ways that mattered, the husband was the baby's father. The wife said, "Physically and biologically, it's sort of an afterthought because it really doesn't matter. It's kind of nice that he looks like him and it would be nice to—if somehow we could prove that it was his, biologically—but really." They had decided to keep the thought alive by not seeking proof one way or the other. By doing so, they could also affirm a decision often made by parents of babies conceived with donor sperm to keep the donation process a secret from their child (Daniels, 1988; Milsom and Bergman, 1982), that is, to not tell their child "the truth, or what could be (but was not necessarily) the truth."

Coming Home and Coming Back

Although having children is neither necessary nor sufficient to initiate or successfully complete the comeback from infertility (Carter and Carter, 1989), comeback work was hastened and intensified in the couples interviewed by the homecomings of the children they had in the course of the study. While infertility was a factor that influenced the early parenting experiences of some affected couples, adoption turned out to be the most significant variable for comeback work of couples in the first three months of homecoming. Adoptive parents had more and different work to do in continuing their transition to parenthood: reinforcing their parental claims, coming to terms with the lack of embodied connection to their children, and contending with societal responses to their unusual parenthood. Adoptive parents sought to reframe adoption by expanding the boundaries of nature while minimizing the importance of biology. Unlike the parents of children conceived with donor gametes, adoptive parents had no gestational tie to bolster their claims or to locate their child within the biological norm, nor did they have the interpretive room to wonder if their child might not in fact be genetically their own. While the experiences of infertile and fertile childbearing couples differed more in degree than in kind, the experiences of adoptive and childbearing couples differed more in kind than in degree, adoption challenging the very substance of conventional notions of having a child.

13. Coming Back

> My infertility resides in my heart as an old friend. I do not hear from it for weeks at a time, and then, a moment, a thought, a baby announcement or some such thing, and I feel the tug—maybe even be sad or shed a few tears. And I think, "There's my old friend." It will always be part of me. (Menning, 1977, p. 117)

As I described in previous chapters, the infertile couples interviewed began the biographical work of comeback in pregnancy and in the preadoption waiting period. They worked to relinquish infertility, or in Strauss and Corbin's terms (1991, p. 367), they engaged in the analytically distinct processes of "coming to terms," "contextualizing," "identity reconstituting," and "biographical recasting" that constitute coming back from illness or disability. Specifically, couples grieved over their losses, worked to make infertility part of but not the whole "fabric" of their lives, regained a sense of wholeness, and envisioned a new "life after infertility" (Leon, 1989, p. 3).

Whether adopting or childbearing, infertile couples engaged infertility's legacy of failure, self-doubt, and accomplishment, and they sought to relocate themselves in "mainstream American family" life. As one father put it after the birth of his twins conceived by in vitro fertilization:

> I feel normal now. And my feeling toward the whole infertility process and everything and what makes that different or special is that it was our attempt to be normal like everybody else and to have a normal life raising kids in a family and that sort of thing. So with the success, that gave us *normality* [emphasis added] to continue on with it. From now on, if we define normal as raising a family, then we've achieved that. That has been corrected.

After the delivery of his child conceived with donor sperm, another man was able to dismiss infertility as an abnormal phase in life. He commented, "The nice thing about pregnancy [is that it] . . . gives you a chance to sort of get back to reality, I think, and to sort of realize that that was just a phase and now things are normal again." And, for a woman who had finally delivered a healthy child conceived by in vitro fertilization after losing her first in vitro pregnancy, normality meant finally having a baby and not having to dread that question of whether she had children and to wonder how to answer it. By achieving parenthood, infertile couples had achieved cultural normality, even if they remained biologically infertile. Their come-back work involved dealing with the fact that their histories and babies were "no ordinary" ones and that only by virtue of their extraordinariness had they achieved the ordinariness they had been seeking.

Integrating Reproductive Pasts

A key component of couples', especially women's, comeback work was coming to terms with infertility "on an emotional level." As I have pre-viously described it, couples themselves distinguished physical from emo-tional fertility. *I-have* infertility—a physical problem that was kept separate from the self—was something different from *I-am* infertile—a state of being where there was a more or virtually complete "fusion" (Corbin and Strauss, 1987, p. 265) of infertility with the self. People with I-have infer-tility, typically men but also women, had considerably less difficulty relin-quishing infertility than the women in the I-am infertile state.

For women, relinquishing infertility on an emotional level involved efforts to divest everyday (arti)facts—the menstrual period, sexual inter-course, pregnancy, the thermometer—of the symbolic meanings they had come to have. For example, most women were able once again to view the menstrual period as a normal fact of life as opposed to a symbol of failed womanhood and even to permit themselves to forget about it. In addition, they were able to view pregnancy less as the symbol of true womanhood.

Yet, these phenomena still had the power to reprise for them the hope and despair of infertility. Three months after the delivery of her daughter, one woman commented:

> The very first time I had my period—well, the first and second time too—those feelings don't go away of disappointment. Even after you have a baby. I thought to myself, "Now why would I still feel like this?" That was a shocker for me to realize that those feelings were still there. . . . Like there inside of you is this little secret wish or thought that maybe it will happen this time. Which is what we had been going

through before the whole time doing the IVF. Still thinking in between times that, well, something would happen. Maybe it could. But
my doctor told me when he did the C-section that my tubes were
blocked and so he told me then that there was no chance that I was
going to get pregnant on my own. And even though I knew that, my
period didn't come for like eight weeks after I had the baby, so—I
don't know—just that little anticipation. So I think it must take years
or awhile for that—to get those feelings to go away. Maybe because
you're used to feeling that way.

Although pregnancy became less important to most of the women as
an experience they had to have or as a route to motherhood, it remained
an important symbolic representation of normal womanhood for some
women even after they delivered their babies. One woman felt "cheated"
that after all of her struggles with fertility drugs and artificial insemination
to achieve pregnancy, it had ended in a premature delivery. Another woman
could not wait to become pregnant again soon after delivering her first
baby conceived by in vitro fertilization. She missed being pregnant and felt
jealous whenever she saw pregnant women. Accordingly, she began to
engage in activities in which she could be involved with pregnant women as
a way of "reliving it all." For this woman and others, whether pregnancy
after infertility was easy or "nine months of stress," it had given her a feeling
of completeness and the sense that she had done what a "woman was
supposed to do." For these women, even if not for most of the infertile
women who became mothers through pregnancy or adoption, it remained
important to "think that [they] could decide next week when [they] ovulate
that [they] could get pregnant."

Relinquishing infertility on an emotional level also meant integrating
two sets of seemingly contradictory conditions: infertility and parenthood,
and infertility and normal adulthood. Especially for the women who had
developed an identity of self as infertile, biographical comeback work
involved the "reconstitution of identity" (Corbin and Strauss, 1987, p. 272)
to incorporate the once- or still-infertile self with the woman or mother self.

Women, as opposed to men, tended to struggle with the paradox
of being both infertile and a mother. Several of the infertile mothers described ways in which they believed infertility had influenced their ability to
mother and had made it difficult for them to see their babies as babies,
instead of as product and symbol of a long and painful struggle. One
woman explained:

I guess because you wait so long to get a baby upfront, and then it takes you the nine months to have it, and you're worried for nine months, and you're just scared to death that something is going to go wrong . . . I don't give [the baby] a chance to just be a baby.

As a consequence of being both an older first-time mother and infertile, this woman, like others, believed she had become less "naive" and more anxious about the possibility of trouble. In her words, she had suffered the loss of self-confidence.

One of the things . . . is how infertile women do lose their self-confidence. I guess, just because we don't feel like we can carry out that basic . . . of what womanhood is about, and I know that's true. Not only in—but in every aspect of your life. I'm nowhere near as self-confident as I was ten years ago. . . . Even in my work and even in my school work, I mean I just do not have—I mean before, just didn't have any doubts about my abilities to do anything and now, I'm always saying, did I do this right? Even when I feel good about something, there's that little nagging thought—maybe it's not right—and so that's carried over into motherhood.

Whether fertile or infertile, women often attributed the successes they had with mothering to the attributes of the child, rather than to themselves; it was the "perfect," "dream," or "good" child who made it "easy" to mother. In times when mothering was hard, though, several of the infertile women looked back at themselves and wondered whether an infertile woman could be a good mother or was meant to have a child at all. One woman remarked that infertility

makes you have a little more doubt when things aren't going well that, well, maybe it really wasn't intended for me to have kids anyway for some reason. Like when she wasn't feeding well, I thought, "Well, maybe I'm not that great of a mother." You know I had those moments where you get a little kooky in your head and wonder if there wasn't some divine intervention that you didn't know about.

Another woman who had lost a previous pregnancy and then experienced a very complicated second pregnancy prior to delivering her first child explained:

I was just having a big letdown sort of like after everything was over. Then I thought, "Oh, now I've got him and I'm not going to be able to take care of him." And I felt so incompetent and just a whole wealth of emotions like I'll never be able to successfully breast feed because we were having so few positive experiences with the whole deal.

As one infertile mother summarized it:

I think I personally have more fears than others do. I think all first-time mothers are really nervous. I agree with that. But I think you have so much more invested in it, or you feel like you do, that it's just overwhelming when something is wrong with them. Like the first time I went and took her to the doctor, worried about her eating. And I made sure I told the doctor—I said, "She's a test-tube baby." I said, "I know that makes no difference as far as her health is concerned, but it might help you understand why I'm so nervous about the fact that I don't think that she's eating right. Not that I think it has anything to do with it. Only it may help you understand why I'm so nervous as a mother." . . . And I think that's a valid point. You've been so nervous through your whole pregnancy that everything wasn't going to turn out okay that once the baby is here, you can't just cut that off. And now that it's actually something that you can see and touch and know what you've been loving all this time, I think you're that much more afraid that something could happen. I think it is also something that you need to *work to overcome*. (Emphasis added)

Women's comeback work, as opposed to men's, often involved regaining a sense of competence and self-worth and maintaining the belief that they deserved and were meant to have a child. Having been infertile for a number of years, it remained hard for some women to feel that they, not somebody else, were a mother and not to feel infertile, even though they had children. Moreover, the "luck" that permitted them, as opposed to so many other infertile women, to have a child imposed its own unique burden. As one adoptive mother put it:

When it takes that long and when you know how many people have tried and you're made to feel like you're special—that you're going to get one of these rare babies—you have this sort of feeling on you like, you have to be a perfect parent at all seconds and not just every day pretty good, but perfect all the time. . . . And I think it's more self-imposed expectations or that you expect everyone to have those expectations of you as opposed to they really do.

It was difficult to admit, or even to find other infertile women who would admit, that the experience of motherhood was not always in line with expectations. In an effort to reassure his wife, one adoptive father explained:

> I think other women probably have the same feelings. . . . They feel like "How can I feel like this? I've longed for this for so long, how can I have these feelings?" So I think they just kind of push them aside or keep them bottled up or keep them separate somewhere, or maybe acknowledge them and don't tell anybody because . . . they get the same thing like you were saying. "No, oh, how can you do that? You waited so long and now you've got what you wanted and you don't like it."

In a sense, infertile mothers wondered how it was possible to feel the same ambivalence toward motherhood that their fertile counterparts often felt; was it possible that they neither really wanted nor ought to be mothers? Remarking on all of the "myths" associated with motherhood, this man's wife was somewhat ashamed to admit her frustrations with her child and said that she had even "twisted things around" to prove what a "bad mother" she was. She also described the "big anticlimax" Mother's Day turned out to be for her. As she recalled:

> I thought that Mother's Day would be from sunup to sundown—I would be revered, honored, and showered with gifts and attention all day [laughs], and I wasn't . . . I had the scenario . . . to go out to brunch. . . . It never occurred to me that with a baby, you probably don't go out to brunch . . . I had thought that I would get flowers and presents and taken out to brunch with my wonderfully behaved child. But we didn't do that. . . . It was kind of like a normal day. . . . It was sort of like for all these years, I held Mother's Day up to be this fantastic day of wonder and it was like every other day almost.

No matter how much they had suffered in the pursuit of a child, most infertile couples proclaimed that it had all been worth it, and many of them had already forgotten many of the details of their struggle soon after their child's arrival home. Infertile couples often experienced a kind of therapeutic amnesia regarding their encounter with infertility, feeling as though it was someone else who had been affected. Infertility was a "bad dream" now that they had their "dream child." What had once seemed so long and so hard now seemed shorter and easier; many felt it was over before they knew it. One woman, who only several months earlier had recalled the hardships of two in vitro fertilization attempts, wondered after the birth of her child, how hard could it have been? Some couples even lauded infertility for bringing them closer together and for serving purposes other than becoming parents to the child they had. For example, one woman suggested that perhaps the fertility tests she had undergone had been necessary to reveal a potentially serious but as yet symptomless gynecological problem. Couples were also pleased and even amazed about what a "good cure" their child was for the "pain and unhappiness" of infertility. The child made infertility "go away" or, at the very least, seem not to have been so bad.

Although most couples found it relatively easy to see their newly arrived children as curative outcomes and even as explanations for their infertility and, therefore, to put the hardships of infertility behind them, not all couples were comfortable reevaluating their past suffering in terms of the joy of finally having a child. For these couples, the child, although loved and wanted, neither had made the struggle "worth it" nor had justified it: having the child was not sufficient for them to relinquish their sorrow and even anger at having had to struggle at all to have a child. One woman who adopted a baby explained:

> People have continued to say, "Oh now, you know, it was worth all the wait," or "She was worth the wait." And my absolute first reaction is defensive. To me, she doesn't have anything to do with the wait. They're very separate entities. The wait was horrible. She, of course, is wonderful. . . . I can't put the two together in my mind yet. Maybe I will one day and maybe I'll look back at this and think, "Oh, God, were you ever callous by not instantly saying that, of course, she was worth the wait. She was worth everything." The wait is what we're used to and she's not what we're used to. And the wait is what we lived.

Her husband agreed that he too could not "assimilate" the two concepts of "daughter" and "worth it." As he further explained:

> I think it just is illogical because that's like saying two babies are twice as good as one. That's not true. . . . When people would say that

she was worth the wait, it made—it kind of slighted what we went through during the wait—like well, the wait was really okay because you got what you want.

This couple believed that it was a "disservice" to everything they had gone through to "dismiss it" so easily by saying "it's all worth it." After all, other infertile people had waited considerably less time than the almost two years they had waited for their baby, and normally fertile people did not have to struggle to conceive for five years. Saying it all was worth it was, to them, like saying that they had to go through all of that to get their baby. Although their baby removed some of the hurtfulness of infertility, the wife could not as yet, or maybe never, fully eradicate its scars.

Another adoptive father found his child "worth it" but did not want to think that God had been so "cruel" as to make them suffer as they had; he preferred to view their struggles as more random. Yet another adoptive father pointed out the similarity in the aftermaths of both a war and a disease like infertility that carried "stigma." As he observed:

> I don't ever want to forget Vietnam. I don't want ever to forget how hard it is for prospective parents to get their child and how hard it is for infertile couples to be going through adoption or going through infertility or both. . . . I'm not saying that I want to rake myself over the coals, I'm just saying that I feel very strongly about those two issues and I don't want to forget it.

For these people, dismissing a traumatic event like infertility too readily would be trivializing what they had survived; for the one father, making infertility part of some divine plan diminished God. In the end, as one adoptive father observed, "We know what it's like and, I mean, we've been there and in some ways, we are always going to be there. I mean, infertility is not something for the most part that goes away."

Projecting Reproductive Futures

Among the most important factors impeding their comeback work were the uncertainty and ambivalence couples had about having additional children. Even if an infertile couple who had a child no longer had to "worry" about getting one, they still had to "worry" about whether they needed birth control; whether, approaching or in their early forties, they would be able to conceive or adopt another child; and whether they even wanted to begin the struggle all over again. Couples with frozen embryos in storage also had to make decisions about their ultimate disposition. In the interests of "biographical recasting" (Corbin and Strauss, 1987, p. 276), couples had to worry about whether they were still infertile and whether they wanted to begin again the infertile round of life.

As I have previously indicated, infertile individuals struggling to conceive, achieving pregnancy, or waiting to adopt a child came to various conclusions about their fertility status, viewing the inability to have a child as a permanent condition, pregnancy and/or parenthood as cures, or themselves as always having been basically fertile. Couples were unsure if they were cured of infertility, if they were essentially fertile or chronically infertile, or, as one woman put it, if they were "in remission."

Contributing to the tentativeness of the conclusions couples reached about their fertility status was the sometimes conflicting advice they received from physicians, friends, and acquaintances, who saw them as alternatively infertile or even hyperfertile, especially if they had delivered twins or triplets. Couples described situations where physicians advised them to contracept just in case or, alternatively, found couples foolish for wanting to do so, and where friends advised them of women's heightened fertility after both delivering or adopting infants. One woman remarked after adopting her child, "Sometimes it comes to my mind that—what a lot of people have said—they say, 'Once you get your baby, you're going to get pregnant.' And so that always sticks in my mind, every once in awhile." Although they generally believed that the probabilities of their conceiving spontaneously were low, infertile couples nevertheless knew of cases where pregnancy had occurred after adoption or where spontaneous pregnancy had occurred after technically assisted pregnancy. That what infertile couples had always resisted as myths or "tales" of infertility, namely, spontaneous conceptions, could themselves be facts (even if not statistically significant ones) served to increase the uncertainty some couples had about their reproductive futures.

Of twenty-five infertile and childbearing couples who provided such information, only seven couples were using or planned to use a form of contraception three months after delivery on the chance they could become spontaneously pregnant, primarily to space their children and, less often, because they wanted no more children. The other childbearing and adopting couples believed it was unnecessary to contracept and/or would not have minded achieving pregnancy, even if soon after the arrival of their first child. (One adoptive mother who was infertile by prescription, or advised not to conceive for health reasons, was contracepting. She anticipated that in a few years, a treatment for her medical condition might permit her to try to have a biological child.) Some women believed that they were knowledgeable enough about their cycles to avoid an unintended pregnancy, or avoided using contraception after the delivery of their babies because they believed that birth control—either intrauterine devices or oral contraceptives—had caused their infertility. For some couples who believed that they were fertile postdelivery (either because they believed pregnancy had cured them or because they had never viewed themselves as infertile), using contraception after an encounter with infertility would be like "looking a gift horse in the mouth" if another child was wanted or, at the very least, using contraception seemed odd to them.

Having successfully delivered or adopted a child, couples typically felt "less pressured about the whole reproductive cycle" and less "desperate" for a child. Resurrecting another myth of infertility—that trying too hard for a child can impede conception—some couples suggested that, whereas they had previously conceived "out of desperation," they might the next time have a baby conceived in liberty and be free of those desperate feelings they came to believe both interfered with but had ultimately led to conception. In addition, as one man stated after delivery of his baby conceived with donor sperm, "we have a baby and we know how to go about getting another one when we are ready." Although couples remained uncertain that the technique or method for getting a child that had worked in the past would work in the future, they, nevertheless, typically felt they knew better where to begin the process the next time around.

Yet couples typically also wanted to avoid falling into the emotional trap of thinking about getting pregnant all the time. One woman admitted that she never wanted to get as "tunnel-visioned" as she had been in her pursuit of a child. In fact, some women were amazed that they no longer knew or cared what phase of their menstrual cycles they were in or that they could hope not to get pregnant. Recalling an incident where she had thought she might be pregnant soon after adopting a child, one woman was both amazed and pleased that the achievement of pregnancy was no longer so important to her. She wanted to avoid "saddling [her adopted baby] with the most typical cliché in the world": pregnancy after adoption. She remembered feeling like she was having "mini strokes" in her brain when both she and her husband wanted her to get her period after years of struggling not to get it. As she put it, "Wait a minute! You hope I get my period? I hope I get my period? What's going on here?" Another adoptive mother also "hoped" she would not get pregnant. As she explained:

> I don't want to be pregnant. I don't want another baby. . . . People will act like, "Well now you can get pregnant and have your own baby." He's my baby. He's as much mine as if I had given birth to him. And I don't have to get pregnant to feel fulfilled anymore. I am fulfilled. But I don't want to get pregnant. He's everything we want.

For these women, achieving pregnancy now would represent a quasi-betrayal of the child they had adopted.

Other couples also wanted to avoid the "I want syndrome" one man described as characterizing infertility and, instead, to enjoy and to attend to the baby they had. Wanting to give both conceptive technology and her baby their proper due, one woman felt "terrible" saying she did not want to do in vitro fertilization again after it had worked in the very first cycle and given her a son. But, as she explained:

> I want to enjoy him. I want to nurse him without having to think I have to stop nursing because I'm trying to get pregnant. I wanted to have this baby . . . I don't want to be so busy trying just to get pregnant. I don't want to spend my whole life just trying to get pregnant, for heaven's sake.

This woman delayed her postdelivery gynecological appointment in order to avoid having to decide about a future pregnancy.

Significantly, couples felt "selfish" or "guilty" both for wanting another child and, less often, for not wanting to undergo treatments again that had worked for them. One man remarked that he did not feel burdened to have a second child. He added, "It's almost kind of like, well—this is a gift. You don't ask for two of them." While infertile couples considered the first child a "necessity," they generally considered any additional child to be a "luxury." One woman who conceived her daughter with a fertility drug explained:

> I would love to have other children, but if I can't, I'm totally satisfied with her. I would love to have another one, but I don't think I would be as disappointed as if I had never had any. Like one isn't really enough, but she's filled in my void. She's satisfied my void.

Moreover, couples considered themselves "lucky" to have succeeded in having the "miracle" children they had. Two weeks after the birth of a baby conceived by in vitro fertilization, one woman expressed a distinctive admixture of survivor guilt, superstition, and lack of entitlement. As she explained:

> When I had the extra eggs and I found out that I was pregnant . . . the first thing that went through my mind [was] how much that would mean to some [other woman] to be able to have these eggs, these fertilized eggs. [I know this woman who] has been through the program twice and produced eggs and they can't get to them. And I felt like it was enough to ask for one miracle—to ask for two was really pushing. Not pushing it, but like it was not something that you should even do. Because you get lucky enough to get a chance at something and you have some eggs left over, then maybe you should let somebody else have a chance for a baby. Maybe they would be happy with just one baby too. So we really haven't decided what we want to do about that. I think that at first, [her husband] didn't like that idea. He thought that we would just try it again. The whole time, I felt like maybe they don't really belong to me and I wouldn't mind giving them away. I just wouldn't want to know the person who got them. . . . It would be our child. But there's no guarantee that they would work for them and there's no guarantee that when we thawed the embryo out, that they would work for me.

Several couples made a special point of lauding the techniques without which they believed they would never have had a baby. A few childbearing couples intimated that it was only after having delivered their babies that they fully recognized the extent to which they shared ownership of their biomedically produced babies with their doctors and how "lucky" they had been to succeed where most couples typically failed. One man, whose wife had conceived by in vitro fertilization, remarked how a doctor they hardly knew commented on all the attention and queries about their baby they were getting in the hospital: "I did not really realize that this is not *your* [emphasis added] baby." Other couples conceiving by this method told stories of consenting or refusing to participate in media coverage of their pregnancies and babies. Emphasizing the rarity of babies born by in vitro techniques, one woman recalled:

[My] doctor kind of surprised me because we were standing there talking and he said, "Well, do you realize just how incredibly lucky you are?" And it was like he was saying more incredibly lucky than they had lead us to believe before we did the procedure.

In fact, this woman discovered after the birth of her child that she had been the first to conceive by the medical protocol used in her case. These couples could never forget how "lucky" they were even to have one child and were, at times, reluctant to tempt fate by trying for another. They also suggested how feeling lucky could interfere with owning both the children and the spare embryos produced with biomedical assistance.

In projecting a future no longer dominated by infertility, couples recognized how much of their married lives had already been devoted to it. One couple found it "odd" not to be working on getting a child when it had been the "total focus" of their marriage. One man, three months after the delivery of his child, remarked that it was the first time that he and his wife were not worrying about having a baby. He said, "It's taken awhile to get used to that." Couples enjoyed the "vacation from infertility" that their newly achieved parenthood had permitted them to take. Yet as one woman observed:

It's kinda scary . . . 'cause we had something to focus on for the last almost four years. And it kept us together real well. I mean we had something to focus on together. Now hopefully, [the baby] will take that place, but who knows? And it's kinda scary to think about now, what's gonna be the glue?

Importantly, couples had to "arrive at a biographical scheme" (Corbin and Strauss, 1987, p. 276) for their lives together that did not have infertility as its focal point.

Legacy

For the couples we interviewed, the legacy of infertility was more or less bitter and sweet. When we left them, they were happy to have survived their ordeal, proud of both their accomplishments and children, and ready to have a normal life again. For couples contemplating having another child, for couples conceiving babies with donor gametes, and for adopting couples, infertility will likely make a "cameo appearance" (Glazer, 1990, p. ix), if not again have a starring role. These couples will likely confront the issue of infertility again when they tell or (in the case of children conceived with donor sperm) decide not to tell their children about their origins, when they approach the end of their reproductive years, and, as Barbara Menning suggested in the opening lines to this chapter, when they least expect it.

In the hospital soon after the delivery of her baby, one of the women I interviewed recalled:

> I started thinking about, and in the last week I've thought about—in fact, it was almost like a movie in my head and it really made me cry. Thinking about the last year, and sort of doing the Pergonal and the insemination and the ultrasounds and seeing the doctor when he came in and told us we were pregnant . . . and the amnio . . . to see if she was okay. . . . It was like I was flashing through all these things that we've been through. . . . Just thinking about all the things really chokes me up because it was such an odyssey. This whole thing was such an incredible odyssey.

14. Intensive Care

Caring is always specific and relational. (Benner and Wrubel, 1989, p. 3)

Over a decade since the rediscovery of infertility as a health and social problem, and despite an ever expanding literature on the ethical, legal, and social implications of new advancements and possibilities in reproductive and parenting partnerships, the question still remains of how to care for infertile people. Both the utopian and dystopian possibilities of contemporary solutions to infertility for society, the family, women, and for embryos/children have been projected. Ethicists, lawyers, theologians, clinicians, social scientists, and social critics have pondered the (il)legitimacy of infertility as a medical problem and of the "brave new babies" produced "between strangers" (Andrews, 1989), and they have considered the (un)naturalness, (im)morality, and (il)legality of noncoital and artificial techniques for reproduction (Blank, 1984, 1990; Chadwick, 1987; Edwards, 1991; Elias and Annas, 1986; Hollinger, 1985; Kass, 1971, 1972, 1979; Macklin, 1991; Overall, 1987; Ramsey, 1972; Rodin and Collins, 1991; Somerville, 1982; Walters and Singer, 1982; Zaner, 1984). The use of donor gametes and surrogate wombs, in particular, has been the subject of considerable controversy, raising issues about the well-being of and nature of the relationships among donors, recipients, and the children produced. Such relationships have been characterized as occupying different points on a continuum between freedom and coercion and have been described in terms of altruistic gift-giving, sacrificial surrender, and contracted service (Despreaux, 1989; Keane, 1981; Novaes, 1989; Raymond, 1990). Other issues frequently raised in relation to the new reproductive and parenting arrangements include the problems of "genealogical bewilderment" (Humphrey and Humphrey, 1986; Sants, 1964), anonymity, and secrecy in situations where there is no biological tie between parent and child (Baran and Pannor, 1989; Clamar, 1989; Rowland, 1985).

Although such discussions illuminate the complex sociocultural context for contemporary practice with infertile couples, they do not necessarily provide direction for everyday practice. By their emphasis on what might be and ought to be, they fail to address the what is—now. By their emphasis on the "possibility of a principled justification for particular actions," they are less attentive to the "concrete experiences of particular individuals" (Lauritzen, 1991, p. 58). If present in these debates at all, the plight of infertile people is often either misrepresented because of stereotypical notions of infertility or politicized in the service of promoting some ideological agenda. The proponents of these agendas seem to care less for infertile couples per se than they care about some project or principle, such as the autonomy of women, the personhood of embryos, the perfectability of the species, or the immorality of secrecy. Although essential to our understanding of possible futures, these discussions often deflect attention away from and even distort the needs of the very people now most directly involved in the reproductive acts critics and futurists seek to interpret and either to laud or protest. Practitioners (principally nurses and physicians but also caseworkers and other professional caregivers) cannot fail to understand these larger social issues, but they can also not afford to be diverted from the personal and present issues of the people in their care. Practitioners often find themselves caught between infertile couples' desire for advice concerning what to do and society's admonitions concerning what should be done.

Although presented in a different context, Tronto's (1989) distinction between caring for and caring about is a useful one in capturing a central dilemma of practice, namely, how to engage persons in the concreteness and immediacy of their present circumstances while engaging the larger social conditions influencing them. How do practitioners care about the issues and problems raised by infertility and care for infertile people? How do they move "upstream"—to take action for social change—while working "downstream" at the level of the individual before them (Butterfield, 1990)? Although the American health care emphasis on the individual as the locus of disease and the target for intervention and change has been criticized for its failure to consider the larger sociocultural factors that constrain individual action and often preclude health and well-being (Williams, D., 1989), caring for must necessarily be individualistic. Caring for implies attending to the needs and circumstances of particular people on the basis of knowledge "completely peculiar to the particular person being cared for" (Tronto, 1989, p. 177). Indeed, such intimate knowledge is both precondition and consequence of caring for (Benner, 1988).

Impediments to Caring for Infertile People

Nurse and physician caregivers especially are challenged in their efforts to care for infertile people because of certain cultural impediments relating to infertility itself and arising from the entrenched and engendered dichotomy between care and cure. In previous chapters, I have described such cultural imperatives as the primacy of the blood tie, the mandate to have children of one's own, and the dependency on physicians and medical technology for the resolution of problems that may serve to constrain caregiving in infertility practice.

There is also the question of what is or what ought to be treated in infertility practice: the biological incapacity to reproduce, or inability to have a child of one's own; the social condition of childlessness; or the social construction of infertility and/or childlessness as disabilities or conditions mandating treatment? These different conceptualizations of the problem(s) engendered by infertility involve very different objectives, necessitate very different courses of action, and necessarily involve very different targets of intervention (Thomas, 1984). For example, when infertility is conceived medically, body parts and processes are targeted for exchange and therapy in order to induce pregnancy or to produce a genetically or gestationally related child. When infertility is conceived socially, the feelings and behaviors of couples are targeted for change to help them become parents to "someone else's" child. When infertility is conceived as a constructed reality, societal attitudes and behaviors concerning gender roles, parenting, and family are targeted for change to make infertility and/or childlessness less of a social handicap.

Other impediments to caring for infertile couples include the (*a*) cultural primacy of cure over care; (*b*) tendency to objectify the infertile people cared for; and (*c*) existence of many candidates in infertility practice who can be valid recipients of care.

CARE AND CURE
A prevailing dichotomy in infertility practice is the culturally engendered distinction that has long existed between caring and curing. To grossly oversimplify complex sociohistorical processes, curing is the more socially visible and valued health service activity by virtue of its association with (male) physicians and high-tech treatments; caring is the less visible and less valued activity by virtue of its association with (female) nurses and low-tech ministrations (Colliere, 1986). While curing is presumably based in the objectivity of science and acquired as a skill only after years of education

and practice, caring is based in the subjectivity of the arts all females presumably possess by nature. While the symbol of curing is technology, the symbol of caring is the female hand. Moreover, although caring is something that is wanted, resources (time and money) are allotted to caring only when caring does not interfere with curing or when no cure is available (Gadow, 1983b).

In contemporary infertility therapeutics, the primacy of curing remains unchallenged as it does in other domains of practice and despite the fact that medical therapies for infertility rarely eradicate or even ameliorate any dysfunction; treated couples typically remain just as incapable of reproduction after therapy as before it. Furthermore, as I have noted previously, neither pregnancy nor a baby necessarily cures emotional infertility.

Couples are, nevertheless, said to be cured when pregnancy is induced, and only the induction of pregnancy and the production of a baby are viewed as cures; *having* to resort to adoption or *having* to resign oneself to childlessness are viewed as failures to cure. In the resolution of infertility, as with virtually every other health or social problem that has become medicalized, success and failure are conceived as mutually exclusive and polar opposites, and they are defined in terms of technical cure.

The primacy of technical cure challenges both couples and their caregivers not to equate abandoning medical therapies with abandoning cure. As apparent in the descriptions of the women and couples in my studies and in the findings of other researchers, both caregivers and their patients may become heavily invested in technical cure. Caregivers' investments in technical cure may make it difficult for couples to invest in other options. Kopitzke and her colleagues (1991) found that couples experienced the decision to begin the adoption process as significantly less stressful than did their caregivers. Some of the couples we interviewed described the public and even media event made of successes—their pregnancies and deliveries—and physicians' difficulties with failures. As one woman remarked, physicians often had problems with infertile people because they reminded physicians of failure. Indeed, programs for assisted reproduction have the dubious distinction of being among those medical programs where failure often exceeds success and where practitioners must develop strategies to deal with recurring failure (Anderson et al., 1989; Appleton, 1990).

THE OBJECTIFICATION OF THE CARED-FOR

A second impediment to care in infertility practice is the inevitable objectification of infertile people (especially women, who typically undergo medical regimens) that is reinforced by technology. Gadow (1984) proposed that the dehumanization often attributed to technology is related to the otherness human beings experience in relation with entities that resist integration into the personal sphere. Technology is not readily assimilated into the individuality of human life because it seems to have a life of its own. In addition, it asserts its otherness because other people are required to deploy, administer, and manage complex technologies.

Conceptive techniques transform human body parts (eggs, sperm, uteri) into medical and marketable products; the body is a "mosaic of detachable pieces" (Braidotti, 1989, p. 152). Body processes, such as ovulation, insemination, and fertilization, become medical acts. As fungible medical/technical goods, a woman's body or an egg or sperm no longer belong to any particular self nor even to any particular time as children are conceived with eggs and sperm previously donated and frozen in time.[1] Experiences such as conception, pregnancy, and childbirth, which are typically lived as flowing and integrated entities, become fragmented into component parts. It is thus an inherent property of reproductive technology that it anatomizes experience and separates self from body. The body is simply the "sum of its organic parts" as opposed to "the threshold for the transcendence of the subject" (Braidotti, 1989, p. 151).

By virtue of this property, conceptive technology perpetuates the long-standing Western conceptualization of the body as reparable machine. Braidotti (1989, p. 149) observed that the "elementary principle of prosthesis animates the whole technological universe." Klawiter (1990) even described reproductive technology as "anti-body" in that it is directed toward the "elimination of the bodily content of existence" (pp. 84–85). In a related vein, Steinberg (1990, p. 75) described the "erasure" of women as whole beings and the "recombination" of their body parts in both the process and the representation of in vitro fertilization. As Gadow (1984) remarked, technology does not itself cause the objectification of the recipient of care, but rather it makes manifest the already existing paradigm of care in which human beings—their bodies and selves—have become objects for scientific theorizing and technical manipulation. Caregivers espousing holistic frameworks for care, therefore, have to work to counter this fragmenting and antiholistic property of technology, a property that is neither necessarily good nor bad, but rather simply itself.

THE MULTIPLE CANDIDATES FOR THE ONE CARED-FOR
A third impediment to care is the dilemma of deciding who the cared-for is and ought to be. In infertility practice, the couple, as opposed to the

individual, is generally conceived to be the one cared-for, as clinicians are repeatedly enjoined to treat the couple as a unit. Yet, like the apparently benign and enlightened idea of the family or the community as patient or client, the idea of the couple as the unit of care can serve to mask the concrete circumstances of the two very different and differently socially positioned individuals who constitute the couple.

By virtue of gender roles and expectations, women carry the greater emotional and social burden of being infertile; by virtue of the largely gynecological nature of infertility therapeutics, women carry the far greater burden in therapy; by virtue of the conventional division of labor in the family, women also carry the greater burden of parenting. These bio-culturally engendered obligations may, accordingly, entitle women to primary status as cared-for whenever conflicts of needs and interests arise. Researchers have emphasized the often conflicting interests that exist between women and men regarding infertility and other issues in the domain of marriage and family that may result in women taking actions against their own good in order to preserve relationships (Lorber 1987, 1989; Thorne and Yalom, 1982).

The "rhetoric of equivalence" (Steinberg, 1990, p. 92) in the conceptualization of infertility as a couple's problem has implications for women similar to the conceptualization of domestic violence as a family problem. Women have traditionally been obliged to keep the family together even at their own mortal expense, and the idea of family deflects attention away from the fact that certain family members are much more likely to be victims of violence while others are much more likely to be perpetrators (Breines and Gordon, 1983). Conceiving the patient as more-than-one may serve in theory only to equalize the unequal relationships of power that actually exist among the individuals who compose the unit of care. Although the couple as unit of care may be appropriate in most cases, there are enough cases in infertility practice where this may be neither an appropriate nor healthful orientation.

Also contributing to the problem of identifying the appropriate unit of care are the many and differently positioned individuals now entering into reproductive and parenting partnerships. Donors of reproductive parts and services and the recipients of these parts and services may have interests that diverge, especially along class lines (Aronowitz and Feldschuh, 1989; Daniels, 1988; Despreaux, 1989; Fidell, 1989). Birthparents relinquishing their children for adoption have interests and needs that are different from couples seeking to adopt (Brodzinsky, 1990; Deykin, Campbell, & Patti, 1984; Millen and Roll, 1985; Modell, 1986; Sorosky, Baran, and

Pannor, 1984). And, the children involved in these transactions may have interests and needs different from or even at odds with their parents.

In an infertility service in which donors are recruited to provide the resources that permit certain procedures to be done, the emphasis is typically on the infertile recipient and less on the donor. It may be a dubious practice at best to have the same caregivers who are charged with the care of women seeking to donate their eggs care also for the woman seeking those eggs to achieve pregnancy. In adoption services, the focus may waver between serving the interests of infertile people who pay for adoption services and the children who must be placed. Caseworkers are obliged both to evaluate couples for their fitness to parent and to provide a climate for couples to authentically express their feelings about their infertility and adoption; yet such authentic expression can operate against couples in the evaluation process.

Although practitioners seek to do no harm to any of the parties involved in the services they provide, they tend to have a primary identification with one party over another in transactions in which someone's loss may unfortunately be someone else's gain. By virtue of who they practice with—infertile people, birthparents, donors, surrogates, children, women, men—practitioners will likely develop a fellow-feeling for and an identification with one party over the other. Indeed, this fellow-feeling seems necessary for caregivers to properly "care-for" (Gadow, 1983a; Scheler, 1970).[2]

A Framework for Care

Practice with infertile couples requires a philosophy of care that can address the distinctive dilemmas that infertility engenders in everyday practice. Caring—as a human trait, moral imperative, affective state, interpersonal interaction, and therapeutic intervention—has been described as the essence of nursing practice (Morse et al., 1991), and so, as a nurse, I draw from philosophies of care espoused in the literature of my profession. Although nurses are not the only individuals concerned with care and nursing cannot claim to be the only caring profession, nursing can rightfully claim to be the paradigmatic public caring practice in Western cultures (just as mothering is the paradigmatic caring practice in the private sphere) (Benner, 1988). The problematic dichotomy between care and cure is more poignantly felt by nurses than other caregivers because of their social position "in the middle": "in between" patient, family, physician, and health care bureaucracy (Bishop and Scudder, 1987; Engelhardt, 1983; Gadow, 1988). Nurses are "ordered to care" in a society that, nevertheless, devalues caring (Reverby, 1987). Nurses and infertile people share the dilemmas of entrenched dichotomy and social marginality.

One of the most beautifully articulated orientations to care is Sally Gadow's (1983a) description of "existential advocacy" as the philosophical foundation of nursing. I interpret existential advocacy necessarily to involve the concrete immediacy and embodied intimacy of attending to the one in one's care. Gadow emphasized the interplay between the unique and "entire self" of the caregiver and that of the cared for that distinguishes existential advocacy from paternalism and consumer advocacy. Unlike paternalistic care, existential advocacy does not involve violating persons' known wishes either for their own good or simply to uphold a moral rule. Unlike consumer advocacy, existential advocacy does not appeal to the principles of autonomy, freedom, and informed consent to justify abandoning people to make important decisions by themselves. For Gadow, existential advocacy involves assisting people to make decisions that are truly self-determined rather than simply not determined by others; it also involves transcending the false dichotomy that persists between the personal and the professional and reconciling the unique—the "I" of the patient—with the typical—the categorizations of science. Caregivers and the cared-for enter a "covenant of care" involving the mutual discovery of truth and the alleviation of vulnerability (Cooper, 1988; Gadow, 1988).

FINDING THE TRUTH
One of the most problematic issues in infertility practice is determining the "truth in information." As a legal mandate, informed consent can only be given by persons who have been provided with the information necessary to make decisions about whether to undergo a procedure and who are both competent and free to make decisions (Jameton, 1984). Threatening the capacity, voluntarism, and autonomy of informed consent for infertility therapeutics are the vulnerability of infertile people to the exploitation of their desire for children, the frequent misrepresentation of the effectiveness of infertility therapeutics, and the coercive (pronatalist, technologically dependent) sociocultural milieu for decision making (Blackwell et al., 1987; Corea, 1985; Soules, 1985). In addition, since many of the short and most of the long-term medical and psychosocial consequences of undergoing new medical therapies for infertility and of entering the new reproductive partnerships remain unexplored, caregivers remain hard-pressed to state what all of the risks of these options are.

Conventional notions of truth in information are based on the assumption that the practitioner (most typically the physician) gives the facts to the cared-for from whom informed consent is then obtained and on the assumption that truth exists independently of meaning and context. Informed consent and the truth-telling integral to it are here conceived as commodities in an exchange between an all-knowing provider and an as yet uninformed receiver. Practitioners are enjoined to provide the most truthful information, or the objective and, if possible, quantifiable facts concerning the benefits and risks of, as well as alternatives to, courses of action as required by law and the ethical standards of health care practice.

Yet, in infertility therapeutics, the putative facts are as open to interpretation as infertility is itself an open-ended condition. For example, couples can be informed of the probabilities (what is likely) and possibilities (what is conceivable) of the success, failure, and risk associated with a course of action. In the case of medical treatment options for infertility, these probabilities and possibilities are necessarily based on some prior accounting of outcomes in other infertile people who may be more or less similar to (in terms of such factors as diagnosis, severity of disease, duration of infertility, and age) the couples receiving this information. Despite the wide variations and rapidly changing protocols in implementing any one therapy, such accountings may be based either on outcomes in categories of therapies (such as ovulation induction and in vitro fertilization) or on outcomes within specific variants of a therapy (such as specified dosages of particular drugs and a specific duration and time for their use to induce ovulation). Physicians may cite average chemical or clinical pregnancy or live delivery rates drawn from syntheses of national or international data on outcomes in a therapeutic category, or they may cite averages of these different rates obtained from data from their own practices or from the institutional setting in which couples will actually undergo therapy.

A couple attending a specific hospital program may, accordingly, be informed of a national live delivery rate of fourteen percent for in vitro fertilization when this rate has yet to be achieved by that hospital's particular program. One group of clinicians (Blackwell et al., 1987) reported that one half of the in vitro fertilization programs in this country had produced no pregnancies; more recently, Medical Research International (1992) reported that over one half of the clinics reporting in vitro fertilization outcomes had produced less than ten pregnancies. Pregnancy rates can be based on all of the women attempting a therapeutic protocol (which tends to deflate these rates) or on only those women who succeed in reaching certain steps in a regimen (which tends to inflate rates) (Bonnicksen, 1988).

In addition, when the outcome of a therapy is presented as either succeeding fifteen percent of the time or failing eighty-five percent of the time, couples are provided with what amounts to the same fact but with what has different interpretive possibilities.

Providing infertile couples with information is hardly the objective fact-giving mission it is often presented as being by experts advising the importance of educating, preparing, and counseling these couples. Indeed, it is more accurately conceptualized as a fact-choosing mission in which practitioners select what truths to tell—what information will be given and how it will be presented.

Adding to the inevitable subjectivity of informed consent is the fact that practitioners in medical treatment programs are less likely to know about and, therefore, to inform couples of alternatives to medical therapy. Two important impediments to pursuing adoption are, for example, not knowing how to begin the process and believing that it is a process that can be easily pursued. One of the women in my studies was advised by her physician to "look in the yellow pages" when she inquired about adoption. The often-cited counsel that "you can always adopt" implies an ease of access and outcome that simply does not exist. Moreover, the longer couples delay pursuing adoption, the more likely they are to reach the age limit beyond which they will no longer be accepted by most agencies.

Jameton (1984) remarked that the lack of in-hospital (or other than physician-centered) alternatives for patients to choose from in seeking counsel for infertility is the "central flaw" of the informed consent process. While informed consent legally mandates a comprehensive discussion of options available, it does not require that the practitioner providing information act in any way to make all options available. According to Jameton, informed consent typically involves "talk about autonomy, not autonomy itself" (p. 189).

Critics of medical solutions to infertility have suggested that informed consent typically involves rhetoric about free choice and truth when coercion and deception actually prevail (Corea, 1985; Spallone and Steinberg, 1987). By virtue of their socialization and work, physicians especially are both psychologically and financially invested in medical solutions to infertility. In the informed consent interaction, they can only offer information about the options they have to offer. Physicians are also challenged as the only practitioners legally privileged and responsible for obtaining informed consent to overcome their typical lack of training and expertise in establishing the kind of interaction necessary to achieve informed consent. By virtue of their enthusiasm for medical therapy, physicians may be least capable of fulfilling either the legal requirement of informed consent or the moral imperative of informed decision making. Hollinger (1985) differentiated the goal of informed consent, to protect the practitioner from liability, from informed decision making, to protect the patients' pursuit of authentic self-determination.

The possibilities for withholding and distorting information are great in infertility practice as infertility has increasingly become big business for physicians, lawyers, and other baby brokers. Yet, there also exist possibilities for giving too much or poorly timed information. Gadow (1983b) has argued that disclosing information solely in the interests of the principle of patient autonomy can also undermine it; indeed, such truth telling can be as paternalistic as deception and outright lying when it involves reifying truth or arming patients with information only to abandon them to make their own decisions. Gadow (1983b, p. 37) observed, "When patients are treated with information for its therapeutic value, irrespective of their wishes, they are addressed as objects, as clearly as when other treatment is administered without their consent." Ethicist Leah Curtin (1979, p. 6) also described the "tyranny of information" some patients are subjected to to achieve a putative informed consent. This kind of truth telling objectifies both truth and the persons to whom it is offered. Moreover, it fails to consider the importance of appraising, by active listening, when couples are ready to receive certain components of information. Ethicist William May (1984, p. 257) emphasized the particular importance to the practitioner of "prudence" and "discretion" in telling the truth. Without these "virtues," a practitioner may tell the truth, and yet not "wholly serve the truth" in the telling (p. 258).

To counter the rather dispassionate view of truth as a thing given by an authoritative practitioner to a supplicant patient, Gadow (1983b, p. 38) proposed a view of truth as

> the most comprehensive and most personally meaningful interpretation of the situation possible, encompassing subjective as well as objective realities, idiosyncratic as well as statistical tendencies, emotional as well as intellectual responses.

Gadow's truth is not independent of persons, time, and circumstances, but rather it is situationally dependent and co- and reconstituted by the caregiver in relation with the cared-for. I have already described how infertile couples variously interpret the statistical probabilities of success in pursuing any one of a number of alternative paths to parenthood in terms of their own idiosyncratic calculus. Other investigators have also found the interpretation of odds and of risk to be highly individualized (Pearn, 1973; Rapp, 1988). The caregiver and the cared-for may not have a "shared meaning" (Faden, 1991, p. 37) of benefit and risk, and there is not necessarily a shared meaning of benefit and risk among infertile couples. If a five percent chance for success with an option is viewed as five times better than no chance by one couple, it will almost certainly be viewed by another couple as virtually equal to no chance at all. A variety of cultural, autobiographical, and temporal factors influences the truths that will be made from information. There is no one nor preexisting truth; truth is not a "finished product" (Gadow, 1983b, p. 38) to be offered, but rather always subject to being remade.

Moreover, informed consent is not reached in a single moment in time, but rather is a process requiring couples to continually appraise their needs and circumstances. Determining what will constitute the truth for any one infertile couple is always an interpretive and moral act and ought to be as relevant as possible to the immediate and concrete circumstances of that couple. Caregivers may better serve couples by assisting them to ask the right questions—of themselves and of their caregivers—rather than by providing them with the putative answers.

Helping people to ask the right questions involves helping them to clarify what they want and value. Gadow (1983a) observed that people can express their individuality and integrity as valuing beings only if the full complexity of their values with all of their contradictions and conflicts is acknowledged and engaged. Yet, as she also noted, this clarity is undermined precisely when it is most needed, such as in cases of personal crisis. In the case of infertility, for example, couples face the necessity of either reframing their desires or reframing their situations according to their existing desires. I have previously described this reframing process as integral to their quest for a child.

The caregiver operating from a philosophical base of existential advocacy helps infertile couples to discern what they want and value and, then, to make decisions that express these reaffirmed or reframed sets of values. This particular expression of caring is especially difficult for caregivers to realize because they inevitably have values and agendas of their own concerning what constitutes appropriate resolutions to infertility.

ALLEVIATING VULNERABILITY

Infertile couples are vulnerable to the losses of esteem, power, and generational continuity associated both with infertility and with available solutions to infertility. Infertility is itself a loss that is not readily acknowledged as one because there is no body to mourn, no repertoire of memories of a physical presence, and no remains to dispose of; infertility is a nonevent in a culture that values "only what is concrete and materially visible" (Savage, 1989, p. xii). In such a cultural milieu, potential parenthood and never-lived childhoods cannot count as losses (cf. Lovell, 1983).

Infertile couples also experience the vulnerability that is an iatrogenic outcome of technical cure. According to Gadow (1988), the very surgical interventions that commonly come to mind as the most dramatic efforts to alleviate vulnerability of disease are the least likely to do so because they achieve their effects through the exercise of power by one person over another; such power inevitably increases vulnerability. For Gadow, all measures directed toward cure require this exercise of power and are the most difficult to include within the realm of care. In infertility practice, power is exercised not only by physician and nurse caregivers, but also by caseworkers overseeing the adoption process who control whether a couple will be accepted or rejected for adoption (Daly, 1989).

Although these disempowering cures for infertility have to be included in the realm of care for them to be considered morally valid and not torture, they can be included only if the powerlessness they create is regarded as a (unwanted) side effect of cure that must itself be treated (Gadow, 1988). Daly (1989), for example, emphasized the importance of empowering couples in the adoption process to offset the loss of control inherent in the process of adoption. For Gadow, it is cure that is morally problematic and that must be justified as a means to care; it is care, not cure, that ought to be the moral end of practice, and only in the context of care can the overpowering of another person and the infliction of pain be justified.

The problem in infertility practice is to expand the notion of therapy to include means other than biomedical conception, to reconceptualize therapy as and redirect it toward healing, and to make care the moral end of practice. This means staying with and being emotionally and physically present to couples and not standing outside the situation or becoming preoccupied with other thoughts or even with someone else's needs (Benner and Wrubel, 1989; Swanson, 1990). One critic of conceptive technology (Williams, L., 1989) admitted to having a "powerful fantasy" in which all of the women professionals around the world involved in in vitro fertilization programs refused to participate any longer in implementing practices that this woman deemed "oppressive" to women. Williams found these women as responsible and guilty as their male counterparts.

Yet, Gadow (1988) proposed that the greatest moral challenge for the nurse is to maintain the "covenantal relationship of caring" in which "no assault is permitted unless it can be redeemed . . . by the immediate, present caring of the nurse who . . . is able to reach across and hold on to patients in their vulnerability." Caregivers who refuse to participate in certain components of infertility practice thus do not care for women but rather abandon them to cure; they intensify couples' vulnerability rather than alleviate it. Moreover, for women practitioners to forego such work will not prevent it from being done by those less inclined and prepared to care and less skilled in caring who have historically been recruited to assist physicians in the achievement of their projects. Such an abandonment presumes that the disempowering and dehumanizing effects of technical cure cannot be countered and, thereby, perversely reempowers technology. As Stanworth (1990, p. 16) asked, "Would it be wise to abandon infertile women to the untender mercies of infertility specialists when a . . . great deal [could be accomplished] to reduce the possible risks to women and their infants?" Would it be wise to deny women the empathic touching that can counter the instrumentality and acquisitiveness of touching in conventional infertility therapeutics and that can reach past the objectivity of treatment to reaffirm women's subjectivity (Gadow, 1984; Wyschogrod, 1981)?

Alleviating vulnerability also means sustaining the faith of couples in their ability to resolve infertility in a healthful and fulfilling way (Swanson, 1990). The very ambiguity of infertility makes such hope work important and problematic. Lange (1978, p. 171) viewed hope as a way of coping with the "uncertainties of the present in anticipation of a . . . more gratifying . . . future." But, as a coping strategy, hope is a "mixed blessing." Lange reminded us that the only thing left in the forbidden box that Pandora opened was hope, and she raised the question whether it was the "antidote" to the world's evils or itself the "greatest evil." Hope can be enabling when it defends against despair (indeed as Werner-Beland [1980, p. 175] proposed, "hope cannot exist except where the temptation to despair also exists") and induces feelings of comfort and control, and it is disabling when it serves only to perpetuate false hopes.

In the case of infertile couples, refusing to give up may not necessarily indicate a nonacceptance of infertility, or an obsession with cure; alternatively, giving up may not necessarily indicate a capitulation to infertility. Drawing from Gabriel Marcel's work on hope, Werner-Beland (1980) conceived acceptance of a condition as a "refusal" to give up. She explained (p. 176); "Hope [is] an acceptance of the problem while also continuing with a forward-looking nonacceptance of all the restrictions that the problem is so apt to imply." By maintaining stereotypical notions of infertile people as accepting or denying their infertility, practitioners in all domains of infertility practice may only disconfirm the specific meaning of and even thwart the hope work of individual couples. For example, Daly (1990) suggested that the common interpretation that couples who are still trying to achieve pregnancy have not sufficiently resolved their infertility to the point of being ready to adopt assumes an often nonexistent linearity to resolution and ignores the different patterns of healthful resolution that infertile couples exhibit. I have also previously described how infertile couples may pursue parallel pregnancy and adoption tracks in order to ensure getting a child. Lange (1978, p. 186) counseled that helping people set "limits on unrealistic expectations" does not entail "kill[ing] hope by imposing the restraints of established experience." Neither does it entail the kind of hope work that merely preserves a medical frame of reference; infertile couples who do not conceive while in medical therapy are not "beyond [medical] treatment" (Perakyla, 1991, p. 427), but rather they are in a position to pursue other treatments.

The Rehabilitation of Care

In a particularly exquisite way, Fox, Aiken, and Messikomer (1990) described the "extraordinary opportunity" to care that AIDS permits nurses who, by virtue of their position in the social order, are often denied the opportunity to implement their vision of care. Because there is unfortunately no cure for AIDS, nurses are freer to call upon and use the entire range of skills that distinctively characterizes nursing. Moreover, in caring for AIDS patients, nurses are freer of the encumbrances of medicine and free not to become absorbed in its technology that often drives a wedge between nurses and patients (p. 230). Nurses have less often to resort to what O'Brien (1989, p. 294) called "guerrilla tactics to force a caring comportment" into health care delivery. Importantly, AIDS is "essentially a nursing disease" (Fahrner, 1988, p. 115).

It appears, however, that the opposite is true in infertility practice. With the advent and continued sensationalization of new conceptive techniques, infertility has become almost exclusively a doctor's disease, with care increasingly subsumed to cure. Perhaps what is needed is to make infertility more like AIDS: not to make it incurable or to deny the progress in medical cure, but rather to liberate it from the encumbrances of cure and to model care for infertile people after programs developed for AIDS patients. The best of these programs conceive of people suffering from AIDS as whole people who are more than their disease but who must live in a world in which they are defined by it and conceive of treatment as comprehensive and multidimensional.

Caring for infertile couples requires not only the rehabilitation of care as the primary moral end of practice but also the revalorization of the narrative of the individual. Descriptions and analyses of infertility and infertile couples have too often failed to tell the individual story; they have presented putatively representative data that fail, however, to be "representative of me" (Viney and Bousfield, 1991, p. 757). Caring for begins with the individual story that both enables the caregiver to have the knowledge that is a precondition for care and empowers the cared-for, thereby also serving to alleviate vulnerability.

Although infertility raises important social issues and highlights important societal failings, infertility is itself ultimately experienced individually (as handicap, as disease, or as no problem at all). Yet caring about the resolution of these social issues and caring for infertile people do not have to be antithetical objectives, but rather can be accomplished from a unifying framework for action that recognizes the very different moral universes in which individuals choose and act. Caring about women as a social group, for example, cannot be achieved by misrepresenting the interests and needs of infertile women or men. Caring about the plight of children without parents cannot be achieved by denigrating the attempts of infertile couples to conceive children. For the practitioner, caring about begins and ends with caring for.

Notes

1. Kovacs and his colleagues (1991) reported the case of three children conceived simultaneously in vitro, two with donor and one with the husband's sperm, but, after freezing, gestated and delivered over a period of five years. Such cases illustrate the new temporal ambiguity associated with new reproductive techniques; are these children triplets or simply siblings?

2. This present work is written from the perspective of the infertile and reflects a fellow-feeling for and identification with them as opposed to other parties, such as gamete donors, birthparents, and children, in infertility practice who are also deserving of such sympathies.

Appendix

Study 1: Women's Experiences of Infertility, 1985–1986

Of the twenty-eight white women in this study, all but one of them were married and all of them had at least a high school education; eighteen of these women had university degrees. The mean age of these women when they were first interviewed was thirty-two (ranging from twenty-five to forty-five). All but five of these women had family incomes over $25,000, and thirteen had incomes over $50,000. Twelve of these women cited female factors contributing to their infertility; one woman, a male factor; and fifteen women, a combination of male and female factors. These women had been trying an average of four years to have a child.

Of the twenty black women in the study, eleven were married and six had not completed high school; only one of them had schooling beyond high school. The mean age of these women at interview was twenty-eight (ranging from nineteen to thirty-six). Only three of these women had family incomes above $25,000, and seven of them had incomes less than $10,000. Nine of these women cited female factors contributing to their infertility; one, a male factor; and the remaining ten women cited no diagnosis. These women had been trying an average of six years to have a child.

We initially selected twenty-two women from private physician practices. These women were interviewed in their homes. These interviews lasted one to two hours, and the women, for the most part, required little direction in telling of their experiences once they were asked to talk about their infertility. We then selected an additional twenty-two women from an infertility clinic in a large public hospital to determine how social background might influence the findings. These women were interviewed in the hospital. These interviews lasted an average of thirty minutes and were more in the mode of question-and-answer; these women generally required prompting to continue. We then interviewed an additional four women and reinterviewed twenty of the private-practice group of women (who were available for this purpose) eight to fourteen months after the first interview to validate findings.

Although I believe we captured something true about the experiences of the women from the clinic, I remain less satisfied with the quality of those interviews than with that of the private practice group. Factors related to differences in class and race between interviewer and respondent and the place of these interviews (the clinic) likely interfered with our getting "private accounts" (West, 1990). Reinharz (1983) suggested that researchers and respondents are not always phenomenologically well-matched.

At the time of the first (or only) interview with the forty-four women recruited in the initial rounds of sampling, twenty-three women had never been pregnant, and the remaining twenty-one women had achieved pregnancy with varying outcomes. Of these twenty-one women, four were pregnant at the time of the interview; sixteen had suffered one or more pregnancy losses; and one woman had undergone an elective abortion. Only twelve of the first forty-four women interviewed had given birth to live infants; one woman had adopted a child prior to becoming pregnant.

By the time of the second interview of twenty of these women, the four women who had been pregnant previously had safely delivered their babies. In the interval between interviews, three additional women had achieved pregnancy; two of these women safely delivered their babies and one suffered an early pregnancy loss. Two women had adopted infants and one woman had undergone a hysterectomy. Three more women were pregnant at the second interview. All of the four women interviewed in the third round had delivered live infants. Overall, we collected 150 hours of interview data over the course of the study.

Study 2: The Transition to Parenthood of Infertile Couples, 1987–1993

Three groups of couples participated in this project: (*a*) infertile couples who were expecting a baby conceived with biomedical assistance or spontaneously; (*b*) infertile couples who were waiting to adopt a child; and (*c*) a comparison group of fertile couples who were expecting a baby conceived spontaneously. We selected recruitment sites that were most likely to have such couples, including private physician practices, hospital infertility clinics, adoption agencies, and infertility and adoption information and support groups. Since couples using these services tended to be white, married, and in a middle-income group, we decided to maintain this homogeneity of race, class, and marital status in our comparison group and sought expectant couples with these same background characteristics but with no history of fertility problems. In contrast, we sought to maximize the variability in fertility status by recruiting couples with a range of fertility and parenting experiences. Accordingly, the couples who participated were demographically similar to couples typically seeking medical services for infertility (U.S. Congress, Office of Technology Assessment, 1988; Henshaw and Orr, 1987; Hirsch and Mosher, 1987) or adopting unrelated children (Bachrach, 1986; Bachrach et al., 1990; Bonham, 1977; Poston and Cullen, 1986).

We contacted couples at comparable points in time in their transition to parenthood. Childbearing (both fertile and infertile) couples who entered the study in the first trimester of their pregnancies were interviewed together in their homes five times: at twelve weeks and then around twenty-two and thirty-six weeks of pregnancy, within one week of the mother's (and usually also the infant's) arrival home from the hospital, and three months after the infant's arrival home. Adopting couples were interviewed together in their homes typically every four months until placement and then within one week and three months after placement. Consistent with the emergent nature of naturalistic studies, our interview schedule was flexible, allowing for variations in the number of interviews conducted in cases where couples entered the study after the first trimester or had pre-term deliveries or where other circumstances merited a change in protocol.

This book is based on the interview data collected in this project. We also collected monthly symptom self-reports from each husband and wife and conducted two systematic observations per couple of mother-father-infant interactions. These data are currently being prepared for analysis and dissemination. The interviews were the mainstay of the project; as principal investigator, I collected half the data and assumed the primary responsibility for its analysis.

The interviews we conducted were intensive, each one lasting about an hour and, at times, up to two to three hours. We sought to create an atmosphere conducive to free expression. I believe that several factors favored our obtaining "private," as opposed to "public," accounts (West 1990). Couples knew that we had no ties to any of the medical services or adoption agencies with which they were working; we had prolonged contact with them typically over a one to two year period (and, in some cases, three to four years); and each couple had the same interviewer throughout the course of the study. In the first interview, we asked couples to tell the story of their infertility and impending parenthood. In subsequent interviews, we asked couples to talk about what had happened to them since the last interview. The wives tended to take the lead, but there were many couples where husbands and wives were equally vocal or where the husband was dominant. Partners typically were supportive of and looked to each other to tell their stories. After couples reached a natural end in their talk and indicated the desire for further direction, we asked them to clarify or elaborate on topics they had raised and that we had determined from our ongoing analytic work were theoretically important.

At the time this book was completed, a total of ninety-four couples expecting or waiting for a child had participated in the Transition to Parenthood study. Additional one-time interviews were conducted with two women several years after they and their husbands had adopted children and with three infertile couples several years after they had had their children by adoption or assisted conception. Overall, we conducted about 450 interviews with ninety-seven couples and two women.

THE ADOPTING COUPLES

Thirty-six couples entered the Transition to Parenthood study waiting to adopt a child. Twenty-three of these couples were waiting to adopt an American child and thirteen couples were waiting to adopt a foreign child typically from Asian or South American countries. All but one of these couples began the adoption process wanting infants and all but three couples were waiting for their first child.

The mean ages and years married of the wives and husbands when they entered the study are shown in Table A.1. These couples had been trying an average of five years to have a child. Factors contributing to their infertility are shown in Table A.2.

THE INFERTILE AND CHILDBEARING COUPLES

Thirty-nine couples entered the study expecting a baby after an encounter with infertility. These couples had undergone diagnostic or treatment regimens for infertility and/or required more than two years to conceive a child. The mean ages and years married of the husbands and wives when they entered the study are shown in Table A.1. Factors contributing to their infertility are shown in Table A.2, while the method of conception is shown in Table A.3. These couples required an average of four years to conceive.

Of these thirty-nine infertile couples, thirty were childless prior to achieving the target pregnancy (the pregnancy observed in the study) and five couples had children in their current marriages. In four couples, three of the wives and one husband had children from a previous marriage.

TABLE A.1.   Means and ranges of ages and years married.

COUPLES AT STUDY ENTRY	YEARS OLD		YEARS MARRIED	
	M	R	M	R
Fertile			5	(1.5–14)
(n = 19)				
Husbands	33	(27–45)		
Wives	31	(26–38)		
Adopting			8.5	(3–18)
(n = 36)				
Husbands	36	(29–46)		
Wives	34	(27–42)		
Childbearing			7	(2–16)
(n = 39)				
Husbands	34	(26–42)		
Wives	34	(24–41)		

A total of forty-four pregnancies were observed among the forty-one infertile couples with wives pregnant in the course of this study. In addition to the thirty-nine couples who entered the study expecting a baby were two couples who entered the study waiting to adopt a child who subsequently achieved pregnancy. Three of the infertile couples lost their pregnancies in the course of the study; one of these couples reentered the study when they achieved a second pregnancy. In addition, two couples who safely delivered their first babies in the course of the study returned when they became pregnant again. One couple withdrew from the study during their preg-

TABLE A.2.   Infertile couples by diagnostic category (N = 75).

INFERTILE COUPLES ENTERING STUDY AS:	FACTORS CONTRIBUTING TO INFERTILITY			
	FEMALE	MALE	COMBINATION	UNEXPLAINED
Childbearing couples (n = 39)	22	2	10	5
Adopting couples (n = 36)	18[a]	4	8	6

[a]Two of the couples who entered the study waiting to adopt a child achieved pregnancy in the course of the study; one couple terminated the adoption process and the second couple adopted an infant in the first trimester of an in vitro fertilization pregnancy.

TABLE A.3. Profile of the sixty-three target pregnancies.

	FERTILE (19 COUPLES)	INFERTILE (41 COUPLES)
Number of pregnancies observed	19	44
Average time to conceive	3 months (R, 0–6)	4 years (R, 1–12)
METHOD OF CONCEPTION		
Spontaneous	19	5
IVF/GIFT	0	17
AIH/drugs	0	9
AID/drugs	0	4
Drugs	0	6
Surgery	0	2
Self-Treatment	0	1

TABLE A.4. Adverse life events prior to research participation.

EVENT	FERTILE (N = 19)	INFERTILE (N = 75)
Divorce	4 (husbands)	24[a]
Widowhood	0	1 (husband)
Pregnancy/infant loss	2	17
Elective pregnancy termination	3	3
Adoption failure	0	8
Serious illness	1[b]	11[c]

[a]Includes 19 couples in which 13 wives and 6 husbands had been divorced, and 5 couples in which both the husband and wife had been divorced. Only 1 divorce was attributed to infertility.
[b]Clinical depression in wife.
[c]Includes anorexia, cancer, heart disease, rheumatoid arthritis, hemothorax and hysterectomy secondary to severe endometriosis, or depression in wife; HSV infection in couple.

nancy. Additional features of these forty-four pregnancies are summarized in Table A.3.

The Fertile and Childbearing Couples

Nineteen couples with no histories of fertility impairments entered the study expecting a child. The mean ages and years married of the husbands and wives when they entered the study are shown in Table A.1. They required an average of only three months to conceive, and included one couple who accidentally became pregnant. Of these nineteen couples, fifteen were childless prior to achieving the target pregnancy; two couples had children in their current marriages. In two couples, two husbands had children from previous marriages.

Finally, as shown in Table A.4, the infertile couples who entered the study experienced more adverse life events both related and unrelated to infertility than the fertile couples. These events included pregnancy loss, adoption failure, divorce, widowhood, and illness.

References

Affonso, D. D., and J. F. Stichler. (1978). Exploratory study of women's reactions to having a cesarean birth. *Birth and the Family Journal* (5): 88–94.

Albert, S. (1984). The sense of closure. In K. J. Gergen and M. M. Gergen (Eds.), *Historical social psychology* (pp. 159–72). Hillsdale, NJ: Lawrence Erlbaum Associates.

Allison, J. R. (1979). Roles and role conflict of women in infertile couples. *Psychology of Women Quarterly* (4): 97–113.

American Fertility Society. (1991). *Investigation of the infertile couple* (pamphlet). Birmingham, AL: American Fertility Society.

Anderson, S., F. Nero, J. Rodin, M. Diamond, and A. DeCherney. (1989). Coping patterns of in vitro fertilization nurse coordinators: Strategies for combating low outcome effectance. *Psychology and Health* (3): 221–32.

Andrews, L. (1989). *Between strangers: Surrogate mothers, expectant fathers, and brave new babies.* New York: Harper and Row.

Andrews, M. C., S. J. Muasher, D. L. Levy, H. W. Jones, J. E. Garcia, Z. Rosenwaks, G. S. Jones, and A. A. Acosta. (1986). An analysis of the obstetric outcome of 125 consecutive pregnancies conceived *in vitro* and resulting in 100 deliveries. *American Journal of Obstetrics and Gynecology* (154): 848–54.

Andrews, R. G. (1970). Adoption and the resolution of infertility. *Fertility and Sterility* (21): 73–76.

Angier, N. (1990, July). The baby-makers. *First,* pp. 35–38.

Appleton, T. (1990). Dealing with failure in an assisted reproduction program. In P. L. Matson and B. A. Lieberman (Eds.), *Clinical IVF forum: Current views in assisted reproduction* (pp. 93–100). Manchester, England: Manchester University Press.

Aral, S. O., and W. Cates. (1983). The increasing concern with infertility: Why now? *Journal of the American Medical Association* (250): 2327–31.

Arditti, R., R. D. Klein, and S. Minden (Eds.). (1984). *Test-tube women: What future for motherhood?* London: Pandora.

Aronowitz, B. R., and J. Feldschuh. (1989). Artificial insemination by donor: Yours, mine, or theirs? In J. Offerman-Zuckerberg (Ed.), *Gender in transition: A new frontier* (pp. 151–61). New York: Plenum.

Ashby, T. A. (1894). The influence of minor forms of ovarian and tubal disease in the causation of sterility. *Transactions of the American Gynecological Society* (19): 260–71.

Atkinson, W. B. (Ed.). (1880). *The therapeutics of gynecology and obstetrics.* Philadelphia: D. G. Brinton.

Australian In-Vitro Fertilization Collaborative Group. (1988). In vitro fertilization pregnancies in Australia and New Zealand, 1979–1985. *The Medical Journal of Australia* (148): 429–36.

Bachrach, C. A. (1986). Adoption plans, adopted children, and adoptive mothers. *Journal of Marriage and the Family* (48): 243–53.

Bachrach, C. A., P. F. Adams, S. Sambrano, and K. A. London. (1990). Adoption in the 1980s. *Advance Data* (From vital and health statistics of the National Center for Health Statistics) (181): 1–9.

Bainbridge, I. (1982). With child in mind: The experience of a potential IVF mother. In W. A. Walters and P. Singer (Eds.), *Test-tube babies: A guide to moral questions, present techniques, and future possibilities* (pp. 119–27). Melbourne: Oxford University Press.

Balin, J. (1988). The sacred dimensions of pregnancy and birth. *Qualitative Sociology* (11): 275–301.

Bandler, S. W. (1920). The instincts, the emotions, and the endocrines in sterility. *Medical Record* (97): 383–91.

Baram, D., E. Tourtelot, E. Muechler, and K. Huang. (1988). Psychosocial adjustment following unsuccessful in vitro fertilization. *Journal of Psychosomatic Obstetrics and Gynaecology* (9): 181–90.

Baran, A., and R. Pannor. (1989). *Lethal secrets: The shocking consequences and unsolved problems of artificial insemination.* New York: Amistad Books.

Barker-Benfield, G. J. (1977). *The horrors of the half-known life: Male attitudes toward women and sexuality in nineteenth-century America.* New York: Harper Colophon.

Bateman, B. G., L. A. Kolp, W. C. Nunley, R. Felder, and B. Burkett. (1992). Subclinical pregnancy loss in clomiphene citrate–treated women. *Fertility and Sterility* (57): 25–27.

Beck-Gernsheim, E. (1989). From the pill to test-tube babies: New options, new pressures in reproductive behavior. In K. S. Ratcliff (Ed.), *Healing technology: Feminist perspectives* (pp. 23–40). Ann Arbor: University of Michigan Press.

Becker, G., and R. D. Nachtigall. (1991). Ambiguous responsibility in the doctor-patient relationship: The case of infertility. *Social Science and Medicine* (32): 875–85.

Bedford, G. S. (1855). *Clinical lectures on the diseases of women and children.* New York: Samuel and Wood.

Beeson, D. (1984). Technological rhythms in pregnancy: The case of prenatal diagnosis by amniocentesis. In T. Duster and K. Garrett (Eds.), *Cultural perspectives on biological knowledge* (pp. 145–81). Norwood, NJ: Ablex.

Beeson, D., and M. S. Golbus. (1979). Anxiety engendered by amniocentesis. *Birth Defects: Original Article Series* (15): 191–97.

Behrman, S. J., R. W. Kistner, and G. W. Patton. (Eds.) (1988). *Progress in infertility,* 3rd ed. Boston: Little, Brown.

Behrman, S. J., and G. W. Patton. (1988). Evaluation of infertility in the 1980s. In S. J. Behrman, R. W. Kistner, and G. W. Patton (Eds.), *Progress in infertility,* 3rd ed. (pp. 1–22). Boston: Little, Brown.

Belle, D. (1982). *Lives in stress.* Beverly Hills, CA: Sage.

Bellina, J. H., and J. Wilson. (1985). *You can have a baby: Everything you need to know about fertility.* New York: Crown.

Benedek, T. (1952). Infertility as a psychosomatic defense. *Fertility and Sterility* (3): 527–41.

Benedek, T., G. C. Ham, F. P. Robbins, and B. B. Rubenstein. (1953). Some emotional factors in infertility. *Psychosomatic Medicine* (15): 485–98.

Benner, P. (1988, October). *Nursing as a caring profession.* Paper prepared for the American Academy of Nursing, Kansas City, Missouri.

Benner, P., and J. Wrubel. (1989). *The primacy of caring: Stress and coping in health and illness.* Menlo Park, CA: Addison-Wesley.

Beral, V., P. Doyle, S. L. Tan, B. A. Mason, and S. Campbell. (1990). Outcome of pregnancies resulting from assisted conception. *British Medical Bulletin* (46): 753–68.

Berg, B. J., and J. F. Wilson. (1991). Psychological functioning across stages of treatment for infertility. *Journal of Behavioral Medicine* (14): 11–26.

———. (1990). Psychiatric morbidity in the infertile population: A reconceptualization. *Fertility and Sterility* (53), 654–61.

Bergum, V. (1989). *Woman to mother: A transformation.* Boston: Bergin and Garvey.

Berkow, S. G. (1937). *Childlessness: A study of sterility, its causes and treatment.* New York: Lee Furman.

Berkowitz, G. S. (1986). Epidemiology of infertility and early pregnancy wastage. In A. H. DeCherney (Ed.), *Reproductive failure* (pp. 17–40). New York: Churchill Livingstone.

Berkowitz, R. L., L. Lynch, U. Chitkara, I. A. Wilkins, K. E. Mehalek, and E. Alvarez. (1988). Selective reduction of multifetal pregnancies in the first trimester. *New England Journal of Medicine* (318): 1043–47.

Berman, L. C., and R. K. Bufferd. (1986). Family treatment to address loss in adoptive families. *Social Casework: The Journal of Contemporary Social Work* (67): 3–11.

Berwick, D. M., and M. C. Weinstein. (1985). What do patients value? Willingness to pay for ultrasound in normal pregnancy. *Medical Care* (23): 881–93.

Bigelow, H. R. (1883). The moral significance of sterility. *Obstetric Gazette* (6): 1–24.

Birke, L., S. Himmelweit, and G. Vines. (1990). *Tomorrow's child: Reproductive technologies in the 90s.* London: Virago Press.

Bishop, A. H., and J. R. Scudder. (1987). Nursing ethics in an age of controversy. *Advances in Nursing Science* (9): 34–43.

Blackwell, R. E., B. R. Carr, R. J. Chang, A. H. DeCherney, A. F. Haney, W. R. Keye, R. W. Rebar, J. A. Rock, Z. Rosenwaks, M. M. Seibel, and M. R. Soules. (1987). Are we exploiting the infertile couple? *Fertility and Sterility* (48): 735–39.

Blackwell, R. E., and M. P. Steinkampf. (1989). Infertility diagnosis and therapy: Appropriate tests and indicated treatments performed in a proper sequence. In M. R. Soules (Ed.), *Controversies in reproductive endocrinology and infertility* (pp. 15–31). New York: Elsevier.

Blackwood, W. R. (1878). Who is to blame? *Philadelphia Medical Times* (9): 1–4.

Blank, R. H. (1990). *Regulating reproduction*. New York: Columbia University Press.

————. (1984). *Redefining human life: Reproductive technologies and social policy*. Boulder, CO: Westview Press.

Blum, H. P. (1983). Adoptive parents: Generative conflict and generational continuity. *Psychoanalytic Study of the Child* (38): 141–63.

Bongaarts, J. (1982). Infertility after age 30: A false alarm. *Family Planning Perspectives* (14): 75–78.

Bonham, G. S. (1977). Who adopts: The relationship of adoption and social-demographic characteristics of women. *Journal of Marriage and the Family* (39): 295–306.

Bonnicksen, A. (1988). Some consumer aspects of in vitro fertilization and embryo transfer. *Birth* (15): 148–52.

Borenstein, R., U. Elhalah, B. Lunenfeld, and Z. S. Schwartz. (1989). Severe ovarian hyperstimulation syndrome: A reevaluated therapeutic approach. *Fertility and Sterility* (51): 791–95.

Bos, C., and R. A. Cleghorn. (1958). Psychogenic sterility. *Fertility and Sterility* (9): 84–98.

Braidotti, R. (1989). Organs without bodies. *Differences: A Journal of Feminist Cultural Studies* (1): 147–61.

Bram, S. (1989). Toward a sense of immortality: Case studies of voluntarily childless couples. In J. Offerman-Zuckerberg (Ed.), *Gender in transition: A new frontier* (pp. 275–83). New York: Plenum.

Brand, H. J., S. S. Roos, and A. B. Van Der Merwe. (1982). Psychological stress and infertility. Part 1: Psychophysiological reaction patterns. *British Journal of Medical Psychology* (55): 379–84.

Brandt, A. M. (1987). *No magic bullet: A social history of venereal disease in the United States since 1880*. New York: Oxford University Press.

Breines, W., and L. Gordon. (1983). The new scholarship on family violence. *Signs: Journal of Women in Culture and Society* (8): 490–531.

Brickman, P., V. Rabinowitz, J. Karuza, D. Coates, E. Cohn, and L. Kidder. (1982). Models of helping and coping. *American Psychologist* (37): 368–84.

Brodzinsky, A. B. (1990). Surrendering an infant for adoption: The birthmother experience. In D. M. Brodzinsky and M. D. Schechter (Eds.), *The psychology of adoption* (pp. 295–315). New York: Oxford University Press.

Brodzinsky, D. M., and M. D. Schechter. (Eds.). (1990). *The psychology of adoption*. New York: Oxford University Press.

Brown, W. M. (1985). On defining "disease." *Journal of Medicine and Philosophy* (10): 311–28.

Bruner, E. M. (1984). Introduction: The opening up of anthropology. In S. Plattner and E. M. Bruner (Eds.), *Text, play and story: The construction and reconstruction of self and society* (pp. 1–16). Washington, DC: American Ethnological Society.

Burns, L. H. (1987). Infertility as boundary ambiguity: One theoretical perspective. *Family Process* (26): 359–72.

Burr, A. H. (1906). The guarantee of safety in the marriage contract. *Journal of the American Medical Association* (47): 1887–89.

Burtchaell, J. T. (1992). The manufactured child. *Second Opinion* (17): 103–7.

Burton, B. K., R. G. Dillard, and E. N. Clark. (1985). The psychological impact of false positive elevations of maternal serum alpha-fetoprotein. *American Journal of Obstetrics and Gynecology* (151): 77–82.

Bury, M. (1988). Meanings at risk: The experience of arthritis. In R. Anderson and M. Bury (Eds.), *Living with chronic illness: The experience of patients and their families* (pp. 89–116). London: Unwin Hyman.

———. (1982). Chronic illness as biographical disruption. *Sociology of Health and Illness* (4): 167–81.

Bush, C. G. (1983). Women and the assessment of technology: To think, to be, to unthink, to free. In J. Rothschild (Ed.), *Machina Ex Dea: Feminist perspectives on technology* (pp. 151–70). New York: Pergamon Press.

Butterfield, P. G. (1990). Thinking upstream: Nurturing a conceptual understanding of the societal context of health behavior. *Advances in Nursing Science* (12): 1–8.

Buxton, C. L., and A. L. Southam. (1958). *Human infertility.* New York: Hoeber-Harper.

Calkins, K. (1970). Time: Perspectives, marking and styles of usage. *Social Problems* (17): 487–501.

Callan, V. J., and J. F. Hennessey. (1989). Psychological adjustment to infertility: A unique comparison of two groups of infertile women, mothers and women childless by choice. *Journal of Reproductive and Infant Psychology* (7): 105–12.

———. (1988). Emotional aspects and support in in vitro fertilization and embryo transfer programs. *Journal of In Vitro Fertilization and Embryo Transfer* (5): 290–95.

Callan, V. J., B. Kloske, Y. Kashima, and J. F. Hennessey. (1988). Toward understanding women's decisions to continue or stop in vitro fertilization: The role of social, psychological, and background factors. *Journal of In Vitro Fertilization and Embryo Transfer* (5): 363–69.

Campbell, H. F. (1888). The infertility of women: The nervous system in sterility. *Transactions of the American Gynecological Society* (13): 423–54.

Campbell, J. (1968). *The hero with a thousand faces.* Princeton, NJ: Princeton University Press.

Caplan, A. L. (1990). Arguing with success: Is in vitro fertilization research or therapy? In D. M. Bartels, R. Priester, D. E. Vawter, and A. L. Caplan (Eds.), *Beyond Baby M: Ethical issues in new reproductive techniques* (pp. 149–70). Clifton, NJ: Humana Press.

Carter, J. W., and M. Carter. (1989). *Sweet grapes: How to stop being infertile and start living again.* Indianapolis, IN: Perspectives Press.

Cassedy, J. H. (1986). *Medicine and American growth, 1800–1860.* Madison: University of Wisconsin Press.

Cassell, E. J. (1978). The conflict between the desire to know and the need to care for the patient. In S. F. Spicker (Ed.), *Organism, medicine, and metaphysics* (pp. 57–72). Dordrecht, Holland: D. Reidel.

Chadwick, R. F. (Ed.). (1987). *Ethics, reproduction and genetic control.* London: Routledge.

Chadwick, R. F. (1987). Having children: Introduction. In Ruth F. Chadwick (Ed.), *Ethics, reproduction and genetic control* (pp. 3–43). London: Routledge.

Channell, D. F. (1991). *The vital machine: A study of technology and organic life*. New York: Oxford University Press.

Charmaz, K. (1987). Struggling for a self: Identity levels of the chronically ill. *Research in the Sociology of Health Care* (6): 283–321.

———. (1983a). The grounded theory method: An explication and interpretation. In R. M. Emerson (Ed.), *Contemporary field research: A collection of readings* (pp. 109–26). Boston: Little, Brown.

——— (1983b). Loss of self: A fundamental form of suffering in the chronically ill. *Sociology of Health and Illness* (5): 168–95.

Chesler, P. (1988). *Sacred bond: The legacy of Baby M*. New York: Time Books.

Child, C. G. (1931). *Sterility and conception*. New York: Appleton.

Childlessness (Editorial). (1939). *Journal of Contraception* (4): 58.

Churchill, J. (1982). Gods, frogs, and sojourns. *Soundings* (5): 206–12.

Clamar, A. (1989). Psychological implications of the anonymous pregnancy. In J. Offerman-Zuckerberg (Ed.), *Gender in transition: A new frontier* (pp. 111–21). New York: Plenum.

Clapp, D. (1989, April). A rite of passage. *RESOLVE National Newsletter* (14): 5.

Clarke, J. N. (1991). Media portrayal of disease from the medical, political economy, and life-style perspectives. *Qualitative Health Research* (1): 287–308.

Clouser, K. D., C. M. Culver, and B. Gert. (1981). Malady: A new treatment of disease. *Hastings Center Report* (11): 29–37.

Cochran, L., and E. Claspell. (1987). *The meaning of grief: A dramaturgical approach to understanding emotions*. New York: Greenwood Press.

Colliere, M. F. (1986). Invisible care and invisible women as health care providers. *International Journal of Nursing Studies* (23): 95–112.

Collins, J. A., J. B. Garner, E. H. Wilson, W. Wrixon, and R. F. Casper. (1984). A proportional hazards analysis of the clinical characteristics of infertile couples. *American Journal of Obstetrics and Gynecology* (148): 527–32.

Collins, J. A., W. Wrixon, L. B. Janes, and E. H. Wilson. (1983). Treatment-independent pregnancy among infertile couples. *New England Journal of Medicine* (309): 1201–6.

Comaroff, J., and P. Maguire. (1981). Ambiguity and the search for meaning: Childhood leukemia in the modern clinical context. *Social Science and Medicine* (15B): 115–23.

Conrad, P. (1987). The experience of illness: Recent and new directions. *Research in the Sociology of Health Care* (6): 1–31.

Cook, R., J. Parsons, B. Mason, and S. Golombok. (1989). Emotional, marital and sexual functioning in patients embarking upon IVF and AID treatment for infertility. *Journal of Reproductive and Infant Psychology* (7): 87–93.

Cooper, M. C. (1988). Covenantal relationships: Grounding for the nursing ethic. *Advances in Nursing Science* (10): 48–59.

Cope, P. M. (1928). The women of "Who's Who": A statistical study. *Social Forces* (7): 212–23.

Corbin, J., and A. Strauss. (1990). *Basics of qualitative research: Grounded theory procedures and techniques*. Newbury Park, CA: Sage.

Corbin, J., and A. L. Strauss. (1987). Accompaniments of chronic illness: Changes in body, self, biography, and biographical time. *Research in the Sociology of Health Care* (6): 249–81.

Corea, G. (1985). *The mother machine: Reproductive technologies from artificial insemination to artificial wombs*. New York: Harper and Row.

Counts, M. L. (1988). *Coming home: The soldier's return in twentieth-century American drama*. New York: Peter Lang.

Cowan, R. S. (1983). *More work for mother: The ironies of household technology from the open hearth to the microwave*. New York: Basic Books.

Cox, B. E., and E. C. Smith. (1982). The mother's self-esteem after a cesarean delivery. *American Journal of Maternal Child Nursing* (7): 309–14.

Cranley, M. S., S. H. Hedahl, and S. H. Pegg. (1983). Women's perceptions of vaginal and cesarean section deliveries. *Nursing Research* (32): 10–15.

Crowe, C. (1985). "Women want it": In vitro fertilization and women's motivations for participation. *Women's Studies International Forum* (8): 547–52.

Curtin, L. (1979). The nurse as advocate: A philosophical foundation for nursing. *Advances in Nursing Science* (1): 1–10.

Curtis, A. H. (1924). Progress in the relief of sterility. *American Journal of Obstetrics and Gynecology* (8): 123–29.

Cutright, P., and E. Shorter. (1979). The effects of health on the completed fertility of nonwhite and white U.S. women born between 1867 and 1935. *Journal of Social History* (13): 191–217.

Daly, K. (1990). Infertility resolution and adoption readiness. *Families in Society: The Journal of Contemporary Human Services* (71): 483–92.

———. (1989a). Anger among prospective adoptive parents: Structural determinants and management strategies. *Clinical Sociology Review* (7): 80–96.

———. (1989b). Preparation needs of infertile couples who seek to adopt. *Canadian Journal of Community Mental Health* (8): 111–21.

———. (1988). Reshaped parenthood identity: The transition to adoptive parenthood. *Journal of Contemporary Ethnography* (17): 40–66.

Daniels, K. R. (1988). Artificial insemination using donor semen and the issue of secrecy: The views of donors and recipient couples. *Social Science and Medicine* (27): 377–83.

Daniluk, J. C. (1988). Infertility: Intrapersonal and interpersonal impact. *Fertility and Sterility* (49): 982–90.

Davis, F. P. (1923). *Impotency, sterility, and artificial impregnation*, 2d ed. St. Louis, MO: Mosby.

Davitz, L. L. (1984). *Baby hunger: Every woman's longing for a baby*. Minneapolis: Winston.

DeCherney, A. H., and T. C. Harris. (1986). The barren woman through history. In A. H. DeCherney (Ed.), *Reproductive failure* (pp. 1–15). New York: Churchill Livingstone.

Demyttenaere, K., P. Nijs, G. Evers-Kiebooms, and P. R. Koninckx. (1991). Coping, ineffectiveness of coping and the psychoendocrinological stress responses during in vitro fertilization. *Journal of Psychosomatic Research* (35): 231–43.

Denber, H. C. (1978). Psychiatric aspects of infertility. *Journal of Reproductive Medicine* (20): 23–29.

Dennerstein, L., and C. Morse. (1985). Psychological issues in IVF. *Clinics in Obstetrics and Gynecology* (12): 835–46.

Denzin, N. K. (1989). *Interpretive interactionism.* Newbury Park, CA: Sage.

Despreaux, M. A. (1989). Surrogate motherhood: A feminist perspective. *Research in the Sociology of Health Care* (8): 99–134.

Deutsch, H. (1945/1973). *The psychology of women,* vol. 2: *Motherhood.* New York: Bantam.

Deykin, E. Y., L. Campbell, and P. Patti. (1984). The postadoption experience of surrendering parents. *American Journal of Orthopsychiatry* (54): 271–80.

DeZoeten, M., T. Tymstra, and A. T. Alberda. (1987). The waiting list for IVF: The motivations and expectations of women waiting for IVF treatment. *Human Reproduction* (2): 623–26.

Donchin, A. (1986). The future of mothering: Reproductive technology and feminist theory. *Hypatia* (1): 121–72.

Dossey, L. (1982). *Space, time and medicine.* Boston: New Science Library.

Downey, J., S. Yingling, M. McKinney, N. Husami, R. Jewelewicz, and J. Maidman. (1989). Mood disorders, psychiatric symptoms, and distress in women presenting for infertility evaluation. *Fertility and Sterility* (52): 425–32.

Drake, T., D. Tredway, G. Buchanan, N. Takaki, and T. Daane. (1977). Unexplained infertility: A reappraisal. *Obstetrics and Gynecology* (50): 644–46.

Drugan, A., M. P. Johnson, and M. I. Evans. (1990). Amniocentesis. In R. D. Eden and F. H. Boehm (Eds.), *Assessment and care of the fetus: Physiological, clinical, and medicolegal principles* (pp. 283–90). Norwalk, CT: Appleton and Lange.

Dunbar, F. (1954). *Emotions and bodily changes: A survey of literature on psychosomatic interrelationships, 1910–1953.* New York: Columbia University Press.

Dunnington, R. M., and G. Glazer. (1991). Maternal identity and early mothering behavior in previously infertile and never infertile women. *JOGNN: Journal of Obstetric, Gynecologic, and Neonatal Nursing* (20): 309–18.

Dunphy, B. C., L. M. Neal, and I. D. Cooke. (1989). The clinical value of conventional semen analysis. *Fertility and Sterility* (51): 324–29.

Eakins, P. S. (Ed.). (1986). *The American way of birth.* Philadelphia: Temple University Press.

Edelmann, R. J., and K. J. Connolly. (1986). Psychological aspects of infertility. *British Journal of Medical Psychology* (59): 209–19.

Edelmann, R. J., and S. Golombok. (1989). Stress and reproductive failure. *Journal of Reproductive and Infant Psychology* (7): 79–86.

Edwards, J. N. (1991). New conceptions: Biosocial innovations and the family. *Journal of Marriage and the Family* (53): 349–60.

Eheart, B. K., and M. B. Power. (1988). An interpretive study of adoption: The interplay of history, power, knowledge, and emotions. *Journal of Contemporary Ethnography* (17): 326–47.

Ehrenreich, B., and D. English. (1978). *For her own good: 150 years of the experts' advice to women*. New York: Anchor/Doubleday.

Ekwo, E. E., J. Kim, and C. A. Gosselink. (1987). Parental perceptions of the burden of genetic disease. *American Journal of Medical Genetics* (28): 955–63.

Elias, S., and G. J. Annas. (1986). Social policy considerations in noncoital reproduction. *Journal of the American Medical Association* (255): 62–68.

Elmer-Dewitt, P. (1991, September). Making babies. *Time* (138): 56–63.

Emerson, J. (1970). Behavior in private places: Sustaining definitions of reality in gynecology examinations. In H. P. Dreitzel (Ed.), *Recent sociology*, no. 2: *Patterns of communicative behavior* (pp. 74–97). New York: Macmillan.

Emotions after infertility. (1952, June). *Science News Letter* (61): 383.

Engelhardt, H. T. (1983). Physicians, patients, health care institutions—and the people in between: Nurses. In A. H. Bishop and J. R. Scudder (Eds.), *Caring, curing, coping: Nurse/physician/patient relationships* (pp. 62–79). Tuscaloosa: University of Alabama Press.

———. (1982). Illnesses, diseases, and sicknesses. In V. Kestenbaum (Ed.), *The humanity of the ill: Phenomenological perspectives* (pp. 142–56). Knoxville: University of Tennessee Press.

Engelmann, G. J. (1901). The increasing sterility of American women. *Journal of the American Medical Association* (37): 890–97, 1532–33.

Erikson, K. T. (1966). *Wayward Puritans: A study in the sociology of deviance*. New York: Wiley.

Estroff, S. E. (1989). Self, identity, and subjective experiences of schizophrenia: In search of the subject. *Schizophrenia Bulletin* (15): 189–96.

Evers-Kiebooms, G., A. Swerts, and H. Van Den Berghe. (1988). Psychological aspects of amniocentesis: Anxiety feelings in three different risk groups. *Clinical Genetics* (33): 196–206.

Faden, R. (1991). Autonomy, choice, and the new reproductive technologies: The role of informed consent in prenatal genetic diagnosis. In J. Rodin, and A. Collins (Eds.), *Women and new reproductive technologies: Medical, psychosocial, legal, and ethical dilemmas* (pp. 37–47). Hillsdale, NJ: Lawrence Erlbaum Associates.

Fagan, P. J., C. W. Schmidt, J. A. Rick, M. D. Damewood, E. Halle, and T. N. Wise. (1986). Sexual functioning and psychologic evaluation of in vitro fertilization couples. *Fertility and Sterility* (46): 668–72.

Fahrner, R. (1988). Nursing interventions. In A. Lewis (Ed.), *Nursing care of the person with AIDS/ARC* (pp. 115–30). Rockville, MD: Aspen.

Farquhar, J. (1991). Objects, processes, and female infertility in Chinese medicine. *Medical Anthropology Quarterly* (5): 370–99.

Farrell, R. A., and V. L. Swigert. (1982). *Deviance and social control*. Glenview, IL: Scott, Foresman.

Fava, G. A., R. Kellner, L. Michelacci, G. Trombini, D. Pathak, C. Orlandi, and L. Bovicelli. (1982). Psychological reactions to amniocentesis: A controlled study. *American Journal of Obstetrics and Gynecology* (143): 509–13.

Fearn, J., B. M. Hibbard, K. M. Laurence, A. Roberts, and J. O. Robinson. (1982).

Screening for neural-tube defects and maternal anxiety. *British Journal of Obstetrics and Gynecology* (89): 218–21.

Fidell, L. S., J. Marik, J. E. Donner, C. Jenkins-Burk, J. Koenigsberg, K. Magnussen, C. Morgan, and J. B. Ullman. (1989). Paternity by proxy: Artificial insemination with donor sperm. In J. Offerman-Zuckerberg (Ed.), *Gender in transition: A new frontier* (pp. 93–110). New York: Plenum.

Fisch, P., R. F. Casper, S. E. Brown, W. Wrixon, J. A. Collins, R. L. Reid, and C. Simpson. (1989). Unexplained infertility: Evaluation of treatment with clomiphene citrate and human chorionic gonadotropin. *Fertility and Sterility* (51): 828–33.

Fischer, I. C. (1953). Psychogenic aspects of sterility. *Fertility and Sterility* (4): 466–71.

Fletcher, J. F. (1988). *The ethics of genetic control: Ending reproductive roulette.* Buffalo, NY: Prometheus Books.

Ford, E. S., I. Forman, J. R. Willson, W. Char, W. T. Mixson, and C. Scholz. (1953). A psychodynamic approach to the study of infertility. *Fertility and Sterility* (4): 456–65.

Fox, R. C., L. H. Aiken, and C. M. Messikomer. (1990). The culture of caring: AIDS and the nursing profession. *The Milbank Quarterly* (68): 226–56.

Frank, D. I. (1990a). Factors related to decisions about infertility treatment. *JOGNN: Journal of Obstetric, Gynecologic, and Neonatal Nursing* (19): 162–67.

———. (1990b). Gender differences in decision making about infertility treatment. *Applied Nursing Research* (3): 56–62.

———. (1989). Treatment preferences of infertile couples. *Applied Nursing Research* (2): 94–95.

Franklin, S. (1990). Deconstructing "desperateness": The social construction of infertility in popular representations of new reproductive technologies. In M. McNeil, I. Varcoe, and S. Yearley (Eds.), *The new reproductive technologies* (pp. 200–229). New York: St. Martin's Press.

Franklin, S., and M. McNeil. (1988). Reproductive futures: Recent literature and current feminist debates on reproductive technologies. *Feminist Studies* (14): 545–61.

Freeman, M. (1984). History, narrative, and life-span developmental knowledge. *Human Development* (27): 1–9.

Freeman, E. W., K. Rickels, J. Tausig, A. Boxer, L. Mastroianni, and R. W. Tureck. (1987). Emotional and psychosocial factors in follow-up of women after IVF-ET treatment: A pilot investigation. *Acta Obstetricia et Gynecologica Scandinavica* (66): 517–21.

Freeman, E. W., C. R. Garcia, and K. Rickels. (1983). Behavioral and emotional factors: Comparisons of anovulatory infertile women with fertile and other infertile women. *Fertility and Sterility* (40): 195–201.

Fry, H. D. (1888). The relative merits of electrolysis and rapid dilatation in the treatment of sterility and dysmenorrhea. *American Journal of Obstetrics and Gynecology* (21): 40–48.

Frydman, R., J. Belaisch-Allart, N. Fries, A. Hazout, A. Glissant, and J. Testart. (1986). An obstetric assessment of the first 100 births from the in vitro fertilization program at Clamart, France. *American Journal of Obstetrics and Gynecology* (154): 550–55.

Gadow, S. (1988). Covenant without cure: Letting go and holding on in chronic illness. In J. Watson and M. Ray (Eds.), *The ethics of care and the ethics of cure: Synthesis in chronicity* (pp. 5–14). New York: National League for Nursing.

———. (1984). Touch and technology: Two paradigms of patient care. *Journal of Religion and Health* (23): 63–69.

———. (1983a). Existential advocacy: Philosophical foundation of nursing. In C. P. Murphy and H. Hunter (Eds.), *Ethical problems in the nurse-patient relationship* (pp. 41–58). Boston: Allyn and Bacon.

———. (1983b). Nurse and patient: The caring relationship. In A. H. Bishop and J. R. Scudder (Eds.), *Caring, curing, coping: Nurse/physician/patient relationships* (pp. 31–43). Tuscaloosa: University of Alabama Press.

———. (1980). Body and self: A dialectic. *Journal of Medicine and Philosophy* (5): 172–85.

Garcia, C. R., E. W. Freeman, K. Rickels, C. Wu, G. Scholl, P. C. Galle, and A. S. Boxer. (1985). Behavioral and emotional factors and treatment responses in a study of anovulatory infertile women. *Fertility and Sterility* (44): 478–83.

Gardner, A. K. (1856). *The causes and curative treatment of sterility.* New York: DeWitt and Davenport.

Garfinkel, H. (1967). Conditions of successful degradation ceremonies. In J. Manis and B. Meltzer (Eds.), *Symbolic interaction* (pp. 205–12). Boston: Allyn and Bacon.

Garner, C. H. (1985). Pregnancy after infertility. *JOGNN: Journal of Obstetric, Gynecologic, and Neonatal Nursing* (14): 58s–62s.

Garrigues, H. J. (1894). *A textbook of the diseases of women.* Philadelphia: Saunders.

Gerbie, A. B., and J. A. Merrill. (1988). Pathology of endometriosis. *Clinical Obstetrics and Gynecology* (31): 779–86.

Gerson, D. (1989). Infertility and the construction of desperation. *Socialist Review* (19): 45–64.

Gibbs, N. (1989, October). The baby chase. *Time* (134): 86–89.

Gidro-Frank, L., and T. Gordon. (1956). Reproductive performance of women with pelvic pain of long duration: Some observations on associated psychopathology. *Fertility and Sterility* (7): 440–47.

Gilman, C. P. (1910/1980). The crux. In A. J. Lane (Ed.), *The Charlotte Perkins Gilman Reader* (pp. 116–22). New York: Pantheon.

Gilman, R. (1987). The waiting since. In H. Bloom (Ed.), *Samuel Beckett's Waiting for Godot* (pp. 67–78). New York: Chelsea House.

Given, J. E., G. S. Jones, and D. L. McMillen. (1985). A comparison of personality characteristics between in vitro fertilization patients and other infertile patients. *Journal of In Vitro Fertilization and Embryo Transfer* (2): 49–54.

Glaser, B. G., and A. L. Strauss. (1971). *Status passage.* Chicago: Aldine.

Glazer, E. S. (1990). *The long-awaited stork: A guide to parenting after infertility.* Lexington, MA: Lexington Books.

Gloger-Tippelt, G. (1988). *The development of the mother's conceptions of the child before birth.* Paper presented at the Sixth Biennial International Conference on Infant Studies, Washington, DC.

Goffman, E. (1969). On face-work: An analysis of ritual elements in social inter-action. In A. R. Lindesmith and A. L. Strauss (Eds.), *Readings in social psychology* (pp. 262–81). New York: Holt, Rinehart and Winston.

———. (1963). *Stigma: Notes on the management of spoiled identity.* Englewood Cliffs, NJ: Prentice-Hall.

Good, B. J. (1977). The heart of what's the matter: The semantics of illness in Iran. *Culture, Medicine, and Psychiatry* (1): 25–58.

Gordon, L. (1977). *Woman's body, woman's right: A social history of birth control in America.* New York: Penguin.

Gorovitz, S. (1982). *Doctors' dilemmas: Moral conflict and medical care.* New York: Macmillan.

Gottlieb, B. (Ed.). (1981). *Social networks and social support.* Beverly Hills, CA: Sage.

Gould, K. (1990, September). Pregnancy after infertility. *RESOLVE National Newsletter* (15): 8.

Gove, W. R. (Ed.). (1980). *The labelling of deviance: Evaluating a perspective,* 2nd ed. Beverly Hills, CA: Sage.

Grabill, W. H., C. V. Kiser, and P. K. Whelpton. (1958). *The fertility of American women.* New York: Wiley.

Green, H. (1983). *The light of the home: An intimate view of the lives of women in Victorian America.* New York: Pantheon.

Green, T. H. (1977). *Gynecology: Essentials of clinical practice,* 3rd ed. Boston: Little, Brown.

Greenfeld, D. A., M. P. Diamond, and A. H. DeCherney. (1988). Grief reactions following in vitro fertilization treatment. *Journal of Psychosomatic Obstetrics and Gynaecology* (8): 169–74.

Gregg, R. S. (1905). Sterility versus fecundity, and the divorce evil. *Milwaukee Medical Journal* (13): 60–62.

Greil, A. L. (1991). *Not yet pregnant: Infertile couples in contemporary America.* New Brunswick, NJ: Rutgers University Press.

———. (1991). A secret stigma: The analogy between infertility and chronic illness and disability. In G. A. Albrecht and J. A. Levy (Eds.), *Advances in Medical Sociology,* vol. 2 (pp. 17–38). Greenwich, CT: JAI Press.

Greil, A. L., and K. Porter. (1988, November). *Explaining "treatment addiction" in infertile couples.* Presented at Annual Meeting of the National Council of Family Relations. Philadelphia, PA.

Greil, A. L., K. L. Porter, and T. A. Leitko. (1989). Sex and intimacy among infertile couples. *Journal of Psychology and Human Sexuality* (2): 117–38.

Greil, A. L., K. L. Porter, T. A. Leitko, and C. Riscilli. (1989). Why me? Theodicies of infertile women and men. *Sociology of Health and Illness* (11): 213–29.

Greil, A. L., T. A. Leitko, and K. L. Porter (1988). Infertility: His and hers. *Gender and Society* (2): 172–99.

Gross, S. W. (1890). *A practical treatise on impotence, sterility and allied disorders of the male sexual organs,* 4th ed. rev. Philadelphia: Lea Brothers.

Grubbs, G. S., H. B. Peterson, P. M. Layde, and G. L. Rubin. (1985). Regret after decision to have a tubal sterilization. *Fertility and Sterility* (44): 248–53.

Guba, E. G. (Ed.). (1990). *The paradigm dialog.* Newbury Park, CA: Sage.

Guzick, D. S., C. Wilkes, and H. W. Jones. (1986). Cumulative pregnancy rates for in vitro fertilization. *Fertility and Sterility* (46): 663–67.

Hales, E. M. (1878). *Diseases of women, especially those causing sterility*. New York: Boericke and Tafel.

Haller, J. S., and R. M. Haller. (1974). *The physician and sexuality in Victorian America*. New York: Norton.

Halpern, S. (1989, January/February). Infertility: Playing the odds. *Ms Magazine*, pp. 147–56.

Hamblen, E. C. (1960). *Facts for childless couples*, 2nd ed. Springfield, IL: Thomas.

Haney, A. F. (1989, October 21). Speech given at RESOLVE/SERONO Conference, Raleigh, NC.

———. (1987). What is efficacious infertility therapy? *Fertility and Sterility* (48): 543–45.

Hanson, F. M., and J. Rock. (1950). The effect of adoption on fertility and other reproductive functions. *American Journal of Obstetrics and Gynecology* (59): 311–20.

Hardyment, C. (1983). *Dream babies: Three centuries of good advice on child care*. New York: Harper and Row.

Harrison, K. L., V. J. Callan, J. F. Hennessey. (1987). Stress and semen quality in an in vitro fertilization program. *Fertility and Sterility* (48): 633–36.

Harrison, R. F., R. R. O'Moore, and A. M. O'Moore. (1986). Stress and fertility: Some modalities of investigation and treatment in couples with unexplained infertility in Dublin. *International Journal of Fertility* (31): 153–59.

Hartford, S. L., P. D. Silva, G. S. DiZerega, and M. L. Yonekura. (1987). Serologic evidence of prior chlamydial infection in patients with tubal pregnancy and contralateral tubal disease. *Fertility and Sterility* (47): 118–21.

Hartmann, S. M. (1982). *The home front and beyond: American women in the 1940s*. Boston: Twayne.

Haseltine, F. P., C. Mazure, W. De L'Aune, D. Greenfeld, N. Laufer, B. Tarlatzis, M. L. Polan, E. E. Jones, R. Graebe, F. Nero, A. D'Lugi, D. Fazio, J. Masters, and A. H. DeCherney. (1985). Psychological interviews in screening couples undergoing in vitro fertilization. *Annals of the New York Academy of Sciences* (442): 504–22.

Hearn, M. T., A. A. Yuzpe, S. E. Brown, and R. F. Casper. (1987). Psychological characteristics of in vitro fertilization participants. *American Journal of Obstetrics and Gynecology* (156): 269–74.

Heilbrun, C. G. (1988). *Writing a woman's life*. New York: Ballantine.

Heimann, M. (1955). Psychoanalytic evaluation of the problem of "one-child sterility." *Fertility and Sterility* (6): 405–14.

Helman, C. G. (1985a). Disease and pseudo-disease: A case history of pseudo-angina. In R. A. Hahn, and A. D. Gaines (Eds.), *Physicians of Western medicine: Anthropological approaches to theory and practice* (pp. 293–331). Dordrecht, Holland: D. Reidel.

———. (1985b). Psyche, soma, and society: The social construction of psychosomatic disorders. *Culture, Medicine, and Psychiatry* (9): 1–26.

———. (1984). *Culture, health, and illness: An introduction for health professionals*. Bristol: John Wright and Sons.

Henshaw, S. K., and M. T. Orr. (1987). The need and unmet need for infertility services in the United States. *Family Planning Perspectives* (19): 180–86.

Hill, A. (1989, April). Infertility as post-traumatic stress disorder. *RESOLVE National Newsletter* (14): 8.

Hirsch, M. B., and W. D. Mosher. (1987). Characteristics of infertile women in the United States and their use of infertility services. *Fertility and Sterility* (47): 618–25.

Hochschild, A. R. (1979). Emotion work, feeling rules, and social structure. *American Journal of Sociology* (85): 551–75.

Holman, J. F., and C. B. Hammond. (1988). Induction of ovulation with clomiphene citrate. In S. J. Behrman, R. W. Kistner, and G. W. Patton (Eds.), *Progress in infertility*, 3rd ed. (pp. 499–511). Boston: Little, Brown.

Hoffman, W. W. (1916). *Sterility and choice of sex in the human family.* Pittsburgh: (no publisher cited).

Hoffmann-Reim, C. (1990). *The adopted child: Family life with double parenthood* (trans. M. Brookman). New Brunswick, NJ: Transaction Publishers.

Hoffmann-Reim, C. (1986). Adoptive parenting and the norm of family emotionality. *Qualitative Sociology* (9): 162–78.

Hollinger, J. H. (1985). From coitus to commerce: Legal and social consequences of noncoital reproduction. *Journal of Law Reform* (18): 865–932.

Holmes, H. B., B. B. Hoskins, and M. Gross. (Eds.). (1981). *The custom-made child: Women-centered perspectives.* Clifton, NJ: Humana.

Hostetter, M., and D. E. Johnson (1989). International adoption: An introduction for physicians. *American Journal of Diseases of Children* (143): 325–32.

Howe, R. S., R. A. Sayegh, K. L. Durinzi, and R. W. Tureck. (1990). Perinatal outcome of singleton pregnancies conceived by in vitro fertilization: A controlled study. *Journal of Perinatology* (10): 261–66.

Hubbard, R. (1985). Test-tube babies: Solution or problem? In A. T. Rottenberg (Ed.), *Elements of argument: A text and reader* (pp. 365–71). New York: St. Martin's Press.

Hull, M. G., C. M. Glazener, N. J. Kelly, D. I. Conway, P. A. Foster, R. A. Hinton, C. Coulson, P. A. Lambert, E. M. Wat, and K. M. Desai. (1985). Population study of causes, treatment, and outcome of infertility. *British Medical Journal* (291): 1693–97.

Humphrey, M., and H. Humphrey. (1986). A fresh look at genealogical bewilderment. *British Journal of Medical Psychology* (59): 133–40.

Hunt, L. M., C. H. Browner, and B. Jordan. (1990). Hypoglycemia: Portrait of an illness construct. *Medical Anthropology Quarterly* (4): 191–210.

Jackson, A. R. (1878). On some points in connection with the treatment of sterility. *Transactions of the American Gynecological Society* (3): 347–62.

Jacobson, E. (1946). A case of sterility. *Psychoanalytic Quarterly* (15): 3300–3350.

Jaffe, S. B., and R. Jewelewicz. (1991). The basic infertility investigation. *Fertility and Sterility* (56): 599–613.

Jameton, A. (1984). *Nursing practice: The ethical issues.* Englewood Cliffs, NJ: Prentice-Hall.

Janoff-Bulman, R. (1979). Behavioral versus characterological self-blame: Inquiries into depression and rape. *Journal of Personality and Social Psychology* (37): 1798–1809.

Jansen, R. (1982). Spontaneous abortion incidence in the treatment of infertility. *American Journal of Obstetrics and Gynecology* (143): 451–73.

Jarrell, J., R. Gwatkin, R. N. Lumsden, K. G. Lamont, G. Boulter, S. Daya, and J. Collins. (1986). An in vitro fertilization and embryo transfer pilot study: Treatment-dependent and treatment-independent pregnancies. *American Journal of Obstetrics and Gynecology* (154): 231–35.

Johnston, M., R. Shaw, and D. Bird, (1987). "Test-tube baby" procedures: Stress and judgements under uncertainty. *Psychology and Health* (1): 25–38.

Johnston, W. I., K. Oke, A. Speirs, G. A. Clarke, J. McBain, C. Bayly, J. Hunt, and G. N. Clarke. (1985). Patient selection for in vitro fertilization: Physical and psychological aspects. *Annals of the New York Academy of Sciences* (442): 490–503.

Jones, H. W., A. A. Acosta, M. C. Andrews, J. E. Garcia, G. S. Jones, T. Mantzavinos, J. McDowell, B. A. Sandow, L. Veeck, T. W. Whibley, C. A. Wilkes, and G. L. Wright. (1983). What is a pregnancy? A question for programs of in vitro fertilization. *Fertility and Sterility* (40): 728–33.

Jones, H., and G. Jones. (1991, October–December). A fertile decade. *RESOLVE of the Triangle* (9): 1, 5–7.

Jordan, B. (1977). The self-diagnosis of early pregnancy: An investigation of lay competence. *Medical Anthropology* (1): 1–38.

Kaledin, E. (1984). *Mothers and more: American women in the 1950s.* Boston: Twayne.

Kamal, S. (1987). Seizure of reproductive rights? A discussion on population control in the Third World and the emergence of the new reproductive technologies in the West. In P. Spallone and D. L. Steinberg (Eds.), *Made to order: The myth of reproductive and genetic progress* (pp. 146–53). Oxford: Pergamon Press.

Kamman, G. R. (1946). The psychosomatic aspects of sterility. *Journal of the American Medical Association* (130): 1215–18.

Kass, L. R. (1979). "Making babies" revisited. *The Public Interest* (54): 32–60.

———. (1972). Making babies: The new biology and the "old" morality. *Public Interest* (26): 18–56.

———. (1971). Babies by means of in vitro fertilization: Unethical experiments on the unborn? *New England Journal of Medicine* (285): 1174–79.

Katz, S. S., and S. H. Katz. (1987). An evaluation of traditional therapy for barrenness. *Medical Anthropology Quarterly* (1): 394–405.

Kaufman, S. R. (1988). Toward a phenomenology of boundaries in medicine: Chronic illness experience in the case of stroke. *Medical Anthropology Quarterly* (2): 338–54.

Kay, T. W. (1891). A study of sterility, its causes and treatment. *Journal of the American Medical Association* (16): 181–84, 222–29, 265–70.

Kaye, K. (1990). Acknowledgment or rejection of differences? In D. M. Brodzinsky and M. D. Schechter (Eds.), *The psychology of adoption* (pp. 121–43). New York: Oxford University Press.

Keane, N. P. (1981). *The surrogate mother.* New York: Everest House.

Kelley, K. (1942). Sterility in the female with special reference to psychic factors, Part I: A review of the literature. *Psychosomatic Medicine* (4): 211–22.

Kermode, F. (1967). *The sense of an ending: Studies in the theory of fiction.* New York: Oxford University Press.

Kipper, D. A., Z. Zigler-Shani, D. M. Serr, and V. Insler. (1977). Psychogenic infertility, neuroticism, and the feminine role: A methodological inquiry. *Journal of Psychosomatic Research* (21): 353–58.

Kirk, H. D. (1988). Integrating the stranger: A problem in modern adoption, but not in that of ancient Greece and Rome. In B. J. Tansey (Ed.), *Exploring adoptive family life: The collected papers of H. David Kirk* (pp. 14–20). Port Angeles, WA: Ben-Simon.

———. (1985). *Adoptive kinship: A modern institution in need of reform,* rev. ed. Port Angeles, WA: Ben-Simon.

———. (1964/1984). *Shared fate: A theory and method of adoptive relationships,* sec. ed. rev. Port Angeles, WA: Ben-Simon.

Klawiter, M. (1990). Using Arendt and Heidegger to consider feminist thinking on women and reproductive/infertility technologies. *Hypatia* (5): 65–89.

Klein, R., and R. Rowland. (1989). Hormone cocktails: Women as test-sites for fertility drugs. *Women's Studies International Forum* (12): 333–48.

Kleinman, A. (1988). *The illness narratives: Suffering, healing, and the human condition.* New York: Basic Books.

——— (1980). *Patients and healers in the context of culture: An exploration of the borderland between anthropology, medicine, and psychiatry.* Berkeley: University of California Press.

Knowles, J. H. (1977). The responsibility of the individual. In J. H. Knowles (Ed.), *Doing better and feeling worse: Health in the United States* (pp. 57–80). New York: W. W. Norton.

Koch, L. (1990). IVF: An irrational choice? *Issues in Reproductive and Genetic Engineering* (3): 235–42.

Kopitzke, E. J., B. J. Berg, J. F. Wilson, and D. Owens. (1991). Physical and emotional stress associated with components of the infertility investigation: Perspectives of professionals and patients. *Fertility and Sterility* (55): 1137–43.

Kornheiser, T. (1983). *The baby chase.* New York: Atheneum.

Kosterman, C. (1987, May). When the stork doesn't come. *Leader,* pp. 6–8.

Kovacs, G. T., B. J. Downing, A. J. Krins, and L. Freeman. (1991). Triplets or sequential siblings? A case report of three children born after one episode of in vitro fertilization. *Fertility and Sterility* (56): 987–88.

Kroger, W. S., and S. C. Freed. (1951). *Psychosomatic gynecology: Including problems of obstetrical care.* Philadelphia: Saunders.

Lacayo, R. (1989, October). Nobody's children. *Time* (134): 91–95.

Lalos, A., O. Lalos, L. Jacobsson, and B. Von Schoultz. (1986). Depression, guilt and isolation among infertile women and their partners. *Journal of Psychosomatic Obstetrics and Gynaecology* (5): 197–206.

Lancaster, P. (1985). Obstetric outcome. *Clinics in Obstetrics and Gynecology* (12): 847–64.

Lange, S. P. (1978). Hope. In C. E. Carlson, and B. Blackwell (Eds.), *Behavioral concepts and nursing intervention,* 2nd ed. (pp. 171–90). Philadelphia: J. B. Lippincott.

Lappe, M. (1984). The predictive power of the new genetics. *Hastings Center Report* (14): 18–21.

Lasker, J. N., and S. Borg. (1987). *In search of parenthood: Coping with infertility and high-tech conception.* Boston: Beacon Press.

Lauritzen, P. (1991). Pursuing parenthood: Reflections on donor insemination. *Second Opinion* (17): 57–76.

Lechtman, H., and A. Steinberg. (1979). The history of technology: An anthropological point of view. In G. Bugliarello and D. B. Doner (Eds.), *The history and philosophy of technology* (pp. 135–60). Urbana: University of Illinois Press.

Leiblum, S. R., E. Kemmann, D. Colburn, S. Pasquale, and A. DeLisi. (1987). Unsuccessful in vitro fertilization: A follow-up study. *Journal of In Vitro Fertilization and Embryo Transfer* (4): 46–50.

Leiblum, S. R., E. Kemmann, and M. K. Lane. (1987). The psychological concomitants of in vitro fertilization. *Journal of Psychosomatic Obstetrics and Gynaecology* (6): 165–78.

Leon, N. G. (1989, June). Nature's beauty: A painful reminder. *RESOLVE National Newsletter* (14): 3.

Leridon, H., and A. Spira. (1984). Problems in measuring the effectiveness of infertility therapy. *Fertility and Sterility* (41): 580–86.

Lilford, R. J., and M. E. Dalton. (1987). Effectiveness of treatment for infertility. *British Medical Journal* (295): 155–56.

Lincoln, Y. S., and E. G. Guba. (1985). *Naturalistic inquiry.* Beverly Hills, CA: Sage.

Lipson, J. G., and V. P. Tilden. (1980). Psychological integration of the cesarean birth experience. *American Journal of Orthopsychiatry* (50): 598–609.

Loftus, V. (1989, September). Infertility and the feelings it creates. *RESOLVE National Newsletter* (14): 7.

Longo, L. D. (1979). The rise and fall of Battey's operation: A fashion in surgery. *Bulletin of the History of Medicine* (53): 244–67.

Lorber, J. (1989). Choice, gift, or patriarchal bargain? Women's consent to in vitro fertilization in male infertility. *Hypatia* (4): 23–36.

———. (1987). In vitro fertilization and gender politics. *Women and Health* (13): 117–33.

Lorber, J., and D. Greenfeld. (1990). Couples' experiences with in vitro fertilization: A phenomenological approach. In S. Mashiach et al. (Eds.), *Advances in assisted reproductive technologies* (pp. 965–71). New York: Plenum Press.

Lovell, A. (1983). Some questions of identity: Late miscarriage, stillbirth and perinatal loss. *Social Science and Medicine* (17): 755–61.

Lumley, J. (1980). The image of the fetus in the first trimester. *Birth and the Family Journal* (7): 5–14.

Macklin, R. (1991). Artificial means of reproduction and our understanding of the family. *Hastings Center Report* (21): 5–11.

Macomber, D. (1924). Prevention of sterility. *Journal of the American Medical Association* (83): 678–82.

Mai, F. M., R. N. Munday, and E. E. Rump. (1972). Psychosomatic and behavioral mechanisms in psychogenic infertility. *British Journal of Psychiatry* (120): 199–204.

Maitland, S. (1978/1980). *The languages of love* (originally titled *Daughters of Jerusalem*). Garden City, NY: Doubleday.

Mandy, T. E., E. Scher, R. Farkas, and A. J. Mandy. (1951). The psychic aspects of sterility and abortion. *Southern Medical Journal* (44): 1054–59.

Mao, K., and C. Wood. (1984). Barriers to treatment of infertility by in vitro fertilization and embryo transfer. *The Medical Journal of Australia* (140): 532–33.

Marbach, A. H. (1961). The study of psychosomatic gynecology and obstetrics. *Postgraduate Medicine* (30): 479–88.

Margolis, M. L. (1984). *Mothers and such: Views of American women and why they changed.* Berkeley: University of California Press.

Marquis, K. S., and R. A. Detweiler. (1985). Does adopted mean different? An attributional analysis. *Journal of Personality and Social Psychology* (48): 1054–66.

Marx, L. (1964). *The machine in the garden: Technology and the pastoral ideal in America.* New York: Oxford University Press.

Mason, C. (1985). The production and effects of uncertainty with special reference to diabetes mellitus. *Social Science and Medicine* (21): 1329–34.

Mason, M. M. (1987). *The miracle seekers: An anthology of infertility.* Fort Wayne, IN: Perspectives Press.

Matson, P. L. (1990). The usefulness of IVF, GIFT and IUI in the treatment of male infertility. In P. L. Matson and B. A. Lieberman (Eds.), *Clinical IVF Forum: Current views in assisted reproduction* (pp. 112–22). Manchester, England: Manchester University Press.

May, E. T. (1988). *Homeward bound: American families in the Cold War era.* New York: Basic.

May, W. F. (1984). The virtues in a professional setting. *Soundings* (67): 245–66.

Mazure, C. M., W. De L'Aune, and A. H. DeCherney. (1988). Two methodological issues in the psychological study of in vitro fertilization/embryo transfer participants. *Journal of Psychosomatic Obstetrics and Gynaecology* (9): 17–21.

Mazure, C. M., and D. A. Greenfeld. (1989). Psychological studies of in vitro fertilization/embryo transfer participants. *Journal of In Vitro Fertilization and Embryo Transfer* (6): 242–56.

McNeil, M., I. Varcoe, and S. Yearley. (1990). *The new reproductive technologies.* New York: St. Martin's Press.

Medical Research International, Society of Assisted Reproductive Technology, American Fertility Society. (1992). In vitro fertilization-embryo transfer (IVF-ET) in the United States: 1990 results from the IVF-ET registry. *Fertility and Sterility* (57): 15–24.

McCormack, T. (1989). When is biology destiny? In C. Overall (Ed.), *The future of human reproduction* (pp. 80–94). Toronto: The Women's Press.

McLane, C. M., and M. McLane. (1969). A half century of sterility, 1840–1890. *Fertility and Sterility* (20): 853–70.

Meaker, S. R. (1934). *Human sterility: Causation, diagnosis, and treatment.* Baltimore: Williams and Wilkins.

———. (1927, November). Two million American homes childless. *Hygeia* (5): 546–48.

Menning, B. E. (1980). The emotional needs of infertile couples. *Fertility and Sterility* (34): 313–19.

———. (1977). *Infertility: A guide for the childless couple.* Englewood Cliffs, NJ: Prentice-Hall.

Miall, C. E. (1989). Authenticity and the disclosure of the information preserve: The case of adoptive parenthood. *Qualitative Sociology* (12): 279–302.

———. (1987). The stigma of adoptive parent status: Perceptions of community attitudes toward adoption and the experience of informal social sanctioning. *Family Relations* (36): 34–39.

———. (1986). The stigma of involuntary childlessness. *Social Problems* (33): 268–82.

———. (1985). Perceptions of informal sanctioning and the stigma of involuntary childlessness. *Deviant Behavior* (6): 383–403.

Miller, R. S. (1978). The social construction and reconstruction of physiological events: Acquiring the pregnancy identity. In N. K. Denzin (Ed.), *Studies in symbolic interaction* (vol. 1, pp. 181–204). Greenwich, CT: JAI Press.

Milne, B. (1988). Couples' experiences with in vitro fertilization. *Journal of Obstetric, Gynecologic, and Neonatal Nursing* (17): 347–52.

Milsom, I., and P. Bergman. (1982). A study of parental attitudes after donor insemination (AID). *Acta Obstetricia et Gynecologica Scandinavica* (61): 125–28.

Mitchard, J. (1985). *Mother less child: The love story of a family.* New York: Norton.

Modell, J. (1989). Last chance babies: Interpretations of parenthood in an in vitro fertilization program. *Medical Anthropology Quarterly* (3): 124–38.

———. (1986). In search: The purported biological basis of parenthood. *American Ethnologist* (13): 646–61.

Moench, G. L. (1927). A consideration of some of the aspects of sterility. *American Journal of Obstetrics and Gynecology* (13): 334–45.

Moghissi, K. S., and E. E. Wallach. (1983). Unexplained infertility. *Fertility and Sterility* (39): 5–21.

Mohr, J. C. (1978). *Abortion in America: The origins and evolution of national policy.* New York: Oxford University Press.

Morrow, P. A. (1909). The relations of social diseases to the family. *American Journal of Sociology* (14): 622–37.

———. (1907). Prophylaxis of social diseases. *American Journal of Sociology* (13): 20–33.

———. (1904). *Social diseases and marriage: Social prophylaxis.* New York: Lea Brothers.

Morse, J. M., J. Bottorff, W. Neander, and S. Solberg. (1991). Comparative analysis of conceptualizations and theories of caring. *Image: Journal of Nursing Scholarship* (23): 119–26.

Mosher, W. D., and W. F. Pratt. (1991). Fecundity and infertility in the United States: Incidence and trends. *Fertility and Sterility* (56): 192–93.

Mosher, W. D., and W. F. Pratt. (1990). Fecundity and infertility in the United States, 1965–1988. *Advance Data* (Vital and health statistics of the National Center for Health Statistics) (192): 1–8.

Murphy, R. F. (1990). *The body silent.* New York: W. W. Norton.

Murphy, R. F., J. Scheer, Y. Murphy, and R. Mack. (1988). Physical disability and social liminality: A study in the rituals of adversity. *Social Science and Medicine* (26): 235–42.

Murray, K. (1989). The construction of identity in the narratives of romance and comedy. In J. Shotter and K. J. Gergen (Eds.), *Texts of identity* (pp. 176–205). London: Sage.

Muse, K. (1988). Clinical manifestations and classification of endometriosis. *Clinical Obstetrics and Gynecology* (31): 813–22.

Napheys, G. H. (1869). *The physical life of woman: Advice to the maiden, wife, and mother.* Philadelphia: George MacLean.

Nash, A., and J. E. Nash. (1979). Conflicting interpretations of childbirth: The medical and natural perspectives. *Urban Life* (7): 493–512.

Nelson, M. K. (1986). Birth and social class. In P. S. Eakins (Ed.), *The American way of birth* (pp. 142–74). Philadelphia: Temple University Press.

———. (1983). Working-class women, middle-class women, and models of child-birth. *Social Problems* (30): 284–97.

———. (1982). The effect of childbirth preparation on women of different social classes. *Journal of Health and Social Behavior* (23): 339–52.

"New bedfellows: Freedom and infertility." (1980, May). *Science News,* pp. 341–42.

Noeggerath, E. (1876). Latent gonorrhea, especially with regard to its influence on fertility in women. *Transactions of the American Gynecological Society* (1): 268–300.

Novaes, S. B. (1989). Giving, receiving, repaying: Gamete donors and donor policies in reproductive medicine. *International Journal of Technology Assessment in Health Care* (5): 639–57.

Noyes, R. W., and E. M. Chapnick. (1964). Literature on psychology and infertility: A critical analysis. *Fertility and Sterility* (15): 543–58.

Nsiah-Jefferson, L., and E. J. Hall. (1989). Reproductive technology. In K. S. Ratcliff (Ed.), *Healing technology: Feminist perspectives* (pp. 93–117). Ann Arbor: University of Michigan press.

Oakley, A. (1986). *The captured womb: A history of the medical care of pregnant women.* New York: Basil Blackwell.

———. (1980). *Women confined: Towards a sociology of childbirth.* New York: Schocken Books.

O'Brien, M. (1989). *Reproducing the world: Essays in feminist theory.* Boulder, CO: Westview Press.

———. (1981). *The politics of reproduction.* Boston: Routledge and Kegan Paul.

O'Brien, M. E. (1984). *The courage to survive: The life career of the chronic dialysis patient.* New York: Grune and Stratton.

Oehninger, S., A. A. Acosta, D. Kreiner, S. J. Muasher, H. W. Jones, and Z. Rosenwaks. (1988). In vitro fertilization and embryo transfer (IVF-ET): An established and successful therapy for endometriosis. *Journal of In Vitro Fertilization and Embryo Transfer* (5): 249–56.

Olive, D. L. (1986). Analysis of clinical fertility trials: A methodologic review. *Fertility and Sterility* (45): 157–71.

Olshansky, E. F. (1988). Responses to high technology infertility treatment. *Image: Journal of Nursing Scholarship* (20): 128–31.

———. (1987). Identity of self as infertile: An example of theory-generating research. *Advances in Nursing Science* (9): 54–63.

O'Moore, A. M., R. R. O'Moore, R. F. Harrison, G. Murphy, and M. E. Carruthers. (1983). Psychosomatic aspects in idiopathic infertility: Effects of treatment with autogenic training. *Journal of Psychosomatic Research* (27): 145–51.

Orr, D. W. (1941). Pregnancy following the decision to adopt. *Psychosomatic Medicine* (3): 441–46.

Overall, C. (1990). Selective termination of pregnancy and women's reproductive autonomy. *Hastings Center Report* (20): 6–11.

———. (1987). *Ethics and human reproduction: A feminist analysis*. Boston: Allen and Unwin.

Overall, C. (Ed.). (1989). *The future of human reproduction*. Toronto: The Women's Press.

Pallen, M. A. (1877). Resume on incision and division of the cervix uteri for dysmenorrhea and sterility. *American Journal of Obstetrics and Gynecology* (10): 364–89.

Palmer, G. (1941, September). Plan for parenthood. *Ladies Home Journal* (58): 28, 54, 56–58.

Paterson, P., and C. Chan. (1987). What proportion of couples undergoing unrestricted in vitro fertilization treatments can expect to bear a child? *Journal of In Vitro Fertilization and Embryo Transfer* (4): 334–37.

Patterson, E. T., M. P. Freese, and R. L. Goldenberg. (1986). Reducing uncertainty: Self-diagnosis of pregnancy. *Image: Journal of Nursing Scholarship* (18): 105–9.

Pauker, S. P., and S. G. Pauker. (1987). The amniocentesis decision: Ten years of decision analytic experience. *Birth Defects: Original Article Series* (23): 151–69.

Paulson, J. D., B. S. Haarmann, R. L. Salerno, and P. Asmar. (1988). An investigation of the relationship between emotional maladjustment and infertility. *Fertility and Sterility* (49): 258–62.

Pawson, M. E. (1981). The infertile patient: Does she always want a baby? In J. Cortes-Trieto, A. Campos Da Paz, and M. Neves-e-Castro (Eds.), *Research on fertility and sterility* (pp. 437–44). Baltimore: University Park Press.

Pearn, J. H. (1973). Patients' subjective interpretation of risks offered in genetic counseling. *Journal of Medical Genetics* (10): 129–34.

Peitzman, S. J. (1989). From dropsy to Bright's disease to end-stage renal disease. *The Milbank Quarterly* (67): 16–32.

Pellegrino, E. D. (1982). Being ill and being healed. In V. Kestenbaum (Ed.), *The humanity of the ill: Phenomenological perspectives* (pp. 156–66). Knoxville: University of Tennessee Press.

———. (1979). The sociocultural impact of twentieth-century therapeutics. In M. J. Vogel and C. E. Rosenberg (Eds.), *The therapeutic revolution: Essays in the social history of American medicine* (pp. 245–66). Philadelphia: University of Pennsylvania Press.

Pepe, M. V., and T. J. Byrne. (1991). Women's perceptions of immediate and long-term effects of failed infertility treatment on marital and sexual satisfaction. *Family Relations* (40): 303–9.

Peppers, L. G., and R. J. Knapp. (1980). *Motherhood and mourning: Perinatal death.* New York: Praeger.

Perakyla, A. (1991). Hope work in the care of seriously ill patients. *Qualitative Health Research* (1): 407–33.

Petchesky, R. P. (1980). Reproductive freedom: Beyond "a woman's right to choose." *Signs: Journal of Women in Culture and Society* (5): 661–85.

Peters, S. (1884). Remarks on the causes of sterility. *American Journal of Obstetrics and Diseases of Women and Children* (17): 841–51.

Peters-Golden, H. (1982). Breast cancer: Varied perceptions of social support in the illness experience. *Social Science and Medicine* (16): 483–91.

Pfeffer, N., and A. Woollett. (1983). *The experience of infertility.* London: Virago Press.

Phipps, S. (1985/1986). The subsequent pregnancy after stillbirth: Anticipatory parenthood in the face of uncertainty. *International Journal of Psychiatry in Medicine* (15): 243–63.

Plough, A. L. (1981). Medical technology and the crisis of experience: The costs of clinical legitimation. *Social Science and Medicine* (15F): 89–101.

Pogrebin, L. C. (1983). *Family politics: Love and power on an intimate frontier.* New York: McGraw-Hill.

Polak, J. O. (1916). A detailed study of the pathological causes of sterility with the end-results. *Surgery, Gynecology, and Obstetrics* (23): 261–68.

Polkinghorne, D. E. (1988). *Narrative knowing and the human sciences.* Albany, NY: State University of New York Press.

Popenoe, P. I. (1948). Infertility and the stability of marriage. *Western Journal of Surgery, Obstetrics, and Gynecology* (56): 309–10.

Popenoe, P. (1926). *The conservation of the family.* Baltimore: Williams and Wilkins.

Poston, D. L. (1976). Characteristics of voluntarily and involuntarily childless wives. *Social Biology* (23): 198–209.

Poston, D. L., and R. M. Cullen. (1986). Log-linear analyses of patterns of adoption behavior: U.S. white women, 1982, 1976, and 1973. *Social Biology* (33): 241–48.

Poston, D. L., and E. Gotard. (1977). Trends in childlessness in the United States, 1910–1975. *Social Biology* (24): 212–24.

Quindlen, A. (1987, June). Baby craving. *Life,* pp. 23–42.

Ramsey, P. (1972). Shall we reproduce? II. Rejoinders and future forecast. *Journal of the American Medical Association* (220): 1480–85.

Rapp, R. (1988a). Chromosomes and communication: The discourse of genetic counseling. *Medical Anthropology Quarterly* (2): 143–57.

———. (1988b). The power of "positive" diagnosis: Medical and maternal discourses on amniocentesis. In K. L. Michaelson (Ed.), *Childbirth in America: Anthropological perspectives* (pp. 103–16). Boston: Bergin and Garvey.

Raymond, J. G. (1990). Reproductive gifts and gift giving: The altruistic woman. *Hasting Center Report* (20): 7–11.

Raymond, J. (1984). Feminist ethics, ecology, and vision. In R. Arditti, R. D. Klein, and S. Minden (Eds.), *Test-tube women: What future for motherhood?* (pp. 427–37). London: Pandora Press.

Reading, A. E., L. C. Chang, and J. F. Kerin. (1989). Psychological state and coping styles across an IVF treatment cycle. *Journal of Reproductive and Infant Psychology* (7): 95–103.

Reed, J. (1984). *The birth control movement and American society: From private vice to public virtue.* Princeton, NJ: Princeton University Press.

Reichlin, S., J. M. Abplanalp, A. H. Labrum, N. Schwartz, B. Sommer, and M. Taymor. (1979). The role of stress in female reproductive dysfunction. *Journal of Human Stress* (5): 38–45.

Reinharz, S. (1983). Phenomenology as a dynamic process. *Phenomenology and Pedagogy* (1): 77–79.

Reiser, S. J. (1985). Responsibility for personal health: A historical perspective. *Journal of Medicine and Philosophy* (10): 7–17.

Reverby, S. (1987). *Ordered to care: The dilemma of American nursing, 1850–1945.* Cambridge: Cambridge University Press.

Rich, A. (1977). *Of woman born: Motherhood as experience and institution.* New York: Bantam.

Richardson, L. (1990). Narrative and sociology. *Journal of Contemporary Ethnography* (19): 116–35.

Riessman, C. K. (1989). Life events, meaning and narrative: The case of infidelity and divorce. *Social Science and Medicine* (29): 743–51.

Robbins, L. L. (1943). Suggestions for the psychological study of sterility in women. *Bulletin of the Menninger Clinic* (7): 41–44.

Robinson, J. O., B. M. Hibbard, and K. M. Laurence. (1984). Anxiety during a crisis: Emotional effects of screening for neural tube defects. *Journal of Psychosomatic Research* (28): 163–69.

Rodin, J., and A. Collins. (1991). *Women and new reproductive technologies: Medical, psychosocial, legal, and ethical dilemmas.* Hillsdale, NJ: Lawrence Erlbaum Associates.

Roh, S. I., S. G. Awadella, C. I. Friedman, J. M. Park, N. O. Chin, W. G. Dodds, and M. H. Kim. (1987). In vitro fertilization and embryo transfer: Treatment-dependent versus -independent pregnancies. *Fertility and Sterility* (48): 982–86.

Rommer, J. J., and C. S. Rommer. (1958). Sexual tones in marriage of the sterile and once-sterile female. *Fertility and Sterility* (9): 309–20.

Rongy, A. J. (1923). Primary sterility. *American Journal of Obstetrics and Gynecology* (5): 631–37.

Rook, K. S. (1984). The negative side of social interaction: Impact on psychological well-being. *Journal of Personality and Social Psychology* (46): 1097–1108.

Rosenberg, C. E. (1989). Disease in history: Frames and framers. *The Milbank Quarterly* (67): 1–15.

———. (1986). Disease and the social order in America: Perceptions and expectations. *The Milbank Quarterly* (64): 34–55.

Rosenberg, E. B., and T. M. Horner. (1991). Birthparent romances and identity formation in adopted children. *American Journal of Orthopsychiatry* (61): 70–77.

Rosenblatt, P. C., P. Peterson, J. Portner, M. Cleveland, A. Mykkanen, R. Foster, G. Holm, B. Joel, H. Reisch, C. Kreuscher, and R. Phillips. (1973). A cross-cultural study of responses to childlessness. *Behavior Science Notes* (8): 221–31.

Rosenfeld, D. L., S. M. Seidman, R. A. Bronson, and G. M. Scholl. (1983). Unsuspected chronic pelvic inflammatory disease in the infertile female. *Fertility and Sterility* (39): 44–48.

Rosenkrantz, B. G. (1979). Damaged goods: Dilemmas of responsibility for risk. *Milbank Memorial Fund Quarterly* (57): 1–37.

Rothbaum, F., J. R. Weisz, and S. S. Snyder. (1982). Changing the world and changing the self: A two-process model of perceived control. *Journal of Personality and Social Psychology* (42): 5–37.

Rothenberg, M. B., and E. M. Sills. (1968). Iatrogenesis: The PKU anxiety syndrome. *Journal of the American Academy of Child Psychiatry* (7): 689–92.

Rothman, B. K. (1989). *Recreating motherhood: Ideology and technology in a patriarchal society.* New York: W. W. Norton.

———. (1988). The decision to have and not to have amniocentesis for prenatal diagnosis. In K. L. Michaelson (Ed.), *Childbirth in America: Anthropological perspectives* (pp. 90–102). Boston: Bergin and Garvey.

———. (1986). *The tentative pregnancy: Prenatal diagnosis and the future of motherhood.* New York: Viking.

———. (1984). The meanings of choice in reproductive technology. In R. Arditti, R. D. Klein, and S. Minden (Eds.), *Test-tube women: What future for motherhood?* (pp. 23–33). London: Pandora Press.

———. (1982). *In labor: Women and power in the birthplace.* New York: W. W. Norton.

Rowland, R. (1987). Technology and motherhood: Reproductive choice reconsidered. *Signs: Journal of Women in Culture and Society* (12): 512–28.

———. (1985). The social and psychological consequences of secrecy in artificial insemination by donor (AID) programs. *Social Science and Medicine* (4): 391–96.

Rozin, S. (1965). *Uterosalpingography in gynecology.* Springfield, IL: Thomas.

Rubin, I. C. (1954). Forty years' progress in the treatment of female sterility. *American Journal of Obstetrics and Gynecology* (68): 324–33.

———. (1947). Unintentional childless marriage. *Hygeia* (25): 196.

———. (1931). Sterility secondary to induced abortion with special reference to the tubal factor. *New York State Journal of Medicine* (31): 213–17.

Rubin, R. (1984). *Maternal identity and the maternal experience.* New York: Springer.

Ruddick, S. (1980). Maternal thinking. *Feminist Studies* (6): 342–67.

Rudkin, D. (1974). *Ashes* (A Play). London: Samuel French.

Rundall, T. G., and C. Evashwick. (1982). Social networks and help-seeking among the elderly. *Research on Aging* (4): 205–26.

Rutherford, R. N. (1965). Emotional aspects of infertility. *Clinical Obstetrics and Gynecology* (8): 100–114.

Rutherford, R. N., A. L. Banks, and H. M. Lamborn. (1951). One pregnancy sterility. *American Journal of Obstetrics and Gynecology* (61): 443–45.

Ryder, N. B. (1969). The emergence of a modern fertility pattern: United States, 1917–1966. In S. J. Behrman, L. Corsa, and R. Freedman (Eds.), *Fertility and family planning: A world view* (pp. 99–123). Ann Arbor: University of Michigan Press.

Sacks, O. (1987). *The man who mistook his wife for a hat: And other clinical tales.* New York: Harper and Row.

Sahaj, D. A., C. K. Smith, K. L. Kimmel, R. A. Houseknecht, R. A. Hewes, B. E. Meyer, L. B. Leduc, and A. Danforth. (1988). A psychosocial description of a select group of infertile couples. *Journal of Family Practice* (27): 393–97.

Sandelowski, M. (1991). Telling stories: Narrative approaches in qualitative research. *Image: Journal of Nursing Scholarship* (23): 161–66.

———. (1984). Expectations for childbirth versus actual experience: The gap widens. *American Journal of Maternal Child Nursing* (9): 237–39.

———. (1984). *Pain, pleasure, and American childbirth: From the Twilight Sleep to the Read Method, 1914–1960.* Westport, CT: Greenwood Press.

Sandelowski, M., and R. Bustamante. (1986). Cesarean birth outside the natural childbirth culture. *Research in Nursing and Health* (9): 81–88.

Sandler, B. (1968). Emotional stress and infertility. *Journal of Psychosomatic Research* (12): 51–59.

Sants, H. J. (1964). Genealogical bewilderment in children with substitute parents. *British Journal of Medical Psychology* (37): 133–41.

Sargent, C., and N. Stark. (1987). Surgical birth: Interpretations of cesarean delivery among private hospital patients and nursing staff. *Social Science and Medicine* (25): 1269–76.

Savage, J. A. (1989). *Mourning unlived lives: A psychological study of childbearing loss.* Wilmette, IL: Chiron Publications.

Schechner, R. (1967). There's lots of time in Godot. In R. Cohn (Ed.), *Casebook on Waiting for Godot* (pp. 175–87). New York: Grove Press.

Schechter, M. D. (1970). About adoptive parents. In E. J. Anthony and T. Benedek (Eds.), *Parenthood: Its psychology and psychopathology* (pp. 353–71). Boston: Little, Brown.

Scheler, M. (1954). *The nature of sympathy* (trans. P. Heath). New Haven: Yale University Press.

Schlaff, W. D. (1991, September). Ethical and practical considerations in treating low-income infertility patients. *Fertility News* (25): 11–12.

Schmidt, C. L. (1985). Endometriosis: A reappraisal of pathogenesis and treatment. *Fertility and Sterility* (44): 157–73.

Schneider, D. M. (1980). *American kinship: A cultural account,* 2nd ed. Chicago: University of Chicago Press.

Schoysman-DeBoeck, A., E. Van Roosendaal, and R. Schoysman. (1988). Artificial insemination: AID. In S. J. Behrman, R. W. Kistner, and G. W. Patton (Eds.), *Progress in infertility,* 3rd ed. (pp. 713–36). Boston: Little, Brown.

Schroeder, P. (1988). Infertility and the world outside. *Fertility and Sterility* (49): 765–67.

Schur, E. M. (1983). *Labeling women deviant: Gender, stigma, and social control.* Philadelphia: Temple University Press.

————. (1979). *Interpreting deviance: A sociological introduction*. New York: Harper and Row.

Schwartz, B. (1974). Waiting, exchange, and power: The distribution of time in social systems. *American Journal of Sociology* (79): 841–70.

Sciarra, J. J. (1989). Infertility: Selected topics of international interest, 1988. In P. Berfort, J. A. Pinotti, and T. K. Eskes (Eds.), *Fertility, sterility, and contraception* (pp. 3–16). New Jersey: Parthenon Publishing.

Scritchfield, S. A. (1989). The infertility enterprise: IVF and the technological construction of reproductive impairments. *Research in the Sociology of Health Care* (8): 61–97.

Seibel, M. M. (1990). *Infertility: A comprehensive text*. Norwalk, CT: Appleton and Lange.

Seibel, M. M., and S. R. Bayer. (1989). Complex forms of ovulation induction. In M. R. Soules (Ed.), *Controversies in reproductive endocrinology and infertility* (pp. 107–29). New York: Elsevier.

Seibel, M. M., M. J. Berger, F. G. Weinstein, and M. L. Taymor. (1982). The effectiveness of danazol on subsequent infertility in minimal endometriosis. *Fertility and Sterility* (38): 534–37.

Seibel, M. M., and S. Levin. (1987). A new era in reproductive technologies: The emotional stages of in vitro fertilization. *Journal of In Vitro Fertilization and Embryo Transfer* (4): 135–40.

Seibel, M. M., C. Ranoux, and M. Kearnan. (1989). In vitro fertilization: How much is enough? (letter to editor). *New England Journal of Medicine* (321): 1052–53.

Seibel, M. M., and M. L. Taymor. (1982). Emotional aspects of infertility. *Fertility and Sterility* (37): 137–45.

Selzer, R. (1982). *Letters to a young doctor*. New York: Simon and Schuster.

Sha, J. L. (1990). *Mothers of thyme: Customs and rituals of infertility and miscarriage*. Minneapolis, MN: Lida Rose Press.

Shaver, K. G. (1985). *The attribution of blame: Causality, responsibility, and blame-worthiness*. New York: Springer-Verlag.

Shiloh, S., S. Larom, and Z. Ben-Rafael. (1991). The meaning of treatments for infertility: Cognitive determinants and structure. *Journal of Applied Social Psychology* (21): 855–74.

Shorter, E. (1982). *A history of women's bodies*. New York: Basic.

————. (1980). Women's diseases before 1900. In M. Albin (Ed.), *New directions in psychohistory: The Adelphi Papers* (pp. 183–208). Lexington, MA: Heath.

Siegler, A. M., J. Hulka, and A. Peretz. (1985). Reversibility of female sterilization. *Fertility and Sterility* (43): 499–510.

Silber, S. J. (1978). Vasectomy and vasectomy reversal. *Fertility and Sterility* (29): 125–40.

Simmons, J. L. (1981). The nature of deviant subcultures. In E. Rubington and M. S. Weinberg (Eds.), *Deviance: The interactionist perspective*, 4th ed. (pp. 226–68). New York: Macmillan.

Simons, H. F. (1984). Infertility: Implications for policy formulation. In M. D.

Mazor and H. F. Simons (Eds.), *Infertility: Medical, emotional, and social considerations* (pp. 61–70). New York: Human Sciences Press.

Sims, J. M. (1868–69). On the microscope as an aid in the diagnosis and treatment of sterility. *New York Medical Journal* (8): 393–413.

———. (1866). *Clinical notes on uterine surgery: With special reference to the management of the sterile condition*. New York: William Wood.

Sjogren, B., and N. Uddenberg. (1988). Decision making during the prenatal diagnostic procedure: A questionnaire and interview study of 211 women participating in prenatal diagnosis. *Prenatal Diagnosis* (8): 263–73.

Slaby, A. E., and A. S. Glicksman. (1985). *Adapting to life-threatening illness*. New York: Praeger.

Slade, P. (1981). Sexual attitudes and social role orientations in infertile women. *Journal of Psychosomatic Research* (25): 183–86.

Smith, D. S. (1979). Family limitation, sexual control, and domestic feminism in Victorian America. In N. F. Cott and E. H. Pleck (Eds.), *A heritage of her own: Toward a new social history of American women* (pp. 222–45). New York: Touchstone.

Smith, J. F. (1983). Parenting and property. In J. Treblicot (Ed.), *Mothering: Essays in feminist theory* (pp. 199–212). Totowa, NJ: Rowman and Allanheld.

Smith-Rosenberg, C. (1973a). The female animal: Medical and biological views of woman and her role in nineteenth-century America. *Journal of American History* (60): 332–56.

———. (1973b). Puberty to menopause: The cycle of femininity in nineteenth-century America. *Feminist Studies* (1): 58–72.

Somerville, M. A. (1982). Birth technology, parenting, and "deviance." *International Journal of Law and Psychiatry* (5): 123–53.

Sontag, S. (1979). *Illness as metaphor*. New York: Vintage.

Sorosky, A. D., A. Baran, and R. Pannor. (1984). *The adoption triangle*. Garden City, NY: Anchor Books.

Soules, M. R. (1985). The in vitro fertilization pregnancy rate: Let's be honest with one another. *Fertility and Sterility* (43): 511–13.

Spallone, P., and D. L. Steinberg. (Eds.). (1987). *Made to order: The myth of reproductive and genetic progress*. Oxford: Pergamon Press.

Special issue: Reproductive and genetic engineering. (1985). *Women's Studies International Forum* 8 (6).

Stack, C. B. (1974). *All our kin: Strategies for survival in a black community*. New York: Harper and Row.

Stanworth, M. (1990). Birth pangs: Conceptive technologies and the threat to motherhood. In M. Hirsch and E. F. Keller (Eds.), *Conflicts in feminism* (pp. 288–304). New York: Routledge.

Stanworth, M. (Ed.). (1987). *Reproductive technologies: Gender, motherhood, and medicine*. Minneapolis: University of Minnesota Press.

Steinberg, D. L. (1990). The depersonalization of women through the administration of "in vitro fertilization." In M. McNeil, I. Varcoe, and S. Yearley (Eds.), *The new reproductive technologies* (pp. 74–122). New York: St. Martin's Press.

Sterility and neurotics. (1952, June). *Time*, pp. 81–82.

Stern, A. (1955). Ambivalence and conception. *Fertility and Sterility* (6): 540–42.

Stewart, E. C., and M. J. Bennett. (1991). *American cultural patterns: A cross-cultural perspective*. Yarmouth, ME: Intercultural Press.

Strauss, A., and J. Corbin. (1991). Comeback: The process of overcoming disability. In A. Strauss, *Creating sociological awareness: Collective images and symbolic representations* (pp. 361–84). New Brunswick: Transaction.

Suls, J. M., and R. L. Miller. (Eds.). (1977). *Social comparison processes: Theoretical and empirical perspectives*. Washington, DC: Hemisphere.

Summey, P. S., and M. Hurst. (1986). Ob/Gyn on the rise: The evolution of professional ideology in the twentieth century, Part II. *Women and Health* (11): 103–22.

Swanson, K. M. (1990). Providing care in the NICU: Sometimes an act of love. *Advances in Nursing Science* (13), 60–73.

Tabor, A., and M. H. Jonsson. (1987). Psychological impact of amniocentesis on low-risk women. *Prenatal Diagnosis* (7): 443–49.

Taeuber, I. B. (1971). Fertility, diversity, and policy. *Milbank Memorial Fund Quarterly* (49): 208–29.

Tagatz, G. (1990). Medical techniques for assisted reproduction. In D. M. Bartels, R. Priester, D. E. Vawter, and A. L. Caplan (Eds.), *Beyond Baby M: Ethical issues in new reproductive techniques* (pp. 89–110). Clifton, NJ: Humana Press.

Takefman, J. E., W. Brender, J. Boivin, and T. Tulandi. (1990). Sexual and emotional adjustment of couples undergoing infertility investigation and the effectiveness of preparatory information. *Journal of Psychosomatic Obstetrics and Gynaecology* (11): 275–90.

Talbert, L. M. (1985). The arithmetic of infertility therapy. In M. G. Hammond and L. M. Talbert (Eds.), *Infertility: A practical guide for the physician* (pp. 9–14). Oradell, NJ: Medical Economics Books.

Taylor, P. T. (1990). When is enough enough? *Fertility and Sterility* (54): 772–74.

Taylor, R. W. (1905). *A practical treatise on sexual disorders of the male and female*, 3rd ed. New York: Lea Brothers.

Taylor, W. C. (1871). *A physician's counsels to woman, in health and disease*. Springfield, MA: W. J. Holland.

Thomas, E. J. (1984). *Designing interventions for the helping professions*. Beverly Hills, CA: Sage.

Thomas, T. G. (1891). *A practical treatise on the diseases of women*, 6th ed. Philadelphia: Lea Brothers.

Thorne, B., and M. Yalom. (Eds.). (1982). *Rethinking the family: Some feminist questions*. White Plains, NY: Longman.

Tolnay, S. E., and A. M. Guest. (1982). Childlessness in a transitional population: The United States at the turn of the century. *Journal of Family History* (7): 200–219.

Tompkins, P. (1950). Editorial: A new journal. *Fertility and Sterility* (1): 1–2.

Toon, P. D. (1981). Defining "disease": Classification must be distinguished from evaluation. *Journal of Medical Ethics* (7): 197–201.

Torres, A., and J. D. Forrest. (1988). Why do women have abortions? *Family Planning Perspectives* (20): 169–76.

Townsend, F. (1889). A report of eighty cases of rapid dilatation of the uterine canal for the cure of dysmenorrhea and sterility. *American Journal of Obstetrics and Diseases of Women and Children* (22): 1271–76.

Trepanier, K. (1985). Infertile couples: Alone in a crowd. *Canadian Nurse* (81): 42–45.

Tronto, J. C. (1989). Women and caring: What can feminists learn about morality from caring? In A. M. Jaggar and S. R. Bordo (Eds.), *Gender/body/knowledge: Feminist reconstructions of being and knowing* (pp. 172–87). New Brunswick: Rutgers University Press.

Turner, B. S. (1987). *Medical power and social knowledge.* London: Sage.

Tymstra, T. (1989). The imperative character of medical technology and the meaning of "anticipated decision regret." *International Journal of Technology Assessment in Health Care* (5): 207–13.

U.S. Congress, Office of Technology Assessment. (1988). *Infertility: Medical and social choices* (OTA-BA-358). Washington, DC: U.S. Government Printing Office.

Van Gennep, A. (1909/1960). *The rites of passage.* Chicago: University of Chicago Press.

Van Hall, E. V. (1984). The infertile couple and the gynecologist: Psychosocial and emotional aspects. In R. F. Harrison, J. Bonnar, and W. Thompson (Eds.), *Fertility and sterility* (pp. 359–68). Lancaster: MTP Press.

Van Horn, S. H. (1988). *Women, work, and fertility, 1900–1986.* New York: New York University Press.

Van Kaam, A. L. (1959). Phenomenal analysis: Exemplified by a study of the experience of "really feeling understood." *Journal of Individual Psychology* (15): 66–72.

Varma, T. R., R. H. Patel, and R. K. Bhathenia. (1988). Outcome of pregnancy after infertility. *Acta Obstetricia et Gynecologica Scandinavica* (67): 115–19.

Veevers, J. E. (1972). The violation of fertility mores: Voluntary childlessness as deviant behavior. In C. L. Boydell, C. F. Grindstaff, and P. C. Whitehead (Eds.), *Deviant behavior and societal reaction* (pp. 571–92). Toronto: Holt, Rinehart, and Winston.

Verjaal, M., N. J. Leschot, and P. E. Treffers. (1982). Women's experiences with second trimester prenatal diagnosis. *Prenatal Diagnosis* (2): 195–209.

Viney, L. L., and L. Bousfield. (1991). Narrative analysis: A method of psychosocial research for AIDS-affected people. *Social Science and Medicine* (32): 757–65.

Waldorf, R. (1990, Winter). Waiting for baby. *Carolina Alumni Review* (79): 17–20.

Walker, J. (1797). *An inquiry into the causes of sterility in both sexes with its method of cure.* Doctoral dissertation, University of Pennsylvania, Philadelphia, PA. (In the Americana Collection at the New York Academy of Medicine).

Wallach, E. E., and K. S. Moghissi. (1988). Unexplained infertility. In S. J. Behrman, R. W. Kistner, and G. W. Patton (Eds.), *Progress in infertility,* 3rd ed. (pp. 799–819). Boston: Little, Brown.

Walters, W. A., and P. Singer. (Eds.). (1982). *Test-tube babies: A guide to moral questions, present techniques and future possibilities*. Melbourne: Oxford University Press.

Ware, S. (1982). *Holding their own: American women in the 1930s*. Boston: Twayne.

Warner, J. H. (1986). *The therapeutic perspective: Medical practice, knowledge, and identity in America, 1820–1885*. Cambridge, MA: Harvard University Press.

We wanted a baby. (1946, March). *Ladies Home Journal* (63): 28–29.

Weinstein, B. B. (1948). The surgical management of the tubal factor in sterility. *Southern Surgeon* (14): 556–61.

Welter, B. (1978). The cult of true womanhood: 1820–1860. In M. Gordon (Ed.), *The American family in social-historical perspective* (pp. 313–33). New York: St. Martin's.

Wendell, S. (1989). Toward a feminist theory of disability. *Hypatia* (4): 104–24.

Werner-Beland, J. A. (1980). Nursing and the concept of hope. In J. A. Werner-Beland (Ed.), *Grief responses to longterm illness and disability* (pp. 169–88). Reston, VA: Reston.

West, P. (1990). The status and validity of accounts obtained at interview: A contrast between two studies of families with a disabled child. *Social Science and Medicine* (30): 1229–39.

White, K. (1981). *What to do when you think you can't have a baby*. New York: Doubleday.

Wilcox, A. J., C. R. Weinberg, J. F. O'Connor, D. D. Baird, J. P. Schlatterer, R. E. Canfield, E. G. Armstrong, B. C. Nisula, (1988). Incidence of early loss of pregnancy. *New England Journal of Medicine* (319): 189–94.

Williams, D. M. (1989). Political theory and individualistic health promotion. *Advances in Nursing Science* (12): 14–25.

Williams, G. (1984). The genesis of chronic illness: Narrative re-construction. *Sociology of Health and Illness* (6): 175–200.

Williams, L. S. (1990). Wanting children badly: A study of Canadian women seeking in vitro fertilization and their husbands. *Issues in Reproductive and Genetic Engineering* (3): 229–34.

———. (1989). The overlooked role of women professionals in the provision of in vitro fertilization. *Resources for Feminist Research* (18): 80–82.

———. (1988). "It's going to work for me": Responses to failures of IVF. *Birth* (15): 153–56.

Winner, L. (1985). Do artifacts have politics? In D. MacKenzie, and J. Wajcman (Eds.), *The social shaping of technology: How the refrigerator got its hum* (pp. 26–37). Philadelphia: Open University Press.

Woliver, L. R. (1989). The deflective power of reproductive technologies: The impact on women. *Women and Politics* (9): 17–47.

Wright, B. (1960). *Physical disability: A psychological approach*. New York: Harper and Row.

Wright, J., M. Allard, A. Lecours, and S. Sabourin. (1989). Psychosocial distress and infertility: A review of controlled research. *International Journal of Fertility* (34): 126–42.

Wyschogrod, E. (1981). Empathy and sympathy as tactile encounter. *Journal of Medicine and Philosophy* (6): 25–43.

Young, I. M. (1984). Pregnant embodiment: Subjectivity and alienation. *Journal of Medicine and Philosophy* (9): 45–62.

Zabielski, M. T. (1984). Giving and receiving in the neomaternal period: A case of distributive inequity. *Maternal-Child Nursing Journal* (13): 19–46.

Zaner, R. M. (1984). A criticism of moral conservatism's view of in vitro fertilization and embryo transfer. *Perspectives in Biology and Medicine* (27): 200–212.

Zelizer, V. A. (1981). *Pricing the priceless child: The changing social value of children.* New York: Basic.

Zerubavel, E. (1981). *Hidden rhythms: Schedules and calendars in social life.* Chicago: University of Chicago Press.

Index

MARGARETE SANDELOWSKI is Associate Professor of Nursing at the University of North Carolina at Chapel Hill.

University of Pennsylvania Press
STUDIES IN HEALTH, ILLNESS, AND CAREGIVING
Joan E. Lynaugh, General Editor

Barbara Bates. *Bargaining for Life: A Social History of Tuberculosis, 1876–1938.* 1992

Janet Golden and Charles Rosenberg. *Pictures of Health: A Photographic History of Health Care in Philadelphia.* 1991

Anne Hudson Jones. *Images of Nurses: Perspectives from History, Art, and Literature.* 1987

June S. Lowenberg. *Caring and Responsibility: The Crossroads Between Holistic Practice and Traditional Medicine.* 1989

Elizabeth Norman. *Women at War: The Story of Fifty Military Nurses Who Served in Vietnam.* 1990

Elizabeth Brown Pryor. *Clara Barton, Professional Angel.* 1987

Margarete Sandelowski. *With Child in Mind: Studies of the Personal Encounter with Infertility.* 1993

Zane Robinson Wolf. *Nurses' Work: The Sacred and The Profane.* 1988

This book has been set in Linotron Galliard. Galliard was designed for Mergenthaler in 1978 by Matthew Carter. Galliard retains many of the features of a sixteenth-century typeface cut by Robert Granjon but has some modifications that give it a more contemporary look.

Printed on acid-free paper.